The South African Connection

RUTH FIRST
JONATHAN STEELE
CHRISTABEL GURNEY

The
South African Connection

Western Investment in Apartheid

TEMPLE SMITH · LONDON

First published in Great Britain 1972
by Maurice Temple Smith Ltd
37 Great Russell Street, London WC1

© 1972 RUTH FIRST, JONATHAN STEELE
       & CHRISTABEL GURNEY
ISBN 0 8511 7029 3

Printed in Great Britain by
Billing & Sons Limited, Guildford and London

Contents

Acknowledgements

We have learnt much from others working on the political economy of apartheid, and this will be clear from our detailed references to sources.

In particular we should like to thank:

Denis Herbstein whose on-the-spot interviews with industrialists in South Africa were invaluable, and who generously made available to us his unpublished notes;

Sean Gervasi who helped with statistics and tables and by placing at our disposal his notes on research in progress;

Harold Wolpe, Vella Pillay and Brian Bunting who read and criticized some of the draft chapters and who helped to clarify our ideas in discussion;

Peter Kellner who was involved in the early stages of the book;

Paul Fauvet who did some of the research on company directorships;

Timothy Smith, Reed Kramer and Tammie Hultman, who made available the material they have collected on the operations of American corporations in South Africa.

Note on exchange rate conversions

In most cases we have converted rands into pounds sterling at the current rate of R1.95 = £1. Where figures refer to capital flows (which are to some extent influenced by the prevailing rate of exchange at the time) we have converted at the rate:

R2 = £1 up to and including 1967
R1.7 = £1 for 1968 to 1971
R1.95 = £1 for 1972 onwards

The 1967 devaluation of the pound occurred in November. We have, however, taken the rate R2 = £1 for the whole of the year 1967. The 1971 devaluation of the rand occurred in December. Again we have taken the rate R1.7 for the whole of the year 1971.

Similarly we have used the following dollar exchange rates:

US $2.80 = £1 up to and including 1967
US $2.40 = £1 for 1968 to 1971
US $2.55 = £1 for 1972 onwards

1   Business and Politics: How They Mix

From a Conservative point of view, it was Reginald Maudling who hit the nail firmly on the thumb. In May 1970 he
launched into an attack on the demonstrators who were
trying to prevent the all-white South African cricket tour.
They were, he argued, putting too much emphasis on one,
relatively minor, aspect of South African life. 'South African
trade and industry', the Conservative deputy leader intoned,
'are just as much based on apartheid as cricket is.'

What Mr Maudling was trying to do, of course, was to
de-fuse the protests with the old formula of 'Why pick on . . . ?'
(cricket, South Africa, Greece, Vietnam, or whatever the
case may be). But inadvertently he had hit on an important
truth; for in spite of all the action by militant radicals
against apartheid, it is only recently that big business corporations have come under direct attack. Demonstrators
have nearly always taken political institutions as the objects
of their opposition, with foreign embassies the favourite
targets. It is surely time to question this approach as a pre-
occupation with the outward symbols of political power and
a lopsided scale of tactical priorities.

This question is probably more important in the discussion
of apartheid than of any other world issue. For, controversial
though the British Government's policy towards South
Africa is, its influence *is* small compared with the effect of
trade and industry. Getting on for two-thirds of all foreign
investment in South Africa is British, and one-third of all
South Africa's exports come to this country. British business
interests spread through almost every aspect of the Republic's
life; it is hard to imagine how some sectors, like banking,
for example, would keep going without British backing.

A*   9

In their reply to the suggestion that this involvement puts a special onus on British firms to help to end apartheid, businessmen generally give one of two answers: the first is that business and politics (like sport and politics) should not be mixed, and the second that apartheid may be objectionable, but that business is 'doing its bit behind the scenes' to change it; the alternative to this reform-by-participation would, after all, be to try to bring down South Africa's regime and consequently her economy. So, let us opt for reform through business rather than for revolution.

The view that business and politics should not be mixed is extraordinarily difficult to uphold; it rests on the argument – a singularly unpersuasive one – that politics and business are autonomous areas of society, and it ignores the widespread and permanent pressure exerted upon governments by those who control industrial, commercial and financial resources. Business and political interests, far from being separate and independent, interact closely with each other, influence each other and each of them relies on this interdependence in its own policy-making.

Manifestly, companies use their influence where they can to further their own interests in both the short and the long term. Sometimes this influence takes the form of special pleading – for instance, the Rolls-Royce appeal to the British Government for a forty-two-million pound subsidy to help the company over short-term difficulties during the design and production of aero-engines for the American market. But the influence is often directed towards more general ends: changes in company taxation; alterations in trade policy; even – as could be seen from the dramatic rise in share prices on 19 June 1970, at the time of Britain's general election – a change of government.

The argument that business and politics should not be mixed comes up against insuperable difficulties in South Africa. The history of the development of the country's economy falls into three main stages: the coercion of black labour into the compounds of the gold and diamond mines; Britain's establishment of Union in 1910 so that centralized state power would control labour in the interests of white capital; and now the stage of apartheid, when the political and economic pressures for cheap labour are intensified; all three tell of the close interdependence of vested political and business interests.

The argument for the defence can shift slightly: some businessmen claim that they cannot be held responsible for supporting apartheid, because they play no part in making the laws which regulate it. 'We would be just as willing', they say, 'to work under a black government in South Africa as a white government.' This argument is not consistent unless it maintains that business should *never* take part in *any* political process. The fact that so many British companies subscribe to the Conservative party, or to other organizations of a rightward persuasion, like the Economic League, suggests that this is not a point of view which many businessmen hold with any conviction.

Now, one man who believes strongly that business and politics cannot be *separated* is Sir Val Duncan. Sir Val is Chairman of Rio Tinto–Zinc (RTZ), the huge international, British-run mining corporation, forty-three per cent of whose profits in 1970 came from its South African subsidiary, Palabora Mining. Two years ago Sir Val headed a Government-sponsored commission to study the future of the Foreign Office. The core of the commission's recommendations was that British missions abroad should be more directly oriented to promoting British commercial interests; indeed, it was felt that in some countries, a full embassy was superfluous: a commercial office would suffice. If there was any disagreement within the British business community with these suggestions, it did not make itself evident. It is more likely that most companies do not, in practice, separate – or even want to separate – business and political considerations, unless it happens to suit them to do so. If this is the case, then the argument that business bears no responsibility for developments in South Africa is sheer hypocrisy, and those who put it forward are really saying that it is in their best interests to keep their mouths shut over politically sensitive issues, and to profit as best they can.

Why maintain the hypocrisy? There is probably a degree of self-deception: few people like to think of themselves as evil exploiters of oppressed black workers. But it cannot be the whole explanation, for any company that wants to make a reasonable return on its capital must understand to a considerable degree the environment in which it operates. Even if the harsh reality of exploitation is softened by such euphemistic phrases as 'cheap labour units' and 'stable workforce', it is inconceivable that any firm with South African interests is ignorant of the country's social and economic system.

The real answer is that there is a vast gulf between the liberal rhetoric and the illiberal actions of advanced industrial societies. The public *persona* which large corporations like to project is one of benevolence, combining a sense of duty towards their employees with one of service towards the community. Such a *persona* is of course, vital for any capitalist society if it is to go on being acceptable to its members. Nothing is more embarrassing to a large company than to find itself confronted with overwhelming evidence that it is, in fact, illiberal. When the evidence is countered with, 'It is nothing to do with us, we are only making money. Blame the politicians, they make the laws', then the gap between rhetoric and reality is recognized, at least by implication, but the blame is shifted.

But we have to deal specifically with the argument used by businessmen in South Africa: that to bring down the economy would make things worse, not better and that, even if the South African subsidiaries of British companies do help the operation of apartheid, they are still doing more good than those who are working for a 'revolutionary' change. This recognizes, again by implication, the need for *some* kind of change. It may even represent the conversion of big business to the principle of non-violence; and that conversion, if it is genuine, must rank as one of the most remarkable developments in this century. However, one or two doubts do come to mind. For one thing, a number of British companies (many with South African interests) quite happily accept arms contracts; for another, the aversion which corporations have for violence manifests itself most strongly when that violence is likely to reduce profits. One of the most consistent supporters of the resumption of British arms sales to South Africa has been the United Kingdom–South Africa Trade Association (UKSATA).

There are grounds for suspecting that behind the argument is the wish to divert attention from what British companies are actually doing in South Africa and to discredit opposition. The speech given by Sir Frederic Seebohm, the Chairman of Barclays Bank DCO, to the company's annual general meeting in January 1971 is an instance. In his speech he said:

. . . There are one or two identifiable political groups in this country who are bent on destroying our society in order to impose their own minority ideologies on the rest of us. . . . One of their objects is to bring about bloody revolution and they see in South Africa a chance to do just this. They believe fervently in a policy of destruction, which is the policy of an empty mind and those who have opted out of civilized society. A racial war in Southern Africa could only result in wholesale slaughter, economic chaos and utter misery for the very people the rest of us want to help.

Such vehement language (which the press naturally reported with glee) was an effective smokescreen for Sir Frederic's defence of Barclays DCO's actual record. He had only one concrete example of any attempt to dent, let alone breach, the defences of apartheid: 'We have recently', he said, 'obtained the South African Government's agreement

13

to the employment of coloured girls outside the coloured areas, and we believe we are the first bank to achieve this.' When he looked towards the future, Sir Frederic did not appear to see a major reforming role for the bank; rather, it would do as well for itself as it could whatever happened – as Sir Frederic put it, rather more delicately, 'When changes come in Southern Africa, as they surely will, the Bank's long and world-wide experience will stand it and all the people there in good stead'.

A detailed discussion of the need, possibilities and prospects for revolutionary change in South Africa is outside the scope of this book, but it is to the point to observe that, until a few years ago, South Africa's black political movements continued to employ non-violent means to seek their rights, as they had done for half a century. They had no support or encouragement from British business interests then, and so it is surely impertinent for those same business interests now to condemn the violence used by people who have no reason to believe that non-violence will work. Moreover, those who argue with such feeling that the victims of apartheid must above all not think of resorting to 'revolution', must prove their case for the possibility of change by reform.

Lord Byers is one of the best examples of those who defend businessmen by saying that they are doing their best behind the scenes to change apartheid. As a director of RTZ he must defend its presence in South Africa; as a Liberal peer he must be seen to be upholding humanitarian views. He maintains that RTZ, by giving skilled jobs where it can to non-whites, is helping to create an African middle class which will in time break down apartheid.

These defensive arguments, however weak they may be, try to remove from the shoulders of companies with South African interests the responsibility for any complicity in apartheid. But a few companies are now beginning to take a different line. In 1970, for example, the building firm, Wates, decided against operating in South Africa, refusing 'to profit from exploitation and ultimately end up with a vested interest in its maintenance'. This decision followed a visit by Neil Wates, the company's Managing Director, to South Africa. However, there were special factors: for one thing, the Wates family has a long Quaker tradition which affects its business decisions; and for another, as a private company it has no fears of a revolt by shareholders who might feel that by the refusal of what was, as Neil Wates admitted 'an excellent opportunity to do business', they would suffer.

While Britain is far and away the largest foreign investor in South Africa and Sterling Area investments (which are almost entirely British) stood at 1,983 million pounds by the end of 1970, nevertheless, the share of the Sterling Area in South Africa's total foreign liabilities declined from 62·4 per cent at the end of 1968 to 58 per cent at 31 December 1970, while the share of Western Europe increased from 18·9 per cent to 24·2 per cent in this period. The EEC countries, notably France, West Germany and Italy, are late-comers on the scene of apartheid. Japan is beginning to appear there. It will be necessary to look at their record and that of the United States.

What explains the sustained and predominant economic involvement of Britain and other Western countries in South Africa? There are reasons of history but clearly we must also look at South Africa's economic system itself. What makes it such a rich investment area? It is common knowledge that South Africa's economic growth and its returns on capital have been spectacular. From the economic point of view, South Africa offers advantages to the investor which few other countries do. Only Malaysia offers higher returns on capital. South Africa has also been relatively free – except in the case of the white minority – of the problem of wages rising faster than productivity. This is exactly what apartheid is all about. It is not a case of whites having gone race mad at the tip of the black continent, or of a specially virulent form of racial prejudice peculiar to Afrikaners, though race mania and bigotry do undoubtedly flourish in this dreadful society. Some people continue to explain the present system of South African rule by the historical tensions that grew up between the African (the black cattle farmer) and the Afrikaner (the white frontiersman who trekked north to found the Boer Republics). They fought prolonged wars over cattle and land, and the aggression that displaced the African from his land is now exercised within an elaborate structure of power controlled by a white minority which claims to be struggling for its physical survival and to be fearful of being swamped by the black majority. Apartheid is thus put forward as a doctrine rising out of the Afrikaner experience and the growth of Afrikaner nationalism; and those who make this interpretation of history and politics explain the policy of Bantustans as a special Afrikaner way of dealing with ineradicable race antagonisms. This explanation is interesting but only as an attempt to accommodate historical and psychological pressures within white racialism; it can even be embellished by the theological justifications for white domination so laboriously produced by the Dutch Reformed Church fundamentalists, who say that it is all written in the Old Testament anyway. The difficulty is that this description of apartheid as the result of a clash between two aggressive nationalisms – African and Afrikaner – does not explain, for one thing, why and how apartheid grew so naturally and effortlessly out of the state policies pursued, not in the *Boer* Republics but in the *British* ones, when South Africa was a colony run from Whitehall; nor does it account for the policies of South African governments before Afrikaner nationalism came to power in 1948. For the striking thing about South Africa is the long continuity between the economic, social and political policies of successive governments, whether they were the instruments of the vested interests of predominantly British, English- or Afrikaans-speaking white groups.

The policies officially known as apartheid, which came formally into being after 1948, when Dr Malan defeated General Smuts in a general election, are distinct only in detail and emphasis from the policy of segregation pursued in the preceding years. The apartheid system is the nub of the matter and one must scrutinize the special mechanisms built into it by law, by the nature of the state, by economic and political policies, which ensure not only impressively high rates of profit for investors, but also the uniquely privileged and prosperous way of life of the white minority. There are in reality not one but two South Africas, one white and the other black, the ruling class of colonizers, as one might say, and the colonized. The difference between this and other colonial situations is that in South Africa colonizers and colonized are present side by side in the same country and it is only colour that marks the difference between the white resident 'army of occupation' and its subject people, the Africans, Indians and Coloureds, all categorized in South Africa's racialist terminology as 'non-whites'. In this way colour is used to conceal class and the existence of a peculiarly intense colonial exploitation.

On the one hand South Africa has all the features of an advanced industrial state. She is, in fact, the only 'developed' country on the African continent. She makes within her borders 30 per cent of the continent's income; she produces not only 43 per cent of the continent's mineral wealth, but also more than twice as much electricity and six times as much steel as the rest of the continent combined. She has reached the stage when she is building up her own armaments industry, exporting both capital abroad and also the products of her industry, and is encroaching politically, economically and militarily on countries to the north. But this expanding and expansionist industrial economy, in which the white minority runs industry, finance, politics, the judicial system, the army and the police, fills all the executive management and skilled jobs, and lives at a standard

17

comparable with that of the industrialized countries of the world, also has the features of a colony. The African areas are stagnant, crowded labour reserves where a debilitated peasant agriculture is unable to support the population; a rigorously controlled system of migrant labour and 'pass' laws – the International Labour Organization called it forced labour – drains cheap labour from the African areas for use in the industrialized sector of the economy and then expels it from urban areas when it is no longer required. It is apartheid which regulates these two ways of life. There is abundant literature about this, some of it serious and exhaustively documented. There are descriptions of the quality of life in South Africa, for Africans perpetually harassed by the fear of breaking the law, and for whites, enjoying prosperity yet troubled by guilt and fear. This book does not set out to deal with these matters but it is necessary to know something of the environment in which British investment thrives.

Figures show that the African workers in South Africa are worse off than ever they were. The wages of African miners have not increased in real terms since 1911. In 1969 Africans, who constituted 67·9 per cent of the population, received only 18·8 per cent of the nation's cash income, whereas the whites, 19·7 per cent of the population, received 73·3 per cent. The gap between wages for black and white workers has not narrowed but widened. There is a serious shortage of skilled workers and a search for (white) immigrants from Britain and Europe, but there is also mass unemployment among Africans: by 1980 the figure could rise to close on four millions out of a working population of ten millions. As we have seen, the principal argument from the 'reform through business' lobby is that economic development in South Africa is naturally and by its own momentum eroding apartheid. In a tug-of-war between ideology (the racialism of apartheid) and economics, it is argued that the latter must win. Thus, the greater the rate of industrial expansion the faster the removal of the colour bar, because, sooner or later, that must be the way to solve the problem of the shortage of skilled labour. And the greater the rate of investment in South Africa, the more trade and economic dealings there are, the more rapid and effective these beneficial consequences of investment will be. This is one case for doing business with South Africa, and investors can enjoy rewarding dividends and a glow of satisfaction that through business and profit one can also do good works. Further discussion must be unnecessary. Apartheid is good for profits; is business not aimed at maximum profit and must companies not justify themselves to shareholders by insuring the best possible returns on investment? So, in place of the 'profit-and-be-damned' argument we have the 'change-through-prosperity' argument: the more business we do the more effectively we undermine apartheid.

This is probably taken less seriously by businessmen whose companies are operating in South Africa than by those conceivably well-intentioned people who are searching for some way of helping to change South Africa from outside, preferably, of course – and this is really implied in the argument – without black revolution, certainly in the immediate future. One of the central questions in this book is whether industrialization is really breaking down apartheid. Is some of the industrial prosperity rubbing off on Africans? Are skilled African workers getting under that utterly 'illogical' but highly profitable colour bar?

General statements of policy are important but particular instances of practice matter just as much. Chapter 8 presents a group of case studies of British business operations in South Africa, based on interviews and questionnaires. British spokesmen in South Africa and this country, like the rulers of South Africa themselves, are becoming uncommunicative. The lives and working conditions of Africans are not easily opened to scrutiny, because even a factual account of them would in itself be an indictment of South African

19

society and those who do business with it. The authors made repeated approaches to companies. The majority were unco-operative.

Denis Herbstein, conducting an investigation for the London *Sunday Times* (18 April 1971) had much the same experience. His investigation took him to Durban, Cape Town, Johannesburg and Germiston, and was originally intended to cover sixteen British-controlled companies, many of them household names. In the end there were ten complete interviews. Three of the firms said 'no' outright or, as Herbstein put it, 'yo-yoed me from pillar to post'. Some were helpful but sceptical of the value of the investigation. One man suggested the article would be so controversial that it might not be loyal to British interests to publish it. Since the Herbstein survey British business in South Africa has grown considerably more surreptitious. What is more, United States business, notoriously susceptible to the questionnaires and interview techniques which are part of the public-relations aspect of American society, has grown strikingly and uncharacteristically discreet during its few years' involvement with apartheid. When the Council on Economic Priorities did its survey in 1969–70 it got replies to questionnaires. Two years later, on-the-spot investigators (Americans, like the men they were trying to interview) more often than not met with silence or evasions. What, then, is the record of those firms about which information *is* available, whether it comes directly from them or from other sources? What do their directors think and say about apartheid, about whether business can influence the South African Government, or whether it can or does evade or resist apartheid regulations? The book discusses liberal experiments to reform industry through participation, like those made by the Oppenheimer empire and the American Polaroid company, and how and why these experiments are bound to fail.

There is discussion, too, of the over-all aspects of British business and British policy. Business is not only making political decisions in the course of its activities in South Africa; business circles are going out of their way to assert – officially through the Department of Trade and Industry and unofficially through UKSATA and the CBI – British *and* South African political interests. This book describes the lobbies and the propaganda machine of British–South African business. It shows, too, how South Africa House, Anglo-South African business interests and important members of the Conservative Party form a powerful political group reaching into the Tory Cabinet and the Civil Service; how business in Britain run by Conservatives is tightly enmeshed in Tory politics; in short, how the claim for the separateness of politics and business is never more frivolous or irrelevant than in its application to apartheid.

Finally, *The South African Connection* deals with the wider dangers of the involvement of British business in South Africa. Trade has always followed the flag in the past. The authors contend that British trade and investment are not following the British flag but the South African one. This is a result of changes that have come about in Britain's policy in Southern Africa since she ceded the region as the stamping ground for apartheid. Rhodesia is a factor in the situation; so is South-West Africa; so too are Lesotho, Swaziland and Botswana, once British Protectorates and now virtually colonies of South Africa. And South Africa's expansion northwards is a new consideration. Some people argue, from the opposite point, that these new policies are symptoms of change for the better under South Africa: the white front is cracking or the Nationalists are coming round to more rational policies. It is said that Bantustans may very well soon be permitted to be independent states as one aspect of the change; an even more marked one is the policy of dialogue which is turning South Africa from her traditional isolationism to a search for good neighbourliness with black states. Is apartheid really changing within and without?

21

What are its larger long-term aims on the whole sub-continent and does Britain share them? Are we seeing a South African effort to contain the area of possible conflict, or the nearing of a confrontation in which Britain will be on the wrong side in a racial, colonial-type war, once more a 'junior partner', as she has been in the war that America has lost for Vietnam? If the latter is the case, then large-scale strategic considerations will take the place of business ones, and these will involve organizations like NATO and other Western alliances. If events do take this direction, and the forces in southern Africa do polarize, at least British official policy will have the merit that it is no longer so hypocritical as to condemn apartheid on moral grounds while shoring it up with cash. But if the change in British policy has resulted in consistency, it has also helped to create the prospect of a prolonged war, involving, of course, not only the British Government and British business, but the British people too.

2 The Foundations of the Partnership

> If you look at the real basis of the relationship
> between Britain and South Africa, which is one of
> mutual self-interest and a recognition of where
> power lies in terms of economic and strategic
> strength, then you will see this relationship is grow-
> ing stronger – *London director of the South Africa
> Foundation, 1970*

No country is tied to South Africa by closer economic links
than Britain. By 1970 Sterling Area investment there totalled
1,983 million pounds or 58 per cent of all foreign investment.
It represented an accumulation of over a hundred years of
British involvement in South Africa, without which the
country and its white minority could never have prospered
as they have.

In spite of the almost world-wide condemnation of apartheid,
the flow of investment to South Africa has been increasing in
recent years. In 1971 more than 500 British companies had
subsidiaries or associates there (listed in Appendix 1). There
can scarcely be a single pension fund, insurance company,
building society or unit trust in Britain which does not have
some of its capital invested in South Africa. Students, trade
unionists or clergymen who complain that their university,
union or church funds are making unwholesome profits out of
a racialist society have only come upon a small crack in the
ground beneath their feet.

What is true for Britain is scarcely less so for the rest of the
Western world. British capital was the first to come to South
Africa, attracted by the country's vast mineral wealth. But as
its economy has grown, and with British help been industrialized, South Africa has become more closely integrated into
the whole Western capitalist system. Since the Second World

23

War it has developed important links with the expanding economies of the USA, the Common Market and Japan. They in turn now have a growing interest in preserving economic and political stability in South Africa, with all the obvious implications for the oppressed majority. In 1969 Dollar Area countries owned 15 per cent of the foreign investment there. There are more than 300 American-owned subsidiaries. Western Europe owned 21 per cent of foreign investment (Table 1).

From 1965 to 1970 South Africa received a net total of 982 million pounds from the West.* The annual average net inflow has risen from 93 million pounds in 1965–7 to 235 millions in 1968–70 and in 1970 itself it reached a record of 328 millions.[1] In 1971, according to *The Times* (supplement on Johannesburg, 11 July 1972) it rose by as much as a third to reach 447 million pounds, and during the first half of 1972 the rate of inflow accelerated even further.

The only period when the Western investment flow temporarily slowed down and was even reversed was in the late 1950s and early 1960s as the African majority launched massive civil disobedience campaigns against apartheid. In 1960, in the immediate aftermath of the Sharpeville massacre, 48 million pounds left the country.[2] For a moment it looked as though the often-predicted explosion in South Africa was imminent. Investors ran for cover. But the 'wind of change' soon blew. By 1965, as the white majority brought in new repressive legislation, outlawed all African political activity and restored physical control, the funds flowed back. A net

* All statistics relating to foreign investment are notorious for undervaluation. This is especially true of the figures of the South African Reserve Bank which calculates direct foreign investment in South Africa by reference to company balance sheets of those firms which are defined as under foreign control. Balance sheet assessments, although they include company reserves, do not include current calculations of assets. Furthermore, the British *Business Monitor* figures of the flow of United Kingdom direct capital are derived from sample surveys of British firms, and the risk of under-valuation here is acknowledged to be considerable.

outflow of 21 million pounds in 1964 became an inflow of 128 million pounds in 1965 (Table 2).

A breakdown of these figures reveals a striking distinction between direct and indirect investment. The flight of capital at the time of Sharpeville turns out to have been almost entirely due to shareholders in the stock market or on the money market pulling out. The large corporations that participate directly by establishing or expanding plants in South Africa continued to support the economy. In 1961 new direct investment from Britain dropped to a low point of 9 million pounds, but it remained a net outflow to South Africa: in other words, more capital was still going out to South Africa than was being withdrawn. Over the whole period from 1961–6, when the South African minority needed every penny of foreign investment as a symbol of the system's stability, British companies sent an average of 28 million pounds of direct investment a year.

This was nothing compared with what was to follow. In 1967–9 the average almost doubled to 53 million pounds and in 1969 Britain sent a record 70 millions (Table 3). American corporations were a little less faithful. In 1960 there was a net US withdrawal of 13 million pounds. But that year was an exception: over the whole 1960–66 period South Africa gained 14 million pounds of American direct investment on average every year and in 1967–9 it gained an average of 20 million pounds. In 1970 the United States sent a massive 41 million pounds (Table 4).

The psychological value of that investment to South Africa cannot be measured. Its economic value was substantial. It provided the capital without which the economy could not have grown. It staved off the recurring danger of balance-of-payments crises by ensuring the country a ready source of foreign exchange. It gave South Africa access to advanced technology as leading Western corporations passed on their findings in research and development to their South African subsidiaries.

25

These immense benefits from the Western stake more than made up for the lessening share, in terms of quantity, of new foreign capital in the economy. With the acceleration in its growth rate and the development of its own money market in the early 1950s, South Africa's economy has been able to provide an increasing proportion of its capital requirements. In the years 1946–9 53 per cent of new capital formation came from foreign inflows.[3] In the early 1950s the share dropped to 19 per cent and is now only about 11 per cent. An important phenomenon now in South Africa's domestic capital formation is that foreign companies already based there are financing expansion through reinvesting their profits. The figures for capital inflows into South Africa therefore undervalue the importance of foreign capital to the economy. Foreign companies are also borrowing locally inside South Africa (Table 5). As a proportion of Gross National Product South Africa's net foreign debt fell from 47 per cent in 1956 to 37 per cent in 1961 and now stands at around 28 per cent.[4] These figures are still high by the standards of developed economies.

But figures alone do not tell in full the part which Western capital has played in the development of South Africa's economy. Its strategic role has been even more important than its volume. At each stage of the country's industrial development since the last war, foreign investment has provided the capital equipment and technological skills which have enabled South Africa to build up new sectors of its economy. In the 1940s and 1950s the key growth sector was engineering and British firms exported the capital, the machinery and the knowledge which gave South Africa this sector. Other firms went into partnership with the Government to provide South Africa with a modern textiles industry. On the base of the explosives industry British technology helped to build up a sophisticated chemicals sector, and also moved into food-processing and canning, chiefly for the export market. In the 1960s the sectors expanding most rapidly were the production of motor vehicles and automobile accessories, and oil prospecting and refining, in which American corporations played a major role. Foreign capital has been crucial to South Africa's economic development because of the technology and skills which it has brought with it. In computers, electronics, chemicals and even nuclear energy this technological 'bridge-building' is linking South Africa with the latest Western trends.

A useful example of this is the old partnership between Imperial Chemical Industries and A E & C I, which is now the country's second largest industrial company. I C I (South Africa), a wholly-owned subsidiary of I C I has a 42·5 per cent holding in A E & C I. I C I's London directors claim strenuously that this minority holding is not enough to give them control over the day-to-day running of the company in South Africa. This argument – a familiar one from boardrooms under challenge – conceals a relationship between British capital and South Africa which is almost a classic model of its kind. The link between the two companies is striking enough to have justified a biography, *The Dynamite Company* by A. P. Cartwright: 'The partnership', he writes, 'has now lasted forty years. It has been of inestimable benefit to South Africa's economy. I C I has no secrets in its exchange of information with its South African associate. As a result some of the best scientific brains in Britain have been at the service of the mining companies, the farmers and the industrialists of South Africa.'

The partnership began in 1930 when I C I technicians went out to build South Africa's first ammonia plant for A E & C I. 'This was an I C I project from start to finish. I C I engineers designed the plant, manufactured a great deal of the equipment and supervised the erection.' By 1950 the company had grown phenomenally and was involved in explosives, superphosphates, paint, cyanide and leather-cloth. In 1950 I C I made a loan of 2 million pounds to A E & C I and two years later, when South Africa began producing uranium oxide,

AE & CI played a part in developing seventeen uranium extraction plants. AE & CI built and operates two munitions factories for the South African Government in the Transvaal in return for an annual fee. In February 1970 the Government took over full technical control of a third munitions plant built for it by AE & CI at Somerset West in the Cape. Cartwright concludes: 'The partnership between AE & CI and ICI has become one of the pillars on which the entire industrial structure of South Africa rests . . . The immense resources of the world-famous British company, its technical skill and all the fruits of its research programmes have always been placed at the disposal of its partner. In almost all the new branches of the chemical industry now established in South Africa ICI acted as the path-finder, so that when the time came to build a factory here most of the trials and errors inseparable from establishing new manufacturing techniques were over and the blueprints were accurate . . . For the past forty years a young country has had some of the best scientific brains in Europe helping it to plan its industrial development.'

Side by side with the technical skill put into the South African economy by Western corporations has gone the technical aid given to South Africa by Western governments. In mid-1970 the chairman of the South African Atomic Energy Board announced that South Africa had developed a new uranium enrichment technique which would enable it to develop energy from nuclear power by 1978: soon after, it was also announced that South Africa would be able to make its own nuclear weapons in five years' time. This is only possible because of technical aid received from the American Government. The reactor at South Africa's research station at Pelindaba is American-made and was purchased and installed through an American corporation, Allis Chalmers. Scores of South African nuclear scientists have been trained at the US Atomic Energy Commission's National Laboratory at Oak Ridge. NASA is another US Government agency which co-operates closely with its South African counterparts. Since 1961 it has operated three space-tracking stations in South Africa and has trained white South Africans to man them. NASA's Deputy Director says that although NASA loses many of its trainees to South African industry, 'We know we're doing the country good and don't mind.'[5]

Governments and corporations are not, of course, doing all this for nothing. In 1970 ICI (South Africa) had pre-tax profits of 4·13 million pounds. More than 60 per cent of these came from its stake in AE & CI which earned for it dividends of 2·6 million pounds.[6] AE & CI's own net profit, from which these dividends were paid, soared by over 30 per cent in 1970, producing a return on capital employed of 17·9 per cent.[7]

Unusually high rates of return are the main inducement to the foreign capital flooding into South Africa. Throughout the 1960s, when industry in Britain failed to expand rapidly because of a shortage of investment, British businessmen were sending funds to South Africa. In spite of South Africa's exclusion from the Commonwealth, Harold Macmillan and subsequent British Prime Ministers did not exclude it from the Sterling Area under exchange control. British capital could and did flow out freely to South Africa. Even when Pretoria imposed severe restrictions on the repatriation of capital from South Africa after Sharpeville, Britain still allowed capital to go into South Africa unchecked. Rates of profit were too attractive.

In the period 1960–68 the average annual rate of return (after South African tax) on direct British investments in South Africa never fell below 10 per cent. Between 1965 and 1968 it averaged 12 per cent. Only Malaysia provided a

AVERAGE RATE OF RETURN ON BRITISH DIRECT INVESTMENT IN SOUTH AFRICA (PERCENTAGE)[8]

1960	*1961*	*1962*	*1963*	*1964*	*1965*	*1966*	*1967*	*1968*
10.3	10.4	12.1	12.9	14.8	12.1	12.8	12.4	11.7

consistently better return for Britain; Ghana produced high but fluctuating profits (Table 6). In the same period Britain was earning more profit from its direct investment in South Africa than from any other overseas area. Between 1964 and 1966 it earned an annual average of 60 million pounds; between 1967 and 1969 the average shot up to 76 million (Table 7). By 1969 British earnings from South Africa had reached 86 millions. More funds were being invested in South Africa than anywhere else except Australia (Table 8).

The rates of return on American capital invested in South Africa were even more striking. The average world rate for direct US investment during 1960–70 was 11 per cent, but capital invested in South Africa earned a phenomenal 18·6 per cent (Table 9).

Historically, the mainstay of the South African economy has been the mines. They continued to produce the highest profits in the early 1960s. In the whole overseas Sterling Area mining investments produced a return of between 25 and 30 per cent.[9] Because of the exceptionally low wages in the South African mines, with average weekly earnings for Africans of about £2, the typical mining investment there has even higher yields.

In the mid-1960s investment in manufacturing overtook the British stake in the mines. The change parallels that in the South African economy. From being almost entirely dependent on the gold-mining industry to earn foreign exchange to buy manufactured goods abroad, South Africa has, since the Second World War, developed its own manufacturing sector. In line now too with the South African Government's plans for expanding northwards, first into the surrounding white buffer states and then into the weaker economies of independent Africa, British capital is beginning to move up from its South African base. Firms are using the profits earned in South Africa to invest in Namibia (South-West Africa), Angola, Mozambique and Rhodesia. British investment has both helped to create the economy of South

Africa and benefited from its expansion, in an interaction
from which British capitalists and the white South have each
profited; Chapter 12 discusses this in more detail. South
Africa is now one of the main outlets for direct British investment, absorbing around 10 per cent of the total. Only
Australia ranks higher in importance (Table 8).

British companies have a substantial shareholding in three
of the ten leading South African ones; ICI's share, already
mentioned, in AE & CI; Associated British Foods' share in
Premier Milling, and British Leyland Motor Corporation's
in Leyland South Africa. Of the country's hundred leading
industrial companies, twenty-five are partially owned by
British corporations, and twelve are direct subsidiaries of
British companies (Appendix 2).

For the Americans South Africa is still considerably less
important as an outlet for capital. In 1970 the United States
sent just over 1 per cent of its total overseas direct investment
to South Africa, but the stake is growing rapidly. It is concentrated in key sectors of the economy. The two American
oil companies, Mobil and Caltex, refine over half the oil
imported into South Africa. American corporations, General
Motors, Ford and Chrysler produce 60 per cent of the
country's cars, and American companies turn out much of
the machinery for the mining and construction industry.

Traditionally, direct investors have been able to exert considerable influence on the economies in which they operate:
he who pays the piper calls the tune. Unlike individual equity
shareholders, who have only a small say, if any, over the
management of the stocks they buy, industrialists who transfer
substantial blocks of funds to open or expand plant have
considerable power. In most developing countries foreign
corporations play a significant economic and political role.
In theory, then, the owners of the huge foreign investment
in South Africa could exert some pressure if they wished. In
practice they have not done so. Increasingly in recent years
British companies in South Africa have been giving up any

potential influence and agreeing instead to operate on the South African Government's terms.

Most British companies have been happy to leave the running of their South African subsidiaries to local managing directors, themselves often South Africans. Head Office in London either did not know or did not want to know, or more frequently did not want to admit that it knew what went on in South Africa. As long as profits are maintained, overseas managements are not likely to lose much sleep over the conditions under which they are made; there is a fuller analysis of company attitudes in Chapter 8.

Nowadays more and more companies are forming joint ventures with South African ones in which they have only minority holdings, albeit large ones. The Bowater Paper Corporation, for example, has gone into partnership with Anglo-American and Johannesburg Consolidated Investments to build what will be one of the most advanced paper mills in the world at Mondi Valley, outside Durban.[10] Bowater holds 8 per cent of the equity of a new firm, Mondi Paper Company. The Plessey Company says that a substantial part of its interests in South Africa is in collaboration with other companies and that it is unable to provide separate statistics for them.[11] In 1969 Fisons merged its interests with those of three South African companies to form Federale Kunsmis Beperk, the fertilizer division of the Afrikaans Federale Volksbeleggings Group.[12] These companies argue now that they have no control. It is interesting to speculate on the motives for this abdication. It is in sharp contrast to the practice in Australia where most British capital is in wholly owned British subsidiaries.

Other companies are offering shares on the Johannesburg Stock Exchange in obedience to the South African Government's request for more participation by local shareholders. The result, as Pretoria knows well, is that if companies did ever think of withdrawing from South Africa one more obstacle has been created to an easy departure. The restric-

tions on capital returning home have a similar rationale. It
is claimed that, once in, foreign capital is stuck. ICI put it
in this way: 'In theory it would be possible for ICI to withdraw from South Africa – at a cost of some £50 million of
investment – but in practical terms it is impossible. Certainly
South African exchange control regulations would make it
very difficult for ICI to withdraw. In addition, where we
are in partnership with South African interests we are
contractually bound to continue those partnerships.'[13]

Despite these blocking mechanisms, companies continue
to offer shares on the stock exchange.

A growing number of companies are prepared to collaborate directly with the South African Government itself.
Pretoria welcomes this development as a way of extending
the State's control of the economy. British Petroleum is linked
to Sentrachem, the chemicals group in which the State has a
financial interest through the Industrial Development Corporation (IDC).[14] The IDC also has an interest in Rossing
Uranium, the company set up by Rio Tinto–Zinc to investigate the huge uranium deposits at Rossing in Namibia.[15] It
also presided over the merger by which Fisons became part
of Federale Kunsmis. The British and Commonwealth Shipping Company is in partnership with the IDC through its
holding in Safmarine. In 1969, under the British Labour
Government, the British Steel Corporation prepared plans
for pooling its substantial interest in three South African
companies with the State-controlled Iron and Steel Corporation, ISCOR; Chapter 8 discusses this deal more fully.

Foreign funds are not used as a means of pressure against
the régime in South Africa: on the contrary, they are helping
it to make itself better able to resist any challenge to apartheid. The more closely South Africa is linked with the
Western economic system, the simpler it will be for the whites
to command political support and sympathy in Washington,
London, Brussels and Paris. Even in 1960 and 1961, the
lowest point in South Africa's recent fortunes, the country

was never really out in the cold: foreign investment continued. A decade later South Africa is so integral a part of the West that apartheid merely looks like one factor in the international economic system.

The link between foreign capital and the South African Government is growing outside the country too. Pretoria has been borrowing extensively in Europe. Since 1969 its foreign debt has trebled, to reach a total in July 1971 of 154 million pounds.[16]

Most of the bond issues which South African public utilities and the Government have offered were snapped up immediately. In October 1970 Pretoria made its first attempt since 1959 to raise money on the London market. It offered bonds worth 5 million pounds. They were so over-subscribed in advance that when the market officially opened it reclosed after ten minutes, sold out. These South African government bonds are guaranteed by almost all the main Western commercial banks. The backers of a further government bond issue of 12 million pounds, repayable in 1986 and promulgated in November 1971, read like a *Who's Who* of European merchant banking: there were over a hundred names, including Hambros, Lazard Brothers & Company, N. M. Rothschild, Hill Samuel, Morgan Grenfell and J. Henry Schroder Wagg.[17]

Foreign governments have also provided substantial transfers of capital to the South African Government. In the five years up to 1968 68 million pounds moved to South Africa although official Government sources obscure the exact nature of these transfers.[18]

Equally valuable for South Africa has been the striking expansion of trade with the West. Britain is still South Africa's main trading partner. In the last ten years the annual turnover has almost trebled from 252 million pounds in 1961 to approximately 650 million pounds in 1971 (Table 10). Although Britain still takes 29 per cent of South Africa's exports – more than any other country – Western Europe now sells more. The United States and Japan have been increasing their trade rapidly and are now close to Britain and Western Europe (Table 11).

Quantitatively this trade is more vital for South Africa than it is for her partners. Exports and imports are each worth at least one-fifth of South Africa's Gross Domestic Product. For Britain the importance of South Africa is relatively much lower. Under 4 per cent of British exports go there.

South Africa still benefits from Commonwealth preferences in spite of her exclusion from the Commonwealth in 1961. In February 1962, as Lord Privy Seal, Mr Heath argued, during the second reading of the South Africa Bill, that these preferences should be maintained since they originated in the Ottawa Agreements of 1932 and not from Commonwealth membership as such.[19] Nearly all South Africa's exports to Britain come in duty free. Some 40 per cent of them are allowed preferences and thereby get tariff protection, compared with the otherwise competitive exports of other countries.

The South African economy used to be even more dependent on British trade than it is now. Over the last forty years Pretoria's aim has been to reduce this dependence, first by a policy of industrialization and import substitution, and secondly by a search for alternative suppliers in the rest of the Western economy. The policy has had some success. Between 1947 and 1967 imports from Britain as a proportion of the Gross Domestic Product fell from 30 per cent to 20 per cent.

In spite of industrialization South Africa's trade has still not changed the traditional colonial pattern apparent in its dependence on the West: the country exports raw materials and food and wine and imports machinery and capital goods. Although South Africa is producing more and more of its capital goods requirements itself it does not yet have a technology sophisticated enough to meet all its needs economic-

35

ally. However, the drive for self-sufficiency is being pushed
hard and foreign corporations that invest in the country and
build up its industry are helping the process. Many States
trying to industrialize fast adopt protectionist policies, but
South Africa has an additional motive. She is afraid that the
pressure for trade sanctions against her may one day mount.
To diversify her markets therefore makes good political sense:
it is a useful insurance policy and it increases the number of
countries who will think twice before embarking on sanctions.

The twin policies of import substitution and diversification
have also been followed in the crucial market for arms. Until
1961 Britain supplied the bulk of South Africa's radar, electronic devices, aircraft and naval equipment and kept up the
flow of spare parts even after the United Nations' arms
embargo in 1963. But as the embargo began to affect the
despatch of new aircraft and warship deliveries, South Africa
turned for supplies to France and Italy. As for small arms,
the Government has embarked on a crash programme of
domestic production which allowed the Defence Minister to
announce in 1971 that South Africa was now self-sufficient
for its internal defence and could start exporting firearms.[20]

The move to find alternative trading partners in Europe
made increasing sense as it became clear that Britain would
eventually join the Common Market. Faced by the prospect
of Britain retreating behind the EEC's Common External
Tariff wall, South Africa anticipated the event by building
up contacts with the EEC countries in advance. When
Britain goes in Europe, South Africa, according to various
estimates, stands to lose 25 million pounds in lost exports
(*Financial Times*) or 100 million pounds (as Lourens Muller,
South Africa's Economics Minister, put it).[21] The drive to
win friends and influence in the EEC took Mr Vorster to
Paris on his first visit to Europe. The EEC's tariff wall poses
more than just a threat to South Africa's exports in Europe.
If, on joining the Market, Britain makes the same sort of
'Associated State' arrangement for the African Common-

wealth countries as France has done for her former colonies, South Africa would face the Common External Tariff in black Africa too. Its design for economic expansion in independent Africa would face an additional obstacle. South Africa has, therefore, started pushing for special concessions from the EEC for itself, and has appointed one of its most experienced negotiators, W. C. Naude, as Ambassador in Brussels. In November 1971 the South African Government asked for a special audience with the EEC's Council of Ministers.[22]

As Britain's entry into the Market became more imminent, South African businessmen and their friends seemed less anxious. The view was expressed that South Africa could even use Britain as a 'springboard' for Europe. The British Government assured them that it did not see that 'entry to the EEC need relegate our valued trading relationship with South Africa'. W. E. Luke, the British Chairman of the United Kingdom South Africa Trade Association (UKSATA) announced that South African businessmen could 'use the outlet they already have in our markets as a means of expanding further in Europe'. The irony is that at the same time British businessmen are using South Africa more and more as a springboard for the rest of Africa. Companies are expanding northwards with investment and sales to the African continent, beyond their South African base. Nothing could better illustrate the growing interpenetration of British and South African business interests.

Although quantitatively trade with South Africa is far less important to the West than trade with the West is to South Africa, South Africa *is* becoming increasingly important to the West as a supplier of vital minerals. The gradual switch in the South African economy from mining to manufacturing should not obscure the fact that South Africa's abundance – and in some cases near-monopoly – of strategic minerals is growing in importance as far as Western corporations and governments are concerned. The West's need for South

37

Africa's gold is well known, but other minerals are assuming greater and greater importance.

The economies of Western Europe have always relied heavily on imports of raw materials. Japan, with its phenomenal industrial growth, has now joined the list of South Africa's best customers. Between 1965 and 1969 South Africa's share in Japan's total imports of asbestos rose from 23 per cent to 36·8 per cent, of chrome from 12 per cent to 30 per cent, of manganese ore and concentrate from 6 per cent to 29 per cent.

The growing American dependence on South Africa has been equally remarkable. The United States used to be self-sufficient in minerals and indeed for the first two decades of this century was an exporter of them. But as the country's economy has developed, domestic supplies of minerals have proved insufficient. The consequences for foreign policy of this development were recognized in 1954 by a specially appointed Presidential Commission: 'This transition of the US from a position of relative self-sufficiency to one of an increasing dependence on foreign sources of supply constitutes one of the most striking economic changes of our time. The outbreak of the Second World War marked the major turning-point of this change.'

Since the Commission's report, American dependence has increased and with it South Africa's importance.[23]

Unlike the period before the Second World War, when Afrikaner capital used the State against foreign capital in order to build itself a stake in the South African economy, today Western economic interests, private South African capital and South African State capital are working together in harmony. The State corporations provide the organizational framework and basic raw materials which attract foreign capital and help it prosper. At the same time the South African mining companies have begun to diversify out of mining and build themselves an industrial base. The clash between mining capital, both foreign and domestic, and the State-led manufacturing sector is disappearing. Old conflicts have been resolved: new conflicts have yet to appear. Meanwhile, the subsidiaries of the great Western corporations, private South African companies and South African State concerns like ISCOR, SASOL and SOEKOR are working together to develop South Africa's economy.

In recent years the technological skills, the experience and the international resources which Western capital has made available to the most advanced sectors of the South African economy have become more important than the capital itself. Because of its race policies and its reluctance to train its black workers, South Africa's industrialization has always depended on using more capital-intensive and technologically advanced methods. It has only been able to do this because of its access to processes developed by the industrial giants of the United States, Britain and Western Europe. In order to grow the South African economy must develop new sectors. Currently these are computers and petro-chemicals in which the leaders are mainly American firms. In order to expand the advanced industries which it already has and to move into new ones in the 1970s, South Africa must continue to be able to draw on Western science and technology.

All the signs are that Western corporations will continue to invest in South Africa. In spite of its problems the South African economy is still an attractive proposition for investors. Its real growth rate has remained steady at between 5 and 7 per cent a year. Inflation is accelerating but at a slower rate than in Britain or the US. The slide in Johannesburg Stock Exchange prices in the twenty months to the end of 1970 which caused some observers to prophesy economic doom for South Africa, changed into a recovery in the first half of 1971. Far from having lost confidence because of the collapse in share prices, foreign investors led the way to their recovery: foreigners made gross purchases worth 37 million pounds on the Johannesburg Stock Exchange in the first quarter of 1971 and were responsible for 41 per cent of all share transactions.[24] South Africa has a chronic balance-of-payments problem and its import/export position has drastically deteriorated in the last two years.[25] But so far this has not deterred foreign investors and the very large amounts of capital which South Africa attracted in 1970 and 1971 went a long way to cushion the impact of the huge trading deficit in South Africa's gold and foreign currency reserves.[26] South Africa is still a magnet for foreign capital and it seems most likely to continue to be so in the 1970s.

3 The Black Poor Get Poorer

> We found everywhere in business circles a refresh-
> ingly free enterprise atmosphere. The economy is
> expanding rapidly in many directions. People want
> unashamedly to make money and spend it, or pile
> up personal fortunes. With low income tax (though
> they do not think it is!) and with no capital gains
> tax that is still refreshingly possible to achieve –
> *Lord Erroll in* The Times *21 October 1968*

One characteristic of South Africa's economy has been its
rapid rate of growth; another is the glaring disparity between
white affluence and black poverty; a third is the continual
decline in African living standards. All three factors are
caused by apartheid. In South Africa, apartheid is translated
as 'separate development'; the International Labour
Organisation has described it as 'a system of forced labour'.
That phrase is apt: apartheid is not primarily about the
separation of races at all, since the economy has always been,
is now, and probably always will be dependent on African
labour; apartheid is a device for making sure that that labour
is in constant supply and total subjection. As the Prime
Minister, Mr Vorster, put it in the House of Assembly on
24 April 1968: 'It is true that there are blacks working for
us. They will continue to work for us for generations, in spite
of the ideal that we have to separate them completely. . . .
The fact of the matter is this; we need them because they
work for us. . . . But the fact they work for us can never
entitle them to claim political rights. Not now, nor in the
future . . . under no circumstances.'

Even under Mr Vorster's predecessor, Dr Verwoerd, the
architect of 'separate development', there was no illusion

B*

41

that whites in South Africa could do without the labour of blacks. Ever since Lord Milner proclaimed at the turn of the century that 'the unskilled labour of this country must be black', the basis of white supremacy has been the same. The nearest that Dr Verwoerd came to a long-term policy of separation was his insistence that by the year 2000 there must be parity in 'white' South Africa, with only one black for every white, and the rest sent off to the reserves.

Africans are controlled by complex legislation designed to make it impossible for them to be anything but cheap labour. Only in the reserves do Africans have even theoretical rights; but the conditions there, the poverty and malnutrition, and the absence of any real prospect of work apart from sub-sistence agriculture, deny them the practical means to a decent existence. The seizure of 87 per cent of South Africa's land for white use has created deliberate overpopulation in the reserves. At present eight million Africans or 60 per cent of the total African population, lives outside the reserves, working for white farmers or in the urban areas. Even the Transkei, the one 'homeland' set aside for Africans that is a geographical unit rather than a cluster of separate small territories, is mountainous over three-quarters of its area. Arable land is scarce, and about 230,000 Africans, or two out of every three people of working age in the Transkei, are absent as migrant workers at any one time.[1] Once they leave the reserves, Africans find themselves without rights and rigidly controlled.

The first law to direct their labour and control their movements by the compulsory carrying of a pass was issued by a British Governor of the Cape in 1809. He issued a proclamation forbidding Coloureds to move from one district to another without a certificate from a magistrate; it was to give them 'an encouragement for preferring entering the service of the inhabitants to leading an indolent life'. Since then the system has been revised and strengthened. In spite of its name, Dr Verwoerd's Natives (Abolition of Passes and

Co-ordination of Documents) Act of 1952 extended the compulsory carrying of passes to African women as well. The pass must contain details of the Government labour bureau permit without which no African may seek work. In most cases an African must accept whatever job is offered to him. He is sent wherever he is needed. If he loses his job and does not return to the reserve he risks being arrested without a warrant and sent to a work colony for up to three years. So the labour bureaux totally regulate the distribution of labour for the State. Any 'surplus' labour is expelled back to the reserves.

In the mid-1960s the Government intensified the scheme for removing 'surplus' Africans from the urban areas. Those who cannot find work, widows, and the chronic sick are being endorsed out of the cities and sent either to the reserves or to so-called 'resettlement areas'. At the same time the Government has steadily whittled away the remaining residential rights which Africans previously 'earned' in an urban area through birth there or through long service with one employer. Henceforth, all Africans will be migrants or temporary sojourners in the cities.

The use of convicts has provided an important extra source of labour where all other measures have been insufficient. In the last two decades in the Western Cape it has expanded considerably. Coloured workers are not subject to the pass laws now and have been moving from the farms into the cities. At the same time white politicians have been reluctant to accept many black workers into the urban area. Farmers have increasingly turned to hiring labour from the thirteen local prisons. Farms are even advertised for sale with a list of amenities and the added attraction 'plus 8 convicts'. The right to use convict labour is estimated to put up a farm's value by about £500 per prisoner.[2]

In the early days when the economy was based largely on mining and agriculture, it was not difficult to implement apartheid, because most Africans lived outside the urban areas. But as industrialization went ahead and the demand for labour grew, extra controls were devised to maintain the supply without letting it interfere with white supremacy. The Bantu (Urban Areas) Consolidation Act of 1945 lays down watertight restrictions on Africans living in the cities. First introduced in 1923 and frequently modified since, the Act stipulates the qualifications which four million urban Africans need to satisfy if they are to be allowed to remain where they are.

The Act provides that no African may remain in an urban area for more than seventy-two hours unless he or she can prove that

(a) he or she has lived there continuously since birth, or

(b) he or she has worked continuously for the same employer there for ten years, or has lived there with official permission for fifteen years, or

(c) she is the wife or he or she is the child of someone who qualifies to be there, or

(d) he or she has special permission from a labour bureau.

Under the Act, no African may move freely from one area to another, or live in one area and work in another, as whites do. Its scope (and that of the pass system) is clear from the number of prosecutions of Africans for violating its conditions. In 1969 there were 1,019,628 prosecutions, an average of 2,800 a day. In December 1971 yet another law was promulgated to channel pass-law offenders through 'aid' centres, instead of through the courts. In time this will lead to a drop in prosecutions but the constraints on labour will remain as severe as ever.

The migrant labour system has always been the basis of the gold- and diamond-mining industries. The system is now being extended to the manufacturing sector, despite the spectacular industrialization of recent years. On 6 February 1968, Mr G. Froneman, the Deputy Chairman of the Bantu Affairs Commission, said in the South African Parliament:

'We are trying to introduce the migrant labour pattern as far as possible in every sphere. This is in fact the entire basis of our policy as far as the white economy is concerned, namely a system of migrant labour.'

As there are two ways of life, one for whites and another for blacks, so there are two labour codes. African workers are not allowed to engage in collective bargaining through the industrial council system, like other workers. The Government is firmly opposed to union membership for African workers; they are barred from joining any registered union and any trade union formed by them is denied legal status and recognition. Disputes between African workers and their employers cannot be resolved between them but must be settled by Government officials. Since the last century every African has been bound by the Master and Servant Laws which make it a criminal offence to be absent from work without lawful cause, to refuse to obey a lawful command, or to try to change one's job before one's contract expires. Strikes by African workers are prohibited under heavy penalties. When 3,000 dock-workers in Durban struck for higher pay in April 1969, armed police moved in, and the employers sacked all the strikers. The authorities gave them *four hours* to get out of Durban. After screening, 450 were given their jobs back but most of the rest lost them, together with their homes and any chance of further work.

Another aspect of the two distinct labour codes is that there is a colour bar in employment. It has its origins in the early days of gold- and diamond-mining. The Mines and Works Act of 1911 which denied skilled jobs in the mines to Africans was the only statutory colour bar until 1951. In that year the Nationalist Government imposed a colour bar in the building industry, closing skilled work to Africans in the urban areas. In 1956 the Minister of Labour was empowered to prohibit anyone from doing a particular job on account of his race. This was described as a 'safeguard against inter-racial competition'. Up to 1971, twenty-six colour bar determinations have been made (two of them were suspended, when employers and the white unions agreed to observe a colour bar independently of the law). But the number of workers affected by these determinations remains small; only 2·99 per cent of the labour force by 1969.

The reason for the limited application of the 'safeguard' is that employers and trade unions usually agree to operate white closed shops anyway. A similar *de facto*, not *de jure* colour bar keeps Africans out of the running for apprenticeships. Although no law denies them the right to training in the skilled trades, Africans are barred from it by an unwritten law observed by employers and white trade unions.

In the matter of wages for African workers, a host of obstacles is put in the way of collective organizing and negotiation. Neither the law nor the white trade unions, strong as they are, could prevent employers from paying Africans higher wages. There is, however, no stampede to do so. (Some white trade unionists, though not the majority, argue in favour of paying the rate for the job regardless of colour, on the grounds that this is the only way to protect white workers in the long run from being undercut by Africans.) In fact, in industry after industry, the wages paid to Africans are below a conservatively estimated poverty line calculated by the Association of Chambers of Commerce (ASSCOM) at the end of 1970 on the basis of a budget for an African family of five in Johannesburg. ASSCOM estimated that to maintain a minimum standard of living, the family would need a monthly income of £37·76 (R73·64).[3] The Association appealed to its members to review their wage scales immediately, but, timely though the appeal was, it had little effect. Some two-thirds of the families in Soweto, the big African township outside Johannesburg, were estimated to be below the poverty line. Average earnings for Africans in manufacturing in March 1971 were £29 a month, only three-quarters of ASSCOM's £37·76. Another study by Professor H. L. Watts, Director of the Institute for Social

Research at the University of Natal, calculated that ASSCOM's budget was unrealistically low and the poverty line for a family of five should be raised by 50 per cent.[4]

Denied the right to take part in collective bargaining, Africans find their wages fixed for them in one of three ways: by the Minister of Labour on a recommendation of the Wages Board; through procedures provided in the Industrial Conciliation Act; or directly by employers. None of these systems is favourable to Africans. Between 1968 and 1970 the Minister of Labour announced twenty-nine determinations made by the Wages Board, all of which applied mainly to blacks. Not one prescribed a weekly wage as high as £9, the minimum needed to reach the poverty line; in nineteen of the twenty-nine cases the minimum weekly wages for African labourers in some areas was fixed at less than £3; not one of them prescribed a weekly wage of £6 for labourers or several other categories of African workers – £6 being the minimum needed by Africans to qualify for protection under the Unemployment Insurance Act:[5] below this level, Africans are left without insurance,* and if they lose their jobs are without income.

Africans fare little better under the Industrial Council system. Nearly half a million Africans have their wages fixed by the arbitrary agreement of employers with white unions. In 1970 twenty-one industrial council agreements were published. The average rate fixed for labourers was £5. Employers sometimes argue that these figures are irrelevant since most firms pay Africans (and indeed whites) above the minimum agreed. The table on p. 48 shows average *earnings* in March 1971; these indicate that in manufacturing and construction the average is below the poverty line.

The worst example of exploitation is found in the mines

* In April 1971 Professor J. L. Sadie, of the Department of Economics at Stellenbosch, calculated that 1,294,500 people were out of work. According to the Department of Labour the average number of white, Coloured, and Asian registered unemployed was only 8,489: so roughly one in four economically active Africans is out of work.

TOTAL NUMBER OF EMPLOYED AND AVERAGE MONTHLY EARNINGS IN SELECTED JOBS, BY RACE, MARCH 1971 (EARNINGS IN POUNDS STERLING)

	Africans: Number employed	Average earnings	Whites: Number employed	Average earnings	Coloureds: Number employed	Average earnings	Asians: Number employed	Average earnings
Mining and quarrying	592,819	9.48	61,782	195.82	6,352	41.90	578	51.46
Manufacture	644,900	29.16	279,700	170.81	201,300	41.16	76,500	43.58
Construction	270,000	28.03	60,800	178.10	47,200	61.74	5,300	79.92
Electricity	14,900	31.94	8,400	185.53	600	41.88	(less than 50)	–
Banking	5,183	94.92	44,551	381.12	1,280	107.77	296	173.25
Building societies	1,429	86.44	8,043	384.34	226	152.03	91	169.06
Universities	4,325	81.45	11,312	489.72	1,471	139.80	338	186.62

Source: Republic of South Africa, Department of Statistics, *Statistical News Releases*, 16 June 1971, 18 June 1971, 13 September 1971.

where average weekly earnings, as the table shows, are less than £2·50. Dr Francis Wilson, a lecturer in the Department of Economics at Cape Town University, studied the wage situation in gold-mining and found that in real terms the cash wages paid to Africans are no higher and possibly even lower than they were in 1911.[6]

AVERAGE ANNUAL CASH EARNINGS IN THE GOLD-MINES

	Whites	Blacks	Whites	Blacks
	current rands		1938 rands	
1911	665.8	57.0	850.0	72.0
1966	3,215.9	182.8	1,241.0	71.0

The mine-owners argue that, as well as their cash wages, Africans get food and lodging and free medical treatment. But the housing consists of walled compounds, the beds are concrete bunks, and married men are separated from their wives and children, and prohibited by law from setting up home outside the compound. The food costs the mine-owners about 9p a day.[7]

Gold-mining at deep levels is one of the most dangerous jobs in the world. In spite of substantial safety measures accidents are frequent. In 1966 762 miners died, most of them in the Orange Free State and the Witwatersrand, where 34 whites and 551 Africans were killed, and 1,903 whites and 24,288 Africans were injured.

Other forms of mining have similarly high injury rates. In the mines of Cape Asbestos 1,309 workers out of a labour force of 9,100 have had to leave their jobs in the last five years after contracting pneumoconiosis, a disease like severe asthma. Of these 27 died. The average monthly wage (excluding food) at the mines is £8·50.[8] Cape Asbestos is 60-per-cent owned by Charter Consolidated, a London-based finance and investment house whose largest single shareholder is Harry Oppenheimer. Chapter 9 deals in more detail with the wages paid in his mines.

African real wages have consistently lagged behind increases in productivity. Mr Harry Goldberg, the President of Bantu Wages and Productivity Association, has stated that in the period 1957–62 the physical output of the African industrial labour force rose by 30 per cent.[9] A more recent study concluded that 'only white wage movements have been inflationary in the sense that they have exceeded the growth in productivity. Black wages, on the other hand, have in many years failed to reach the productivity growth line and have exceeded it not at all.'[10] Rising African productivity, therefore, brings benefits not to Africans but to white wages and corporation profits.

Taking average African incomes over all, the evidence is that these have declined in recent years. It has been calculated that the total income of wage-earners and peasants in 1970 was 801 million pounds compared with 497 millions in 1958. This is an increase in money terms of 61 per cent, and in real terms of about 20 per cent. However, during the same period the African population has risen by 40 per cent.[11] So, *per capita* incomes have fallen. The *Financial Mail* reported that the *per capita* figure for African workers was £4·12 a month in 1969; average white income per head was £55·88 a month.[12]

The absymally low figure for Africans suggests that conditions in the 'homelands' must be barely enough for subsistence. The last major Government study of these areas, the 1954 Tomlinson Commission, reported that they were capable of supporting 2·1 million people at subsistence level. It estimated that by 1980, with agricultural modernization and the creation of one and a quarter million new jobs outside agriculture, the reserves could support seven million people, so, by inference, by 1970 the tolerable figure would be five millions. But there are already one million more people than that in the 'homelands' and the Commission's predictions about an increase in jobs have come nowhere near to being met. In fact, only 70,000 new jobs have been created. On the Commission's assumptions, this means that there are now approximately two million more Africans in the 'homelands' than they can support even at bare subsistence.

The obvious consequence is starvation. By 1960 a UNESCO report was already quoting surveys showing that sixty to seventy per cent of African children suffered from malnutrition.[13] Two years later the South African Institute of Race Relations referred to findings that four out of every five unskilled labourers in the urban areas showed signs of undernourishment, caused by lack of food in the first years of their lives. Even in Soweto, where average African incomes are probably higher than anywhere else in South Africa, the daily consumption of milk per person is only half an ounce.[14]

It is impossible to find accurate statistics for the number of Africans suffering from malnutrition: if South African society were interested in collecting statistics on such matters, it might also be doing something about the problem. In fact, nothing is being done. But, then, of course, in 1970 Mr M. C. Botha the Minister of Bantu Administration, claimed that 'there is not one starving African in South Africa . . . the Nationalist Party would not allow it.'[15]

However, even without complete statistics, the general picture can be seen. Two of the most frequent symptoms of malnutrition and protein deficiency are kwashiorkor and gastro-enteritis. Often they interact and are referred to as a single complaint – protein–calorie malnutrition (PCM) and about 40,000 cases of this are treated annually in South Africa. Most of them are children. The Department of Paediatrics at Cape Town University recently estimated that for every case of PCM which is attended to by doctors, approximately forty others are never reported or seen.

Doctors are almost powerless in the face of such a problem. In Cape Town, medical facilities for Africans were worse in 1971 than they were ten years before, according to Dr Stewart Truswell, a lecturer at Groote Schuur, the hospital made famous by Dr Christian Barnard's expensive heart transplants.[16] 'It is well known', Dr Truswell says, 'that patients come into the non-white wards of our Cape Town hospitals with more serious and advanced forms of illness and disease like tuberculosis and malnutrition which are rarely seen in white patients.' There were only seven convalescent beds for Africans in the entire Cape Town area in 1971. Africans in South Africa are ten times more prone than whites to tuberculosis. Much illness could be prevented by a relatively small outlay of money: for example, taking a third of a pint of milk a day (at a cost to the State of some 40 pence a month) could forestall kwashiorkor.[17] The money is not forthcoming.

Scientific work on the effects of prolonged malnutrition in children has shown that it can lead to mental retardation. A child born to an undernourished mother is likely never to develop fully. Kwashiorkor can cause irreparable brain damage: because the brain cells grow fastest in the first two years of life, adequate food is particularly essential then. Many children do not survive. Two doctors who conducted extensive research in one African reserve, Sekhukuniland, concluded that half the children born did not reach the age of five.[18] In the Transkei 40 per cent of the children die before the age of ten.[19] And the situation is scarcely any better in or near towns; for example, in 1969 the Medical Officer of Health for Port Elizabeth reported that one of every three African babies died before their first birthday. The infant mortality rate there was fifteen times higher than that for white babies. In Durban the rate is somewhat lower: 10 per cent of babies die in the first year, a rate five and a half times higher than that for whites. These children are not dying miles away from white society in the 'homelands': they are babies whose fathers may well be working for foreign companies in the most industrialized parts of South Africa.

These and similar data have led one highly qualified observer, Professor John Reid, Professor of Physiology at the University of Natal, to the conclusion that, as regards

malnutrition and child mortality rates, the position in South
Africa is as bad as or worse than in many other countries with
a lower *per capita* income. It is because of apartheid that
malnutrition is more widespread in South Africa than it
might otherwise be. The South African Government glosses
over this point with the argument that Africans in South
Africa at least have a higher income than Africans in independent Africa to the north, but the argument is irrelevant:
poverty has to be judged by the resources available to a
country and by the way its wealth is shared, rather than by
what its neighbours may be doing or failing to do.

GROSS DOMESTIC PRODUCT *PER CAPITA* (AT CURRENT
MARKET PRICES) IN SELECTED AFRICAN COUNTRIES IN
1968 (IN US DOLLARS)

Zambia	345	Cameroon	175
Ivory Coast	317	Mauretania	175
Liberia	312	Gambia	151
Ghana	288	Central African	
Mauritius	277	Republic	128
Senegal	266	Kenya	127
Congo (People's		South Africa:	
Republic)	215	Africans*	118
Swaziland	201	Whites*	1717
Sierra Leone	177		

Financial Mail, Johannesburg, 18 April, 1969.

Source: *UN Survey of Economic Conditions in Africa,* Part 1, 1971.

Even at its face value, the Government's claim is of very
doubtful validity. The average African income in South
Africa was about £50 in 1959.[20] As the table above shows,
there are a dozen independent African countries south of
the Sahara which have higher figures than that. Income
data can, of course, only be approximate for countries where
statistics are inadequate. The table shows figures for Gross

Domestic Product *per capita* – a measure not completely equivalent to *per capita* income. It could not be used accurately to compare highly urbanized industrial countries with peasant economies, but for the African countries in the Table, which, apart from Zambia, have no significant white expatriate group and no wide divergence of incomes, the measure is an acceptable one. Even if one accepts the South Africans' propaganda figure for African incomes, their claim that Africans are better off in the Republic is seen to be invalid. In a *Reader's Digest* article written after a sponsored visit to South Africa (paid for by the South Africa Foundation), Selwyn Lloyd, a former Conservative Foreign Secretary, said that the average African income was 210 dollars a year and claimed that 'the Bantu enjoy the highest standard of living in Africa.'[21] The table shows the figure bettered by seven independent States. (Mr Selwyn Lloyd's article was published in September 1970, but the position of African incomes is highly unlikely to have altered significantly between 1968/9 and 1970.)

Bald comparisons between countries in money terms may conceal real differences in standards of welfare. The more town-dwellers and wage-earners a country has, the higher their incomes must be to pay for rent and transport, and for the packaging and distribution of food, which subsistence farmers have 'free'. South Africa has the highest proportion of wage-earners (thirty per cent) on the continent. Zambia, with ten per cent, is the only country that comes near this. In welfare terms South Africa's income figure is therefore overstated. Africans in South Africa are living no better than Africans with an average income in the countries in the lower half of the Table.

South Africa devotes a smaller proportion of its national income to African education than almost any other African State, as the table on p. 55 shows, and that proportion is lower now than it was in 1953. A memorandum prepared by the South African Institute of Race Relations shows how

much it has gone down since the Bantu Education Act was
applied in 1955.[22]

	Percentage		Percentage
1953–1954	0·57	1961–1962	0·42
1958–1959	0·49	1963–1964	0·39

Since 1963 figures cannot be calculated on the same basis as
before because education in the Transkei is treated separately, but the following amounts were given in the House of
Assembly in 1971 by the Minister:

1968–1969	R40,864,000
1969–1970	R48,649,850
1970–1971	R58,881,000

As a percentage of national income this works out approximately as: 1968 – 0·42 per cent, 1969 – 0·45 per cent, and
1970 – 0·49 per cent.

EXPENDITURE ON EDUCATION AS A PERCENTAGE OF NATIONAL INCOME

Ivory Coast	6.5 (1962)	Liberia	3.4 (1964)
Zaire	5.3 (1964)	Senegal	3.2 (1964)
Uganda	5.2 (1964)	Zambia	3.2 (1962)
Kenya	5.1 (1962)	(Africans	
Tanzania	4.5 (1962)	only)	
Ghana	4.1 (1964)	Gabon	2.9 (1962)
Mauretania	4.1 (1961)	South Africa	0.39 (1963-4)*
Malawi	3.9 (1960)	(Africans only)	

Objective Justice, Vol.3, No. 3, July-Sept 1971 p.31, published by
the UN.

Source: *UN Compendium of Social Statistics,* 1967, p.380 (latest
issue available).

The purpose of the Bantu Education Act as Dr Verwoerd, then Minister of Native Affairs put it, was to ensure 'that Natives will be taught from childhood to realize that equality with Europeans is not for them'. Race relations 'cannot improve if the result of Native education is the creation of a frustrated people who have expectations in life which circumstances in South Africa do not allow them to fulfill'. The Government accordingly set up a different (and inferior) syllabus for Africans. Schooling for whites is free of charge and compulsory. For Africans it is neither. In 1970 the State spent £117 on each white child's education, and £10 on the education for each African.[23]

In the political field restrictions have continually been tightened. African Nationalist Parties are banned. Multi-racial political parties are illegal. Throughout the 1950s and 1960s the Government extended its repressive legislation to outlaw all forms of political activity. In 1950 the Suppression of Communism Act defined a Communist as anyone the Government defines as a Communist: 'If you were a Communist forty years ago,' as Lord Gardiner, the former Lord Chancellor put it, 'you are a Communist today . . . whether you are a Communist or not, you are a Communist if the State says so.'

In 1953 the Criminal Law Amendment Act provided for a sentence of three years and a whipping for any offence, however minor, 'committed by way of protest or in support of any campaign . . . for the repeal or modification of any law'. Nine years later the Sabotage Act made it an offence punishable by death to contravene any law and 'enter upon any land or building to further or encourage the achievement of any political aim, including the bringing about of any social or economic change in the Republic'. Under the Terrorism Act of 1967, death by hanging may await anyone convicted of performing any act 'likely to have had the result of embarrassing the administration of the affairs of the State'.

Both the Sabotage Act and the Terrorism Act shifted the burden of proof to the accused. The Terrorism Act provides for indefinite detention without trial. A detainee can be held incommunicado, in solitary confinement and with no access to family, friends or legal representation.

Neil Wates has said that 'the climate [in South Africa] is designed to demoralize and maintain an industrial helotry. . . . 'There is virtually no communication between the races . . . the rule of law has been abolished . . . all the ingredients are there for a legal reign of terror within the country.'[24] Since he said this, in August 1970, the police have made the largest swoop in the country's history, searching more than a hundred people of all races in one night, the Dean of Johannesburg was sentenced to five years' imprisonment (the sentence was subsequently set aside by the South African Supreme Court in April 1972), and yet another political detainee, Ahmed Timol, has died in mysterious circumstances while in the hands of the security police.

Over the years the ever-increasing political repression has been well publicized. Yet, surprisingly, in spite of the background of terror and the Government's manifest contempt for African interests, the claims of South African propaganda, that economic progress is benefiting all races, have often gone unchallenged. The truth is that South Africa must be one of the few countries in the world – perhaps the only one – where the majority of the population has become poorer during the last decade. Africans in South Africa are not only worse off now, by comparision with whites, than they were ten years ago: they are worse off by comparison with their own standard of living ten years ago. And this development has occurred in spite of boom conditions in the economy and a growth rate at constant prices of roughly 6 per cent per annum. It has also happened during a period of rapid urbanization. This state of affairs is paradoxical for how can an economy which, by all the usual criteria – rapid industrialization, fast growth, urban development – must have passed the point of take-off, in fact be going backwards as far as the majority of people is concerned? And what has happened to the business argument that behind-the-scenes investment is pushing for reform?

4 The Floating Colour Bar

> Smuts's original policy was political separate
> development combined with economic integration.
> The signs are that South Africa is moving towards
> that concept faster than at any time since 1948.
> Give it a chance! – *Sir Colin Coote in the* Daily
> Telegraph, *15 April 1971*

Inevitably and irreversibly, the pressures of economic
growth and the requirements of a sophisticated industrial
society are undermining apartheid. So goes the refrain to
be heard increasingly loudly in the 'corridors of power'
in the Western world. Heckled by shareholders at annual
general meetings, company chairmen argue that they are
being misunderstood: they are acting as agents of peaceful
change in South Africa. Politicians plead for gradualism,
and for critics to be patient. Apartheid will die of attrition
beneath the weight of economic logic. In the space between
the advertisements in the supplements on South Africa in the
'quality' press, the editorial copy rams the message home.

At his meeting with President Kaunda of Zambia over the
British sale of arms to South Africa, Mr Heath is reported to
have used the same argument. To show how internal forces
were eroding apartheid, the Prime Minister referred to a
briefing about a recent congress of Afrikaner businessmen,
who had recognized that, within two years there would be a
shortage of 65,000 skilled white workers but a surplus of
98,000 black ones. Train them and the country could avoid
a grave lack of labour and a serious brake on its future
expansion. The moral of Mr Heath's story was that even
Afrikaners now see that continuing economic growth
requires a relaxation of the absurd apartheid labour laws: the

59

Nationalist Party itself is at last becoming aware of the economic facts of life.

For Britain and other foreign countries the inference is clear and attractive. The more you invest in South Africa, the more you undermine apartheid from within. Profit and principle go hand in hand. There is no need for pressure against South Africa from outside. Conversely, those who argue for a boycott of trade or a withdrawal of investment are only strengthening the irrationality of the present system.

The evidence for the 'peaceful change' theory rests mainly on two factors: South Africa's need for more semi-skilled and skilled workers, and for an expanding internal market. Only the Africans, the argument goes, can supply the solution. In the early days, when a large section of the white population still lived on farms, employers could always fill their vacancies with 'poor whites' moving into the cities, and for additional labour, the country could call on white immigrants from abroad. Now both these sources are inadequate for the rate of expansion which South Africa needs to sustain. The white community has become largely an urban one, and immigration, even though it is now at a record level, is insufficient. A long-term prediction by the Prime Minister's Economic Advisory Council revealed that if the economy continues to grow at an annual rate of 5·8 per cent (the rate achieved between 1965 and 1969), by 1980 South Africa will be short of half a million skilled workers.[1]

As for the internal market, the argument is that South Africa's economy is now more and more an industrial one, based on the manufacturing sector rather than on mining. If it is to sustain the current momentum, it must find outlets for its products. At the moment, because of low wages, Africans are producers but not consumers. A controlled policy of raising African wages is essential to allow Africans to create the internal demand for goods without which the economy will stagnate. A larger market would also give

60

industry the chance of obtaining economies of scale from mass production.

If this is the theory, the evidence must be there to back it up. Those who are looking for it claim now to have found it. More and more businessmen are demanding exemptions from the job-reservation provisions which prevent them from hiring African workers. White trade unions are agreeing to drop the colour bar and accept Africans into previously all-white jobs. It is said that wages for Africans are being increased. A few industrialists and trade union leaders have even started to call for a policy of equal pay for equal work, regardless of race.

At a political level, the debate within the Nationalist Party over the future of apartheid is said to have reached a new pitch. The most conservative elements within the Afrikaner community, the so-called '*verkrampte*', formed a breakaway party at the last election and were soundly beaten. The Government is now prepared to sit down with black political leaders from neighbouring African states and from the Bantustans inside South Africa. The erosion of apartheid from within seems, it is said, to be taking on the dimensions of a landslide.

How significant are these changes, and do they really weaken apartheid? In spite of the existence of a colour bar in law and in practice, Africans have always been allowed to filter into some semi-skilled and even skilled and white-collar jobs – though nearly always at lower wages than those which would be paid to whites. Sometimes this promotion has been in violation of the law. Sometimes the Government has acquiesced, however hypocritically. In Maritzburg, for example, African workers on a housing project were allowed to use garden trowels to lay bricks (with the full knowledge of the Department of Labour) because if they had used builders' trowels, it would have counted as skilled work, and that is reserved for white bricklayers.

In 1956 the Government made a sweeping amendment

61

to the Industrial Conciliation Act, empowering the Ministry of Labour to extend the colour bar to any branch of any industry. The move was intended to protect the white working class and guarantee it full employment in each industrial sector. Significantly, as Legassick[2] has pointed out, although the legislation extended the colour bar, it was much less specific than the legislation for a mining colour bar, passed in 1911 and reinforced in 1926. This showed that the Government recognized that with growing industrialization the economy needed the flexibility to 'recognize the level at which the white/non-white divide should come'. Given the small white work-force, and an expanding economy, too rigid a demarcation would rapidly produce shortages in the white sector. To counteract this, jobs have been reclassified in recent years in a gradual readjustment, 'at first covert but now more openly espoused, so that white workers move upwards into more skilled or supervisory posts while the jobs they vacate are "diluted" into a large number of less skilled tasks and are filled by non-white workers at lower wages. . . .'[3]

The process has given rise to occasional tensions between employers and the Government: the former complain of white labour shortages and inflated white wages and the latter takes its time about accepting the reclassifications. But these are minor frictions. Reclassification of jobs is understood by both sides to be a way of shifting the colour bar as economic conditions change: Africans move into more jobs – and more skilled jobs – and may receive marginally higher wages, but the whites move even further upwards.

Legassick argues that the heart of the system of racial discrimination is 'the state's role in regulating the non-white labour force, the inhibitions on African bargaining power, and the differential access to education. So long as these institutions exist, the gap between white and non-white wages even in manufacturing industry is likely to increase.

And, even more starkly, the gap between white prosperity and the declining real wages, malnutrition, poverty, and starvation of Africans on the mines, on white farms and in the reserves will grow apace: growing development under the forced labour economy producing growing under-development.'[4]

Legassick concludes that an attempt to pay equal wages for equal work, as one or two American and British companies have now promised to do, will, in the present over-all framework of apartheid, simply produce greater mechanization and fewer employees – with blacks rather than whites being dismissed first.

This gradual shifting of the colour bar is an old factor in the South African economy. It has not been a threat to the whites because the number of skilled jobs of an administrative and technical nature has been increasing, and the whites continue to control these new high-status jobs. Wolpe[5] has argued from these data that the requirements of the South

WHITE AND AFRICANS IN VARIOUS OCCUPATIONS (EXCLUDING FARMING) AS A PERCENTAGE OF THE ECONOMICALLY ACTIVE POPULATION OF EACH RACE GROUP

Occupation	1921		1936		1946		1951		1960	
	W	A	W	A	W	A	W	A	W	A
I–IV	31.3	0.8	33.1	0.9	38.4	1.9	44.4	1.9	49.4	2.4
VI–VIII	6.2	28.3	6.5	24.6	14.0	28.0	19.3	35.9	29.0	43.9
IX	7.3	33.1	8.8	33.2	18.0	36.0	14.6	27.1	16.5	25.0

I–IV Professions, technical, managerial, administrative, executive, clerical, and sales
VI–VIII Miners, transport workers, unskilled and skilled industrial workers
IX Service, sports, entertainment, etc.

Source: Adapted from the 1960 South African Census (calculated by H. Wolpe[5]).

African economy are changing so that, instead of needing a cheap, unskilled black labour force, its demand now is for a substantial section of this force to provide cheap semi-skilled and skilled labour. In other words, the levels of skill change, but the cheapness remains. In the 1960s, as industrialization gathered pace, the moving of blacks into more skilled jobs probably increased at a faster rate than before. But this conclusion can only be shown piecemeal (see p. 63) since the May 1970 Census figures on occupations have not yet been published.

The test of any lessening of the colour bar would be a narrowing of the wage gap between black and white. In 1968 the 13,000,000 Africans constituted 67·9 per cent of the population but received only 18·8 per cent of the nation's cash income; whites, who made up only 19·2 per cent of the population, received 73·3 per cent.[6] Yet if that gulf seems wide, it has become wider since 1968, and is still growing.

The most spectacular differentials are to be found in the mines, where the ratio of white to black wages was 11·7 to 1 in 1911, had reached 17·6 to 1 by 1966, and by early 1971 was 20·3 to 1. In manufacturing over the decade 1957–67, according to a study published in the *Rand Daily Mail*,[7] the difference between average white and African wages increased from R120 to R194 a month:

	1957	1967	Percentage increase
Whites	R146 (£75)	R238 (£122)	61·4
Africans	R26 (£13·34)	R44 (£22·56)	59·0

The author of this survey pointed out that to prevent the gap from widening further, the percentage of future pay increases for Africans would have to be five and a half times greater than that for whites. In fact, the gap continued to grow. By 1969 average white earnings had gone up by 19 per cent in 1967 while African earnings were only up by 13·6 per cent.[8]

By March 1971 the ratio of white to African earnings in manufacturing had risen to 5·85 to 1 compared with 5·1 to 1 in May 1966. In spite of some cash wage increases, African real earnings in the urban areas declined substantially because of the sharp increases in inflation and the cost of living. The average (percentage) increase in African incomes per head between 1948 and 1970 was just under 5 per cent, almost identical with the rate of increase in the African cost of living over the same period, but if the increasing number of wage-earners per household is taken into account, the trend appears to have been adverse.[9] Over the boom years of South Africa's development the expansion of the economy and of white profits has thus been financed in part by the Africans through a fall in real wages. The traditional and ever-widening gap between white and black income has not altered.

At least three sets of mechanisms have been devised to filter Africans into jobs formerly closed to them, without undermining the status of white workers. All three rest on the principle of cutting costs and paying Africans less for work that would otherwise be done by whites. The first method is simply to promote a white man and hire an African to do his job, usually changing the job's name in the process. The second consists of the 'dilution' or 'fragmenta-tion' of skilled jobs and the redefinition of work processes in industrial agreements. This means, for example, that a job in which one white man previously performed a range of operations will be subdivided with the white man retaining the most skilled (and best paid) part while the less intricate parts are given to semi-skilled Africans at lower pay. The third mechanism is the creation of 'border areas' near the African 'homelands' to which industrialists are encouraged to move their plants. The incentive here is the availability of an even greater reserve of cheap labour, and the opportunity to pay lower wages than in the urban areas.

Since the impetus behind the changes comes from employers worried by the shortage of labour and constantly on the lookout for ways of cutting wage costs, it is not surprising that white workers are encouraged to see African workers, not as allies in the industrial struggle, but as a threat to their own jobs. Paradoxically, perhaps, the leadership of the Trade Union Council of South Africa (TUCSA), from which Africans are barred, has argued in favour of equal pay for equal work. The contention is that this will prevent Africans from undercutting whites and will better preserve jobs for whites, for whom, in any case, the discriminatory educational system will ensure the best positions.

LESS PAY FOR EQUAL WORK

A policy of equal pay for equal work goes against employers' traditional practice, especially in an economic system founded on the exploitation of cheap labour. Employers have therefore sought to replace white workers with lower-paid Africans while reassuring the whites that the scheme can allow 'everyone to take one step up the ladder', as Mr Vic Robinson, the chief technical adviser to the Chamber of Mines, has put it. Mr Harry Oppenheimer, the chairman of the Anglo American Corporation, and one of the best-known advocates of a wider use of African labour, has called it 'floating up'. In June 1970 he said it should be understood that if the white man was replaced, it meant that he would be free to do more interesting and higher paid work: 'We are in the position that we can maintain this system and allow the whole structure to float upwards so that everybody benefits.'

'Everybody benefits', but, as we have said, some benefit more than others. The advantage which this system offers for employers can best be illustrated from AE & CI, South Africa's second largest industrial company, which is also chaired by Mr Oppenheimer. In January 1971 the company negotiated an agreement with its 1,800 white workers to give them an average ten per cent pay rise in return for a relaxation of some of the barriers against black workers. In addition, white workers received an increased holiday bonus, and long-service increments. By using more lower-paid Africans, the company stood to benefit substantially. The Johannesburg *Sunday Times* reported that the scheme was a follow-up to a similar one brought in in 1967, which gave the factories a 25 per cent increase in production 'without increasing the total wage bill'.[10]

On an industry-wide basis, the Bantu Wage and Productivity Association discovered, after a comprehensive survey, that as a result of the substitution of Africans for whites in 1970 productivity had gone up by 20 per cent. Describing the survey in an article in 'Commercial Opinion', the Association's President, Mr W. L. Campbell-Pitt discussed a particular firm where this had happened: 'This change was made after full consultation. No white operator lost his job – they were upgraded and transferred to other departments.'[11]

In other industries some white workers have lost their jobs. In June 1967 the Minister of Labour authorized the employment of Coloureds in various categories of work in the distributive trades. His change of policy merely ratified a situation in which employers were already illegally using black labour, allegedly because whites were unavailable. But in welcoming the Minister's decision, the President of the National Union of Distributive Workers declared that, in spite of the Minister's condition that no white workers should be displaced by Coloureds, this was actually happening. The reason, he said, was that Coloureds were being employed at lower rates of pay than whites for the same job.[12]

A similar complaint was made in the electrical engineering industry, where Coloured workers were given white jobs at lower rates of pay. Mr R. Cowley, the General Secretary of the South African Electrical Workers Association complained that the number of white women in the trade had dropped by 1,000 in two years. Even though white women were available, they were being told 'Sorry, no vacancies', he said.

In other parts of the engineering industry a slightly better-disguised form of cost-cutting has operated. Since 1967 the Government has accepted an Industrial Council agreement whereby skilled jobs in the industry are reserved for employees eligible to join unions recognized under the Industrial Conciliation Act of 1956. This excluded African workers but allowed Coloured and Indian workers, in addition to whites, to join. As a result, a growing number of Coloureds and Indians have been recruited into skilled jobs. Employers pay them the statutory minimum wage. There is nothing apparently wrong in that, except that, as TUCSA's Natal Organizer pointed out, whites doing the job previously were getting well *above* the minimum. In an article in the *Rand Daily Mail*, one of TUCSA's officials, Mr Derek Smith, wrote: 'There is hardly a white in commerce or industry today being paid the rates laid down. The actual figure in many cases is double the official rate and the gap is still widening.'[13]

The building industry, with its large number of fiercely competitive, small firms has, as one might expect, produced a whole maze of cost-cutting. Spot checks have revealed that hundreds of Africans employed as labourers are doing semi-skilled and skilled work reserved by law for whites, and doing it at lower rates of pay.

Discrimination in the building industry is laid down by two sets of legislation. One is the Bantu Building Workers Act (No. 27 of 1951) which prohibits Africans from doing skilled work in 'white' areas and limits their employment to African townships and reserves. Their wages are determined by the Minister of Labour, and not by negotiation with employers. The best they can hope for is about one-third of the earnings of white artisans.

Two job reservation determinations apply to the building industry in the urban areas of the Transvaal and Orange Free State, and in the whole of the Cape Province and Natal, to keep out other black groups. But as the economy expanded, white workers began to be more choosy about working in the building industry, particularly in the 'wet trades', bricklaying and plastering. By 1970 Africans constituted 69·4 per cent of the labour force in the industry, and Asians and Coloureds 13·9 per cent. In spite of a campaign to bring in white immigrants (between 1965–69 the country took in 11,570 white immigrant building workers), the proportion of white workers in the industry had dropped to 16·7 per cent in 1970, compared with 25·2 per cent in 1945.

The Ministry of Labour started to grant occasional exemptions to allow employers to take on blacks in semi-skilled and skilled work. Some of these exemptions produced farcical distinctions. Africans in the Transvaal were allowed to apply first coats of paint, though not the second or third. And always, to preserve the status of the white jobs, the Africans were given different titles. Painters became 'painting operatives', plasterers were 'plastering operatives', and so on. Then in February 1971 the Minister gave permission for employers on the Witwatersrand and in Pretoria to hire Coloured bricklayers and plasterers. (As usual, this was not a general change in policy: employers still had to make individual applications which the Ministry would consider on merit.) The result again was that some employers used the exemption to cut costs at the same time. Coloureds were given the area minimum of R1·19 (61p) an hour, which whites refused to work for.[14]

In September 1971 the Minister made a new exemption, this time for Africans, who were allowed in Maritzburg and parts of the Natal Midlands to work on plumbing, painting, blocklaying and carpentry jobs. A new category of 'building assistant' was created, subdivided into Class One and Class Two ratings. The two classes were to get 46 cents (23½p) and

37 cents (19p) an hour for doing work for which artisans were previously paid R1·02 (52p) an hour. As a reward for allowing Africans to come in beneath them, white artisans had their basic minimum raised to R1·10½ (56½p) an hour, i.e. more than double the Africans' pay.[15] Naturally the building employers reacted to these various exemptions with jubilation: when the bar on Coloured bricklayers was lifted, a spokesman for one big Johannesburg company told a reporter: 'This is great news. This decision will stabilize spiralling costs and wages.'[16]

The Government and local authorities have benefited from the policy of less pay for equal work. The fate of blacks in the Post Office has produced a revealing cycle. Like other Government departments, the Post Office has always kept blacks to a minimum and only employed them in menial jobs. Soon after the Nationalists took over in 1948, under a scheme to restore 'a civilized labour policy', 1,290 Africans were replaced by whites, at much higher rates of pay. But by the mid-1960s a shortage of white labour and rising costs forced a reversal. Africans were taken on, first only for tele-graph deliveries, and then a little later as postmen, although officially only 'on a temporary basis'. Once again the wage rate dropped.

On the railways during 1971 the Government's attempts to bring in more black workers produced a near-crisis with the white unions. The Railways Administration wanted 'to promote whites to better paid and more responsible work and to fill in at the bottom of the labour scale with non-white workers'. That move was only the latest one in a series which had started several years before. By 1970, 30,500 Africans had been trained to handle harbour cargo, to do maintenance work in the mechanical workshops, and work as booking clerks and barrier attendants (serving black passengers, of course). The Minister of Transport had made it clear in 1968 that 'with the approval of staff and on condi-tion that the wages, status, and standards of living of the whites are protected, I am already employing non-whites in work previously done by whites.'

For the whites the reward was generous: in May 1970 white railway artisans received increases of up to 24 per cent for conceding that blacks could come into jobs traditionally held by whites. The blacks worked at a lower wage.

In Randburg the Town Council employed Africans to drive municipal vehicles because of the difficulty of finding whites and because of their low productivity. Although officials were reported to estimate that African drivers' productivity was four times that of whites, they received R100 (£51) a month for work which whites had done for a minimum of R180·90 (£92·82) a month.

JOB DILUTION

Job dilution (or fragmentation) is the process enabling an employer to hire two or three Africans to do the work of one white man and still to cut costs. Where simple substitution of black workers for white workers is not possible, job dilution is being used increasingly to shift the colour bar in South African industry. In mines, in motor assembly plants, in the steel industry and on the railways, job dilution is going ahead fast.

The process is straightforward: a job previously done by a white man on his own is subdivided so that he continues to do the most skilled (and best-paid) part of the work while Africans are brought in to do the rest, By 1971, for example, the labour shortage in the State Railways had reached to the category of artisans, and the management and the Artisan Staff Association (ASA) opened negotiations to find an acceptable form of job dilution. Under a plan worked out by ASA's negotiator, J. H. Liebenberg, a new category of 'artisan assistants' was devised. It was estimated that an artisan and four assistants could in a short while do the work of 3·5 artisans.[17] Although the idea was to try to recruit white assistants in the first instance, it was soon recognized that the bulk of the assistants would be Africans. In 1970 the ratio between average annual wages for whites and Africans in the railways was $5\frac{1}{2}$:1. By bringing in four African 'assistants' to replace 2.5 white artisans, therefore, the railways stood to cut their wage costs by approximately two-thirds.

Even more flagrant was the job dilution scheme worked out in the wide-ranging iron, steel, engineering, and metallurgical industry. The industry makes almost everything from plastic cups to railway coaches and marine boilers, and employs a quarter of the total manufacturing labour force. In February 1968 a new industrial agreement was worked out between the employers and eight registered trade unions, representing the white, Coloured and Indian workers – although three out of every four workers in the industry are African, they were unrepresented. The agreement resulted in considerable pay increases for the whites, a guaranteed closed shop at the top, and a fragmentation of the skilled jobs to allow Africans to do them at a lower wage.

Work schedules were revised into ten new categories, the first four reserved for members of registered trade unions, mainly the white workers, with lower sub-divisions of these categories for Coloured workers. The last category was an unskilled grade. In the course of the revision, the semi-skilled categories were fragmented and down-graded. In return for workers' acceptance of these changes, the employers – the Steel and Engineering Industries Federation of South Africa – offered pay rises all round. At the bottom of the scale the rises were small, in any case, but as a result of down-grading some Africans got almost no increase at all: a man earning $18\frac{1}{2}$ cents ($9\frac{1}{2}$p) an hour, for example, should have received a wage of 22 cents ($11\frac{1}{2}$p) under the new schedule, but because his job was downgraded, he actually got 19 cents (10p), a rise of $\frac{1}{2}$ cent an hour. This was the common experience. In the steel industry most of the African workers (approximately 150,000) got increases of $\frac{1}{2}$ cent to

2 cents an hour. At a wage of 19 cents (10p) an hour for a 45-hour week, an African's monthly pay amounted to R37.24 (£19), which was well below the current poverty datum line of R52.32 (£27.34) a month, calculated by the Johannesburg Non-European Affairs Department for a family living in Soweto, the city's African township, at the end of 1967. At the white, high end of the scale, meanwhile, the rise was 9½ cents an hour plus new holiday bonuses and other benefits.

The effects of job fragmentation have been well described by E. H. McCann, General Secretary of the Amalgamated Engineering Union: 'This is the process whereby one part of a skilled artisan's work is given to a less skilled individual who as a result can be paid slightly more than he was receiving as a pure labourer. In this way we have helped to create a large force of semi-skilled workers whose pay is substantially less than that of skilled workers. Take two cases. . . . Those for automatic machines and the fly or manual pressing job. Automatic lathes and drilling machines are turning out work previously done by a skilled artisan paid at the rate of 86·5 cents (44p) an hour. Now the manufacturers are getting the same job done for only 22 cents (11½p) an hour.'[18]

Small wonder that after analyzing the figures in the agreement, the *Financial Mail* commented that 'the employers are playing the old South African trick of giving the White worker a leg up – on the back of the Black man.'[19]

Until 1968 the motor assembly industry, which is entirely dominated by foreign companies, was covered by a job reservation Determination (No. 16) made by the Minister of Labour. But in 1968 Ford, General Motors and Volkswagen broke away from the National Industrial Council for the industry and set up a local council. This allowed the three companies to obtain total exemption from Determination No. 16 and to make their own deals about racial quotas with the union. Far from objecting, the South African

Government prefers unions and employers to make their own racial agreements.

The employers' motives for the change were to overcome the labour shortage, and to cut costs through job fragmentation. In return for better pay, the white unions were prepared to see more use of blacks. In October 1970 the three car companies asked for a new agreement. As the *Rand Daily Mail* reported: 'The unions are demanding higher basic pay and improved fringe benefits. The employers in an effort to contain increased costs within reasonable limits are striving for a greater labour dilution.'[20]

Nowhere is there greater pressure for job fragmentation than in the gold mines. African wages in the mines have always been the lowest in any part of the South African economy, apart from agriculture. Employers have consistently tried to hold them down, and also to extend the range of jobs open to Africans, so as to replace better-paid whites by low-paid Africans.

But union resistance to the 'encroachment' of Africans has traditionally been as stubborn as employers' attempts to introduce job dilution. A statutory colour bar was laid down in the Mines and Works Act of 1911, and the mine-owners' plan to circumvent it in 1922 produced a general strike. But by 1965, after considerable (and tempting) pressure from the Chamber of Mines, the white Mine Workers' Union itself proposed a plan whereby whites would get more pay in return for delegating some of their duties to African 'boss-boys'. Together they worked out an experimental scheme which was approved by the Government Mining Engineer.

In a few selected mines, 'boss-boys' were chosen for a special course of training. On passing, they were given the extraordinary title of 'competent non-scheduled persons'. They were allowed to take charge of the transporting of unopened cases of explosives and they could set gangs to work underground although, once a shift, they would still be inspected by a white supervisor. Limited though the scheme was, it caused a split in the white union on the ground that it was the thin end of a wedge, and it had to be abandoned. Everyone reverted to his original rate of pay, at least for a time. Some weeks later white daily-paid workers got an extra 25 cents per shift.

By 1967, pressure was brought to bear again and the Federation of Mining Unions signed a productivity agreement with the Gold Producers' Committee of the Chamber of Mines; as a result, whites received an average eleven per cent rise in return for allowing Africans to drive the smaller underground locomotives and do some other previously all-white jobs.

The mine-owners have always been able to keep African wages down more easily than other employers. The mines have been allowed to get round the pass-law system; workers in rural areas may not go freely to industrial areas, but they can always, if they are fit, get to the mines simply by applying at the nearest recruiting office. Equally importantly, under the contract labour system, the mines have been given permission to use migrant labour from the rest of Southern Africa. As the gap between black mine wages and the pay offered to black industrial workers in South Africa has widened, the mines have not been able to find South African black workers so easily, and more and more workers have come in from the client States round South Africa, like Lesotho and Mozambique.

Since there is this cheap pool of labour, and since the average white pay in the mines is £205 a month compared with £10 a month for Africans, employers are still trying to replace whites by blacks wherever possible. By 1969 the proportion of Africans among the country's 400,000 gold miners was up to 90·2 per cent. In an article in *The Banker* in September 1971, Mr Graham Hatton, the Economics Editor of the *Financial Mail*, commented: 'Looking ahead, mine managements believe the only way to keep their wage

75

bills under control will be to further increase the ratio of black to white workers. Plainly with black wages so much lower than white ones, the managers are on to a good thing.' He went on to report that the next move by the managers will be to offer whites a shorter working week in exchange for more job fragmentation: 'The President of the Chamber of Mines spelt it out recently in his regular annual address: "We would now ask the white mine-worker to take a step or two up the ladder of responsibility and allow the non-white to do the same; the white man would assume a more supervisory role and would release to the non-white the remainder of the tasks he formerly carried out. As time goes on, further steps could be taken. In asking union men on the mines [i.e. whites] to agree to changes on these lines, the industry has offered to guarantee that no white employees will be retrenched as a result of such changes." ' Mr Hatton went on to say that 'Obviously, since the blacks under the proposal would be doing only part of the operations previously carried out by whites, they would not, according to the employers, need to be paid the same.'

This view is echoed by Mr Harry Oppenheimer, who is not only the largest employer of labour on the mines, but also the largest single employer in the whole of South African industry, apart from the Government itself. In the 1970 review of the Anglo American Corporation he wrote: 'Nor should it be thought that better jobs and better pay for the African majority would be bought at the expense of the European workers. On the contrary, African advancement could certainly make possible much more rapid advancement for the Europeans also.'

In the late 1960s it was sometimes argued that the gold mines are an exceptional industry, because the selling price of monetary gold was for years fixed at 35 US dollars to the ounce, and that if the world price were raised African wages could be improved. The result of the rise in the gold price in sales to Britain in 1949 from R17·3 to R24·8 per ounce, when sterling was devalued, did not bear this out. Black workers shared little of the windfall. By 1959 average white earnings per shift were 81 cents higher than in 1948, whereas black earnings were only up by 4½ cents.[21] When a rise in the gold price on the free market finally came at the end of 1970, Africans again had little benefit. In the *Financial Times* (23 February 1972), Graham Hatton reported that in 1971, when the industry earned an extra 59 million pounds in revenue because of an average price increase of $4 an ounce, the companies only gave black workers an extra 2·6 million pounds in wage increases, bringing average pay to £2·50 a week.

Mr Oppenheimer's notion of 'floating upwards' (p. 66) is now widely shared throughout South African industry: 'What the trade unions must strive for is to upgrade the white artisan to a technologist,' said the editor of *Volkshandel*, the journal of the Afrikaans Chamber of Commerce. It is already happening. Whites are moving into the professional, technical, administrative and managerial grades, and Africans are entering semi-skilled and even some clerical jobs. The change is obvious to any businessman, politician or journalist returning to South Africa after five years. But it does not mean that the colour bar is being broken down. All that is happening is that the threshold is rising. The discrimination based on colour which is intrinsic in a system of white supremacy remains – in work allocation, in work roles and, above all, in rates of pay.

THE BORDER AREAS

The border-area programme has been described as 'of major importance as the means of maintaining economic prosperity without loosening the white grip on the levers of power'.[22] Instead of African labour being channelled into the industrialized parts of the country, industry is being resited, close to the Africans.

The Government offers firms a host of inducements to go

to the border areas: tax rebates, loans from the Industrial Development Corporation, preferential water, power and rail rates, and other benefits. But the main attraction for industrialists is the opportunity to pay lower wages than in the urban areas; trade union activity is forbidden, and employers are left to pay their African workers whatever they like. Where the Government has designated as a border area a place which is already covered by national wage determinations or collective bargaining agreements, it has also immediately waived the arrangements and adjusted wages to suit employers.

The result is that African wages in the border areas are significantly lower than elsewhere. In May 1971 the General Secretary of the Garment Workers' Union complained that wages paid in some border-area clothing factories were only 29 per cent of those paid in Johannesburg.[23] In the border area of Hammarsdale a machinist earned £5·40 a week compared with £7·70 in Durban and £9 in Port Elizabeth and East London. In the Rustenburg border area of the Transvaal wages in the textile plants were 36 per cent of the rates in the major centres. The Government has also authorized wages below the statutory minimum in motor, engineering, and canvas goods factories in border areas.

Higher-paid workers in the cities have complained that the low-wage policy adopted in the border areas endangers their livelihood. In reply the Government has given assurances that it will not be applied 'in such a way that it prejudices the employment position of white workers in a white area'. In fact, it is black workers who are being affected by finding their jobs down-graded in the border areas. And urban employers are using the wage rates in these border areas to argue for and carry out, on a basis of comparison, a reduction in urban wages. Even if there were no ban on African trade unions, wages in the border areas would be likely to remain low because rural Africans face chronic unemployment in the reserves and have no freedom to seek work in the cities. They have to accept jobs on whatever basis they find them.

Foreign companies and their subsidiaries have been no less ready than their South African counterparts to take advantage of this artificially-created pool of cheap labour. The Reed Corporation of South Africa, a wholly-owned subsidiary of the British company, Reed International, has built a 4 million pound mill to make corrugated cardboard in a border area at Rosslyn. Tyre manufacturers seem particularly to favour border areas: Firestone is building a new plant at Brits in the Transvaal; Dunlop South Africa, the 70 per cent owned subsidiary of Dunlop, is building a 10·3 million pound tyre factory in another of these areas, near Ladysmith in the Orange Free State.

When Dr Verwoerd first propounded the idea of border areas, the general impression was that factories would be going up in remote rural areas near the large reserves. In practice, however, the designated border areas are adjacent to the country's smaller pockets of 'non-white' land, and these are near the white urban areas. Long-established white towns, like Durban, Newcastle and Ladysmith, now turn out to be near border areas. Anomalies arise: Pretoria is a 'border' area but nearby Johannesburg is not; East London is, but Port Elizabeth is not.

This curious situation is a good illustration of the way the theory of apartheid and the practice of industrialization, far from working against each other, complement each other to the advantage of the white minority. The Government gets its concept of border areas adopted, and industry gets its cheap labour concessions conveniently near the existing urban centres.

The whole argument that industrialization undermines apartheid rests on a simplistic vision of apartheid. The notion of a complete territorial separation between black and white races, while put forward to give a theoretical logic to South Africa's racialist policies, is recognized by

Nationalist Party spokesmen as untenable in practice. The white economy will always require black labour, even if the Government chooses to make it – or at least call it – 'migrant' labour. The suggestion that apartheid is a coherent political theory which, if it is undermined in one place by the 'logic' of industrialization, will collapse like a house of cards, to be replaced by a 'rational' economic system, is therefore wide of the mark. The example of the border areas is only one more confirmation that apartheid is an extremely flexible device for using Africans in the white economy while denying them political power. Mr Harry Oppenheimer put it well when he said: 'There is no evidence so far that economic integration has led to any improvement in political or social integration.'[24]

5 The Place of Foreign Capital

> The bigger the existing scale of investment and hence
> commitment of resources, the stronger the compul-
> sion to further investment to protect the commit-
> ment – *Ralph Horwitz in* The Political Economy of
> South Africa

Some time between 1964 and 1965 one of the most significant
milestones in the history of foreign investment in South Africa
was reached. The manufacturing sector overtook mining as
the main recipient of foreign capital. The goose that had laid
the golden eggs of South Africa's economic development for
so long was relegated to second place. Foreign businessmen
and shareholders were putting more money into manufacturing. As an industrial economy South Africa had arrived.

By 1968 investment in manufacturing constituted 31 per
cent of total private foreign investment in South Africa.[1] In
1966, the last year for which the South Africans have given
complete statistics, investment in manufacturing at 29 per
cent was just ahead of mining at 28 per cent. The shift must
have occurred a year or so before.

The distribution of British investment in South Africa has
probably paralleled this development closely. Its shift from
mining into manufacturing can be traced in the figures which
show the growing importance of direct investment by British
firms in South African subsidiaries over indirect investment in
mining shares. In 1963 direct investment, of which the bulk
went into manufacturing industry, some into distribution,
banking and insurance and only a small part into mining,
already formed 72 per cent of total British investment:
indirect investment, most of which was purchases of shares
in the South African mining finance houses, was 28 per cent.

81

By 1966 the proportion formed by direct investment had
risen to 75 per cent and indirect investment had fallen to
25 per cent. By 1969 direct investment by Sterling Area
countries, by far the largest part of which came from Britain,
formed 78 per cent and indirect investment only 22 per cent.[2]

BREAKDOWN BY SECTOR OF TOTAL PRIVATE FOREIGN INVESTMENT IN SOUTH AFRICA (IN MILLIONS OF POUNDS)

	1956	%	1961	%	1966	%
Mining	454	37	435	33	497	28
Manufacturing	303	25	349	26	515	29
Wholesale and retail trade	149	12	179	14	240	13
Insurance	30	2	39	3	47	3
Other finance	197	16	233	18	365	20
Other industries	102	8	89	7	125	7
Total	1235		1324		1789	

Sources: J.C. du Plessis, Foreign Investment in South Africa in Litvak
and Maule, *Foreign Investment: The Experience of Host Countries.*
Figures for 1956 taken from South African Reserve Bank *Quarterly
Bulletin of Statistics,* December 1958. Estimates for 1961 and 1966
provided by the Economics Department of the South African Reserve
Bank.

More precise figures are available: in the mid-1960s British
direct investment in South Africa was heavily concentrated
in manufacturing industries and the biggest single concentra-
tion was in engineering: in 1965 investment in electrical and
mechanical engineering accounted for 11 per cent of direct
total investment and vehicles and shipbuilding accounted for
4 per cent. Altogether nearly 70 per cent of direct investment
was in manufacturing, 11 per cent in distribution and 10
per cent in insurance, banking and other service industries.

In the last few years the engineering industry has continued to absorb about 12 per cent of total new direct investment from Britain, although the share absorbed by other manufacturing industry has fallen slightly. The mines have begun to receive direct investment now, and so has the banking sector which accounted for a considerable part of the increase in the net flow of British direct investment to South Africa to a record 70 million pounds in 1969.[3]

VALUE OF BRITISH DIRECT INVESTMENT IN SOUTH AFRICA
BY SECTORS, 1965 AND 1969 (BOOK VALUES)
(IN MILLIONS OF POUNDS)

	1965	Percentage	1969	Percentage
Mining	16.8	4	64.6	10
Electrical and mechanical engineering	44.1	11	72.6	11.7
Vehicles and shipbuilding	16.1	4	*	
Other manufacturing	214.6	55	328.2	50
Construction	5.6	1.4	9.9	1.5
Distribution	42.5	11	88.1	13.4
Transport, communications and ship-building	7.5	2	*	
Other (including insurance and banking)	39.7	10	54.2	8.3
Total	391.7		585.6	

Source: *Board of Trade Journal,* 19 July 1968 and 23 September 1970 *Business Monitor,* Miscellaneous series, Overseas Transactions, M4. 1970, Department of Trade and Industry.

*Figures not available

A look at the industrial composition of the 512 British firms which had subsidiaries or associated companies in South Africa in 1971 shows the same concentrations as the figures for the amount of capital invested. 175 ,or just over one-third of the total, are in engineering; 36 are in distribution and 45 are insurance or finance companies. The very high proportion formed by engineering firms – a much higher one than the proportion of *total* direct investment formed by engineering – is partly the result of the relatively small size of the typical engineering firm. In mining, on the other hand, only 21 British companies have South African subsidiaries – although mining accounts for 9 per cent of total British direct investment in South Africa – because mining companies are usually much bigger. Of other companies with South African subsidiaries in the manufacturing sector, 47 are in the chemical industry, 41 are in textiles, 24 manufacture building materials and 19 are in food processing. Appendix 3 (p. 324) gives a more detailed classification.

American investment in South Africa has in the past been very different from Britain's. Unlike Britain, the United States had only a small stake in South African mining shares before the Second World War; the large influx of American capital into South Africa came after the war and took the form of direct investment in US subsidiaries. In 1963 74 per cent of American investment in South Africa was direct investment. By 1969 the proportion for the Dollar Area had risen to 80 per cent. Unlike British subsidiaries, American subsidiaries in South Africa are wholly owned by their parent US corporations.

American investment has shown the same shift from mining into manufacturing as British investment. In 1959 the American stake in manufacturing was 34 per cent of total US direct investment, with mining and smelting at 27 per cent. By 1970 it had grown four-fold by 183 million pounds, or 50 per cent of the total, while mining investment was down to 10 per cent. Petroleum accounted for 20 per cent and the remaining 20 per cent was dispersed over other industries.[4]

The huge inflow of Western funds into South Africa since the Second World War has given foreign investors a substantial stake in key sectors of the economy. The following sections examine the contribution that Western capital is making in some of them.

MINING: THE MAGNET FOR THEM ALL

Gold first put South Africa on the road to economic development. Gold first attracted foreign capital. Gold is still the country's largest single export item. Gold still makes some handsome profits.

Anglo American Corporation, the biggest of South Africa's 'Big Seven' mining finance houses earned working profits from its gold mines of over £9 million in 1970. Consolidated Gold Fields, 41 per cent of whose assets are in South Africa, mainly in gold, reported a group profit before tax of nearly £28 million in 1970, 'a new record and an increase of about 19 per cent over the previous year'. Historically most foreign capital in the gold mines has come through indirect investment via the Stock Exchange or money market in London, New York or continental Europe. Of the seven major mining houses only Consolidated Gold Fields is registered outside South Africa.

As South Africans themselves have put more money into mining stocks the proportion of foreign to local capital has declined. The proportion of mining dividends paid abroad has been decreasing almost uninterruptedly from 82·5 per cent in 1918 to 47·6 per cent in 1945 and 26·9 per cent in 1965,[5] but 42 per cent of shares in Anglo American are still held in Britain and other European countries.[6] And in absolute terms foreign shareholdings have greatly increased. J. C. du Plessis, formerly of the South African Reserve Bank, writes of 'the large amounts of foreign private capital still flowing into gold shares, although manufacturing has since supplanted gold mining as the major investment field for foreign capital in South Africa'.[7] New money has been vital in helping the mines to expand. Since 1946 the volume of capital raised by the gold and uranium companies is in the order of 500 million pounds.[8] Over the years the ownership of these shares has shifted. Instead of private individuals buying stock, much of the new portfolio investment is coming from financial institutions – unit trusts, pension funds and insurance companies.

In 1970 gold still accounted for 53 per cent of South Africa's total mineral production.[9] Earlier forecasts four or five years ago that gold had reached its peak and might soon cease to be a unit of international currency have not yet been borne out. South Africa had a windfall from the Western countries' decision to set up a two-tier price system for gold in March 1968. Previously the eight major buyers used to operate what was known as the London Gold Pool. Through this they undertook to sell from their own stocks of gold whenever the price on the free market, which caters for private and industrial buyers, looked like rising above $35 an ounce. But in 1968 they stopped intervening and the free market price rose sharply as demand exceeded supply. Speculators also hoped for a rise in the official price for gold and a devaluation of the dollar. During the second quarter of 1969 the free price averaged around $41 and reached a peak of $44. But when the member countries of the International Monetary Fund agreed to extend each other extra credit through special drawing rights, the crisis over the shortage of world liquidity temporarily abated and speculation about a devaluation of the dollar dwindled again. Under an agreement between South Africa and the IMF in December 1969 South Africa, which had been trying to push the price still higher by hoarding some of its newly-mined gold, was forced to abandon this practice. This was no great loss to South Africa since demand for gold for industrial purposes and for jewellery exceeded supply. The free market price averaged $38·40 an ounce for the first nine months of 1971 and by the beginning of January 1972 it had risen to $47. It was estimated that 78 per cent of South Africa's total gold production was sold on the free market in the 1970/71 financial year.[10]

The United States' dollar devaluation of December 1971 brought about the long-awaited rise in the official price of gold. Though the increase was quite small – the price rose to $38 an ounce – South Africa will benefit from being able to fall back on this increased floor price. In the meantime the free market price went on soaring. In the very long-term the country will still have to reduce its dependence on gold, but for the foreseeable future gold will remain a major foreign currency earner.

Apart from the Soviet Union and the United States, South Africa has the largest and most varied mineral resources of any country in the world. As well as gold and diamonds it has copper, nickel, tin, manganese, asbestos and zinc. It has one-third of the world's known reserves of uranium, it produces more than 80 per cent of the non-Communist countries' production of platinum and it has the largest known reserves of chrome and vanadium. It produces antimony, fluorspar, titanium and vermiculite. It also has extensive reserves of coal and iron ore. The only important minerals of which it is not known to have large deposits are oil, bauxite and molybdenum.

These metals are now taking their place with gold and diamonds as major export commodities. Platinum, copper, uranium, asbestos, manganese, vanadium, iron, antimony, nickel and chrome have become important foreign currency earners. In 1970 sales of base metals rose by 18·8 per cent, exactly double the average annual growth rate of the 1960s, while total sales, including gold, but excluding gold premiums, rose by only 6·7 per cent. (These figures were given in the president's address to the annual general meeting of the Chamber of Mines of South Africa, held in June 1971.)

In the growth of production of base metals the South African mining finance houses have led the way. Johannesburg Consolidated Investments operates the world's biggest platinum mine at Rustenburg. South Africa's other big Impala platinum mine is controlled by Union Corporation. In copper Anglo-Transvaal Consolidated Investments has a big stake in the copper/zinc mine at Prieska in the northern

87

Cape, sited on a copper reef which may turn out to be the richest in the world.

Uranium production began in the early 1950s as a gold-mining by-product. After a boom which lasted till the mid-1960s world demand for uranium fell and the companies were forced to stock-pile. Demand is now picking up and uranium is once again making a substantial contribution to gold-mining company profits.

Other British and American companies have shared in the boom in base metals. US Steel has a 30 per cent interest in African Triangle, the group operating the Preieska copper mine and controlled by Anglovaal. Lonrho has opened up a platinum mine in partnership with Falconbridge Nickel of Canada.

Overseas interests also provide technical expertise in the processing of minerals. Rustenburg's platinum is processed by the British metals company Johnson, Matthey. Union Corporation's Impala platinum mine depends on its link with International Nickel of Canada and Engelhard Minerals and Chemicals (see p. 132). The Union Carbide Corporation processes its South African vanadium into a refined metal known as carvan, which competes with Highveld Steel and Vanadium Corporation's vanadium.

Historically, Western investment in South Africa has taken the form of investment in the share capital of South African mining finance houses. However, since the last war share purchase has been overtaken by direct investment by multinational corporations and mining, as an outlet, has been overtaken by manufacturing industry. Now, as South Africa's boom in base metals gets underway, and the West, especially the United States, becomes more and more dependent on South Africa for its supplies of strategic minerals, the wheel turns full circle and mining is once again an expanding area for Western investment in South Africa.

BANKING AND INSURANCE: FUND-RAISERS FOR
APARTHEID

Banking in South Africa has traditionally been dominated
by British institutions. Two-thirds of the commercial banks'
assets which totalled 1,962 million pounds at the end of
1970 were controlled by the two biggest banks. Both were
subsidiaries of British companies: Barclays National Bank
Ltd, a subsidiary of Barclays Bank International (the former
Barclays Bank DCO), and the Standard Bank of South
Africa Ltd., a subsidiary of the Standard Bank in London.
Both had grown fast. In August 1961 Barclays had 340
branches in South Africa and Namibia (then South-West
Africa). By 1969 it had 963. The Standard Bank over the
same period increased its number of branches from 350 to
822.

The Afrikaner community and the Nationalist Government have taken two steps to try to lessen foreign control
while continuing to welcome foreign capital. The first move
was the deliberate policy of setting up Afrikaner banks and
encouraging Afrikaner businesses to use them. In 1941 the
Volkskas was set up, and in 1955 the Trust Bank. By the
end of 1970 these two banks had become the third and fourth
largest in South Africa. But with assets, respectively, of 350
million pounds and 270 million pounds they were still a long
way behind Barclays with assets of 688 million pounds and
Standard with assets of 600 million pounds.[11]

The second step taken to reduce foreign control has been
the Government's insistence that foreign-owned banks must
gradually allow South Africans a share in them. In 1971 a
Government-appointed committee, the Franzsen Commission, recommended that 'over a reasonable period' foreign
banks must reduce their shareholdings to 50 per cent. In
line with the Commission's findings Barclays took the first
steps in October 1971 by incorporating its South African
operations into a separate local company which was later to
be quoted on the Johannesburg Stock Exchange. The

Standard Bank had already floated off its South African operations into a separate company at the end of 1967 though it retained almost 90 per cent of the shares.

Merchant banks started late in South Africa. As the economy has expanded rapidly however, several of them have been set up to encourage foreign investors to take advantage of profit opportunities in South Africa, and in order to raise local capital. From the South African Government's point of view, anxious as it is to attract foreign investment at a time of international pressure at the UN and elsewhere, the merchant banks have played the key role in the banking sector. They are more important than the commercial banks, which concentrate mainly on servicing local consumer and business needs.

Inevitably British capital has taken its share in their development. The first merchant bank in South Africa was formed in 1955. Called Union Acceptances Ltd, it was established by the Anglo American Corporation and Lazard Brothers, and now includes a minority share owned by Barclays. It has now been overtaken in size by the Central Merchant Bank Ltd (Senbank), in which the Standard and Chartered Banking Group has a minority holding. The Hill Samuel group, a subsidiary of the British bank of the same name, is the fourth largest merchant bank in the country.

Hill Samuel makes no bones about its role in bringing foreign capital into South Africa. In an advertisement in a special survey on South Africa, published by *The Banker*, it declared: 'Project yourself into the South African profit picture. The net capital inflow into South Africa in 1970 was a record 557 million Rand [347 million pounds] – an indicator of the confidence foreign investors have in South Africa's immense growth. Hill Samuel – international merchant bankers with six South African branches – have the financial expertise and local knowledge to advise you on the best methods of obtaining a lion's share in this profitable market.'[12] The company was smart enough to show its faith in South Africa early by anticipating the Franzsen Commission's recommendations. In 1969 it sold 23 per cent of its holdings to the South African public. As the Chairman, Sir Kenneth Keith, commented in his 1970 report: 'This local interest should help to consolidate our position as an important element in the financial life of South Africa.'

The next stage, and it has already been reached, is for the merchant banks to start raising South African capital for investment abroad. As South Africa pushes on with its 'outward-looking' policy of penetrating the countries to the north, this development is likely to gather pace. In September 1971 Alan Williams, the Deputy Chairman of Union Acceptances, said that his bank had become 'increasingly active in international markets'. It had already successfully arranged revolving credits in currencies other than the rand for South Africa's imports and exports and participated in the financing of capital projects at home and abroad. 'This exciting field has every prospect of keeping us increasingly busy in the years to come,' he said.[13]

The commercial banks have been operating in the rest of Southern Africa for some time. In its accounts Barclays treats the area as a whole. Taken together, South Africa, Namibia, Botswana, Lesotho, Swaziland and Rhodesia made up 35·75 per cent of the total geographical spread of the deposits of Barclays Bank DCO when the company changed its name in October 1971. It was the largest single area of the Bank's operations.[14]

Since the Unilateral Declaration of Independence in Rhodesia, Barclays' branch activities there have continued. The Rhodesian board includes Sir Frederick Crawford whose passport was confiscated by the British Government on the grounds that he was one of the Smith régime's 'active supporters'. In 1971 the bank sold its business in Mozambique to a Portuguese-controlled bank, the Banco Comercial de Angola. During 1970 and 1971 Barclays came under fire for its part in supplying credit for the construction of the strategic

Cabora Bassa dam in the Tete province of Mozambique. Barclays was not part of the consortium of banks that is financing the dam, but it was giving facilties in what the bank called 'the normal course of buisness to an established customer involved in a subcontarct for part of the pre-liminary work on the dam.'[15]

In the hire purchase field the largest institution in South Africa is again a British subsidiary – the National Industrial Credit Corporation, a subsidiary of the Standard and Chartered Banking Group. Taking all the different types of bank together, merchant banks, commercial banks, general banks, and hire purchase houses, British banks have majority holdings in four of the top twenty and substantial minority holdings in another four of them.

American banks have played a special role in South Africa. As commercial banks they have not been important. The Chase Manhattan Bank, for example, which entered South Africa in 1959, had only three branches until it bought a 15 per cent stake in the Standard Bank in 1965. Chase Manhattan has now merged all its branches with Standard. The First National City Bank which preceded Chase Manhattan into South Africa /by one year has only six branches.

Throughout the post-Sharpeville period Chase Manhattan and First National were part of a consortium of ten American banks which supplied the Government with a 40 million dollar revolving loan. The consortium was formed and administered by Dillon, Read, and Co., one of whose senior partners, Douglas Dillon, was President Kennedy's Secretary of the Treasury. Other South African Government institu-tions have received smaller loans from US banks.

The South African Government has also been warmly helped by the World Bank, which is strongly influenced by American and Western capital – its president has always been an American. During the whole postwar period the Bank played a major part in financing South Africa's economic development through loans for power and transport. Between 1947 and 1962 the Bank lent South Africa 220 million dollars. It gave the state-owned Electricity Supply Commission three loans, 30 million dollars in 1951, 30 million in 1953, and 14 million in 1961. Seven loans were made to the South African Railways and Harbour Board totalling 147·8 million dollars. In 1966 a further 20 million dollars was lent to ESCOM.

Another vital sector where foreign capital, particularly British capital, has operated is insurance. 'One of the important factors in the growth of the South African economy in the past decade', wrote a leading official of the South African Mutual Life Assurance Society in 1970, 'has been the rapid growth of the South African life assurance industry and the crucial role it has played in encouraging personal savings and investment.'[16] To back his point up he emphasized that the income raised by premiums was running at the rate of about 140 million pounds a year. This was equivalent to 19 per cent of South Africa's total net investment by both private and Government enterprise. In 1958 the comparable percentage was only $11\frac{1}{2}$.

Several British companies have won significant stakes in the life insurance market. Although the three biggest firms are South African (SA Mutual, Sanlam, and Southern Life) Britain was represented in nine of the top twenty firms in 1970. The biggest company was the Legal and General with total assess of 74 million pounds, and a net premium income of 9·5 million pounds. It was the fourth largest life insurer in South Africa.

This income was invested in every branch of the South African economy. As well as contributing to industrial and mining investment much of it went into South African Government and local authority stocks. The South African Eagle Insurance Company, a 59 per cent subsidiary of the Eagle Star Insurance Company, had an investment portfolio with a market value at the end of 1970 worth 14·5 million pounds. Over 40 per cent of this was in South African Government stocks or municipal loans, mortgages and debentures.

Insurers have been moving into equities and investment-linked policies. The official of SA Mutual, already quoted above, pointed out that 'a feature of the current life assurance scene is the rate at which insurers are combining with other financial institutions to form enlarged organizations offering financial services of many kinds.' South African Eagle provides a good illustration of the important bridge-building role which insurance companies can play in the South African financial scene. Its Deputy Chairman is Dr F. C. J. Cronje, Chairman of the Netherlands Bank of South Africa, of the Netherlands Finance and Investment Corporation and of South African Breweries, and an executive trustee of the South Africa Foundation. Other directors include P. H. Anderson, Chairman of Rand Mines Ltd, and a director of Middelburg Steel and Alloys, and of the National Finance Corporation of South Africa; C. S. Barlow, Chairman of Thos. Barlow and Sons, a director of the Standard Bank and of the American–South African Investment Corporation, and a Vice-President of the South Africa Foundation; M. Menzies, President of Hill Samuel Incorporated, New York, and a member of the South African Boards of Barclays Bank International: M. D. Moross, Chairman of the Investment Corporation of Africa Ltd; John Schlesinger, Chairman of the Schlesinger Organization, and E. R. Symons, Chairman of the Allied Investment Corporation Ltd.

For short-term accident insurance South African Eagle is the biggest company in the South African market. Indeed, there is probably no other sector of the economy where United Kingdom subsidiaries are so dominant. After SA Eagle the next biggest short-term insurers are both British affiliates: the Royal Insurance Co., in which Britain's Royal Insurance has a minority interest, and Commercial Union. Other British subsidiaries in the top twenty in 1970 were:

Protea (sixth), a subsidiary of the Sun Alliance and London Assurance Co. General Accident (ninth), Norwich Union (eleventh), National Employers (twelfth), and Pearl Insurance (sixteenth).

Much of the British investment in South African insurance is recent. Among companies which have set up subsidiaries there since 1968 are Edward Lumley and Sons, Phoenix Assurance Co., and Willis Faber and Dumas (Holdings). Insurance brokers have found South Africa particularly profitable, and most of the British firms have subsidiaries there. A *Financial Times* writer spotted this significant trend at the end of 1971 when he commented: 'Invisible exports were the great discovery of the 1960s . . . it is only recently that insurance has come to play the lead role among the many services that make up the U K invisible portfolio.'[17] Between 1965 and 1970 British net overseas insurance, including portfolio investments, rose from 80 million pounds to 281 millions.

A slight shadow fell upon the profitable South African business scene in 1971 with the report of the Franzsen Commission. In addition to its recommendations on banking, the Commission argued that no insurance company should be allowed to register for business in South Africa if it were more than 10 per cent foreign-owned. Existing companies would be allowed at least ten years to reduce their 'foreign ownership'. However, the *Financial Times* reported that 'this chauvinistic recommendation' is unlikely ever to become law.[18]

THE MOTOR INDUSTRY: IN GEAR WITH THE GOVERNMENT

Motor vehicle manufacture and assembly was recently described by a leading South African business economist as 'the Government's chosen instrument for achieving the crucial sophistication of industrialization in South Africa over the next decade, when gold-mining is expected to decline in significance.'[19] Attracted by the prospect of high profits and an expanding but still undivided market, the world's major car producers went to South Africa with few doubts about meeting the Government's wishes. Throughout the world the industry is still more competitive than are most other sectors of the Western economy, in which a few big suppliers have monopolized the major share of the market. The car companies had to fall in with Pretoria or risk seeing business pass to rivals.

The first car assembled in South Africa, in February 1924, was a Model T Ford, but it was an exception. Before the war most cars in South Africa were imported models, assembled and packed abroad. Gradually the Government brought in tariff protection, obliging companies to import components and put them together in South Africa. Further tariff changes made it cheaper for companies to manufacture components in South Africa. In 1960 the Government decided to intervene: from that time it gave favoured treatment in the allocation of import permits for components to firms making a certain proportion of the vehicle (by weight) locally.

This programme of increasing the 'local content' of the 'South-African-made car' became a major feature of official 'forced industrialization' policy. By 1 January 1971 when 'Phase Three' of the programme came in cars had to be 55 per cent South-African-made and there are plans for raising this to 66 per cent by the end of 1976.

In 1961 only $12\frac{1}{2}$ per cent of all materials for the vehicle industry were locally made. But the companies on the whole went along smoothly with the Government's requirements. Within days of its announcement of new conditions for importing engines, Ford and General Motors announced plans, involving 4 million pounds and 10·5 million pounds respectively, to start building engine-assembly and machining plants. As Phase Three began programmes totalling over 100 million pounds were announced by various companies.

The largest single programme was that of Leyland Motor Corporation which prepared to double its existing stake of 16·5 million pounds. At Uitenhage in the Eastern Cape Volkswagen launched a 7·5 million-pound scheme.[20] By January 1971 there were fifteen assembly plants in South Africa, three of them dealing only with lorries and other commercial vehicles.

As the car industry developed, its location shifted because companies took advantage of lower labour costs. The country's first plants were sited in Port Elizabeth, near the import port and in an area of 'poor white' workers, where cars could be assembled by 'civilized labour'. Then plants moved to Durban and the Western Cape, where labour was mostly Coloured or Indian. Now African labour is increasingly used. The Chrysler Corporation, for example, is moving its operation from Cape Town to the Silverton industrial area near Pretoria. The site is handily within walking distance of an African location. On it, at a cost of 15 million pounds, Chrysler has 'built the most modern automobile plant in Africa and indeed in the whole of the Southern hemisphere', as one of Chrysler's advertisements boasts. 'Why? Because this is the fulfilment of Chrysler's faith in South Africa. Faith so strong that it is backed by every resource that Chrysler can bring to bear.'[21]

With an average wage for its African workers of £7·25 a week, Chrysler's 'faith' may conceivably have been based on its managing director's long-term expectation of a 'reasonable' annual rate of return of 15 to 25 per cent. At all events it chimed well with the Government's plans for 'forced industrialisation'. For Pretoria the policy had several benefits: it saved foreign exchange; it gave a stimulus to the whole economy; it was useful for a country that wanted military independence – fast. For the car industry and its associated plants have obvious strategic value: 'In times of emergency or war each plant could be turned over rapidly to the production of weapons and other strategic requirements for the

D

defence of Southern Africa', according to the *Financial Gazette*, referring to Ford and General Motors.[22]

By 1970 the last stage had been reached in the process of creating the 'South-African-made car' – exports. Benefiting from South Africa's low wages, the companies started to export products to the industrialized West. Car workers there faced a new threat of redundancy in the future. In September 1970 General Motors South Africa announced that the first South-African-made car was going abroad. Designed and developed in South Africa, the Ranger was sent for sale to Europe. General Motors' subsidiaries in Europe supplied the engine but the body-parts were South African. The company promised that it would be a major foreign exchange earner for Pretoria.

Between them the three American companies (Ford, General Motors and Chrysler) supplied nearly 44 per cent of the total South African car and vehicle market in 1970. Other major manufacturers are Leyland, Volkswagen, Toyota-Rambler and Datsun-Nissan.

Foreign participation in industries connected with car production is substantial. The leading tyre manufacturer in South Africa is Firestone, and with Goodyear Tyre and Rubber Company, which controls one-third of the South African tyre market, it is collaborating with the Synthetic Rubber Company of South Africa to make the local rubber industry less dependent on external producers.

TEXTILES: THE BENEFITS OF CHEAP LABOUR

More than any other South African manufacturing industry, the textile industry owes its existence to Government policy and Government aid. Unlike many other recently industrialized countries South Africa did not develop a textiles industry at an early stage of its industrialization. Before the Second World War it only produced blankets woven from imported yarns. During the war the manufacture of clothing (including army uniforms) from imported materials boomed and the cost of textile imports shot up until it became a major factor in South Africa's deteriorating balance of payments. The Government stepped in to reduce the import bill by promoting a local textile industry and so took another important step in encouraging South Africa's all-round industrialization.[23]

Since the Nationalist Party came to power in 1948 the Government has had another special interest in the development of the textiles industry. Because textile manufacture is labour-intensive it has been a 'key instrument' in the implementation of the Government's 'separate development' policy.[24] By siting new textile mills in 'border areas' the Government has tried to decentralize industry and move it to areas where it can employ African workers who live in a Bantustan, only leaving it to go to work, and so to stem the influx of Africans into 'white' cities. The inducements the Government offers to firms to persuade them to set up shop in the 'border areas' are the suspension of the labour laws which lay down minimum rates of pay for Africans and the provision of labour at an even cheaper rate than it is elsewhere in South Africa.

The two instruments used to promote the textiles industry have been massive tariff protection and the provision of capital and initiative through the Industrial Development Corporation. Between 1940 and 1962 it put 9·5 million pounds into 25 textile and clothing undertakings.[25] From the start it looked abroad for technical knowledge and for foreign capital which it could take into partnership. One of its earliest coups was to draw the British Calico Printers Association into a fifty-fifty partnership in the Good Hope Textiles Company which set up a mill in the border area of Kingwilliamstown. Calico Printers was bought out by the IDC in 1968. Near Kingswilliamstown, in a border area round East London, the IDC persuaded Cyril Lord to set up a poplin mill at a time when Britain's textile industry was contracting and hundreds of textile workers were being

99

thrown out of work. (Cyril Lord South Africa and Good Hope Textiles have since been merged in the South African-controlled Da Gama Textile Group.)

Between 1949 and 1965 the value of South African textile production rose from 12 million to 42 million pounds a year and the number of textile factories rose from 62 to 163.[26] But by the mid-1960s the rate of increase of production was slowing down. The industry has only continued to expand in the last few years because it has been able to move ahead into new processes and to develop new modern fibres, synthetics like nylon and terylene, knitted yarns and, most recently, non-wovens.

The role that overseas companies have played in this latest phase of textiles development is even more striking than their part in helping to set up South Africa's woollen and cotton mills. South Africa was given the basis of a synthetic fibres industry in 1951 when Courtaulds joined with the IDC to set up the South African Industrial Cellulose Corporation (SAICCOR) to produce rayon pulp. Since 1951 SAICCOR has gone from strength to strength and is now a major exporter to Britain, Canada and the United States. In 1969 it completed a 1·5 million-pound expansion at its plant on the Natal coast.

With the setting up of South African Nylon Spinners at Bellville in the Cape by ICI, South Africa became the only country in Africa with a nylon-spinning plant. The IDC and Anglo American were quick to take up shareholdings in Nylon Spinners, to patriotic applause. ICI's shareholding in Nylon Spinners is now a minority one of 37·5 per cent.

South Africa's own Alexander Sagov Holdings, and its holding company, Sidcor, dominate the knitted fibres sector. In many fields Sagov owes its leadership to franchises held for processes developed by British and American firms. In 1968, for example, it acquired the franchise for the manufacture of crimplene by taking over Nylon Processors, a subsidiary of the British company, Carrington and Dewhurst, in return giving Carrington and Dewhurst a holding in Sagov.

From being a late starter the textiles industry has become one of South Africa's most technologically advanced sectors. With an economy that is many times smaller than the advanced industrial economies of Britain, the United States and Western Europe, South Africa has access to processes they develop. South Africans buy the latest man-made fabrics only a few years after they first appear in the countries where they have been developed. At the same time, the South African Government has been very wary of allowing overseas interests to exercise financial control over textiles companies, and technical expertise has been acquired mostly by encouraging overseas firms to take up minority holdings in companies that are South African controlled. The textiles industry illustrates the pattern which is growing in South Africa of an economy in which foreign capital is allowed entry and accepts it on the Government's terms and as a junior partner.

CHEMICALS: THE GIANT THAT NEEDS A MARKET

'The chemical industry must be regarded as one of the utmost importance for the growth and stability of the South African economy,' declared Dr Nico Diederichs, the Minister of Finance, in November 1971.[27] He had reason to be pleased about its past performance. In the words of the *Financial Mail*, the 1960s were for the industry 'a decade of astonishing expansion'.[28] In a few years it has grown into a giant employing 26,000 people and with a total investment of approximately 300 million pounds.

The industry is dominated by two firms, A E & C I and Sentrachem, which between them account for 80 per cent of total chemicals production, and by two products, explosives and fertilizers. A E & C I is jointly owned by I C I and Anglo American, each having a 42·5 per cent share: the remaining 15 per cent has been sold to the South African public.

Sentrachem is the result of an IDC-sponsored merger between National Chemical Products, Klipfontein Organic Products, several smaller South African companies and BP Chemicals. BP retains a 19 per cent stake and the British Government also has an indirect interest through its holding in BP. Sentrachem represents a pooling of South African private capital from both the English and Afrikaans-speaking communities, British private capital and South African and British state capital.

The chemical industry has real structural problems. It is a highly capital-intensive industry which benefits from economies of scale: for some basic products one plant ten times the size of another may cost only four times as much to build. But South Africa does not have the market. Even with an equitable distribution of wealth and the expansion of purchasing power which would follow that, it could not sustain plants on the scale of those in the United States or Western Europe. As things are, its market is tiny.

Where it has built giant plants it has been heavily dependent on foreign technical knowledge. According to one chemical engineer, 'When we get an inquiry, there is not time to start any fundamental development work or research. It's a matter of finding an overseas company which has the necessary knowledge of the process and buying its know-how.' According to another chemicals man, 'We rely on Europe and America for fundamental research but the sort of product produced there is not always automatically correct for conditions here.'[29]

One of the answers to the industry's problems is for it to build up export markets. Dr Diederichs made the speech in which he stressed the importance of the industry at the opening of a new subsidiary of Ciba–Geigy, one of the largest chemical manufacturers in the world. He referred also to the plant's potential for export: 'The activities of Ciba–Geigy in South Africa have already led to substantial exports to neighbouring territories such as Angola, Mozambique,

Malawi, Mauritius, Madagascar and the like.' AE & CI already does a substantial export trade.

Pharmaceuticals is a section of the industry where the size of South Africa's market does not justify local manufacture of many products. Pharmaceuticals and medicines account for 18 per cent of total chemical output. Most of the components of pharmaceutical products are imported from abroad and the industry 'still has the character of an assembling rather than a manufacturing industry'. Sophisticated drugs must also be imported from abroad. According to Bert Sachs, the President of the Pharmaceuticals and Chemicals Manufacturers' Association of South Africa, 'Even if overseas supplies of pharmaceutical chemicals were cut off and the Government decided to make them all here, it would cost more than the Government's entire annual revenue to do so.'[30]

The chemicals industry shows within itself different stages of dependence on outside capital and outside links. The sophisticated basic chemicals sector needs technical knowledge while the pharmaceuticals sector needs partly finished goods. The industry demonstrates that, even as South African industry develops new capabilities, it increases its dependence on the outside world.

OIL: THE ACHILLES HEEL

Oil is the one vital raw material which South Africa does not possess. Ninety per cent of the country's supplies have to be imported from potentially hostile sources in the Persian Gulf. The rest is made through the expensive oil-from-coal process started after the Second World War by the State-owned South African Coal, Oil and Gas Corporation (SASOL).

In spite of a UN resolution of November 1963 urging member states to refrain from supplying this strategically vital material to South Africa, American, British and French companies are busy prospecting for oil in South Africa, as well as refining and marketing her oil imports. American companies are the leaders and they make no bones about the value of their operations to South Africa. Caltex (which is jointly owned by Texaco and Standard Oil of California) ran a series of advertisements in Johannesburg newspapers, one of which read 'Ahead of Caltex lies many years of search and perhaps disappointment . . . or the discovery which will free South Africa for all time from dependence on outside oil supplies.'[31]

In 1970 American companies were operating six on-shore and eleven off-shore concessions up and down the coast of South Africa and Namibia (South-West Africa). Companies include Amoco, Mobil, Chevron-Regent, Esso Exploration, Placid Oil, Gulf Oil Corporation, Syracuse Oil Company and the Superior Oil Company of Houston. The British oil company, BP, is also engaged in off-shore drilling through the BP Development Corporation of South Africa. It joined a consortium with Shell and the French company Total, to prospect a large area off the Cape coast up to the border of the Transkei. Together with Shell, it has another large concession in Namibia on which £150,000 had already been spent by the spring of 1971.[32]

The fruits of all this searching have so far been meagre. In 1969 South Africa announced a petroleum gas strike by the Superior Oil Company in the continental shelf off Plettenberg Bay in the Cape, but little has developed since then. However, the nearby town of Mossel Bay has become the centre of operations. In hopeful anticipation of a big strike, two major shipping companies, the British Cayzer, Irvine & Company (whose Chairman is Sir Nicholas Cayzer, President of UKSATA) and Safmarine, the partly State-owned South African company, have formed a joint operation, Southern Africa Offshore Services, which has won a large contract from the Government exploration agency to set up a fully equipped oil base at Mossel Bay.

The three American companies Caltex, Mobil and Esso

control roughly 44 per cent of the market for all petroleum products in South Africa; the market leader, with 25 per cent, is still Shell. It has an investment in marketing facilities alone of some 24 million pounds and is pumping another 30 million pounds into joint enterprises like the Shell/BP refinery, an adjacent lubricating plant and a giant, single-buoy-mooring tanker terminal at Reunion, a few miles south of Durban.

The Shell/BP refinery (known as Sapref) at Reunion has the biggest single output of any of the four commercial South African refineries, although it is now being overtaken by the huge state-controlled Natref (National Refinery) which was opened by the Prime Minister, Mr Vorster, in May 1971. Of the other three refineries two are American.

The most striking feature of the Western oil companies' operations in South Africa has been their flaunting of the UN sanctions, and their deliberate policy of linking themselves to South African capital. The Caltex refinery at Milnerton in the Cape was opened in 1967 and planned only a few months after the UN urged its members to impose an oil embargo on South Africa. The Shell/BP lubricating plant at Reunion was partly financed by the raising of just under 3 million pounds in loans on the South African capital market. The plant is now half owned by the Afrikaans group Trek Beleggings. This is a complex interlocking financial device, since Shell and BP themselves hold a 17 per cent interest in Trek.

Thanks to the foreign companies, South Africa was able to test the effectiveness of international oil sanctions in the 'trial run' created by the UN imposition of mandatory sanctions against Rhodesia. In November 1967 the UN reported: 'In spire of sanctions . . . Southern Rhodesia is still receiving sufficient oil to meet its industrial and other needs. The origin of such oil should be emphasized. It was no secret that the United Kingdom and the United States companies, such as Caltex, were the main suppliers through their subsidiaries in South Africa. . . . In order to be able to do this more efficiently Caltex was reported to have extended its storage tank facilities in August 1966.'[33] In 1966 Shell and Mobil co-operated to finance a 100,000 gallon oil depot at Messina in the Transvaal, within easy reach of the Rhodesian border.

Collaboration with the foreign policies pursued by the white minorities in Southern Africa cannot be separated from the economic collaboration which the oil corporations willingly embark on the minute they apply for concessions to the State-owned exploration agency. The profits are certainly there. The *Financial Mail* commented in March 1971 that 'A stake in the South African market is of great benefit to the oil "majors" for it is a lucrative one and ripe for expansion.'

COMPUTERS: THE MOST ADVANCED SECTOR OF THEM ALL

The computer industry in South Africa has been growing at a furious rate. In 1964 the country had 105 computers. In 1968 there were 341 and by 1971 this had risen to approximately 500.[34] Spending on computers had by then reached 60 million pounds.[35] As might be expected in so advanced a field, the whole of the country's supply comes from abroad. International Business Machines is reported to hold nearly half the computer market in the country.[36] Another third is held by International Computers Equipment Finance Corporation (South Africa) (ICLEF) in which the British ICL has a substantial holding.[37] The company finances the marketing of the ICL 1900 range and the English Electric System 4 range.

IBM was established in South Africa in 1952. It began to market computers there in 1960. The exact stake which the company has in South Africa is not known since the head office in the United States does not release any figures on the percentage of its turnover and profits which is generated in the Republic. But if its profits are as high as ICLEF's, then IBM must be pleased with its operation.

In its first five years, from 1965 to 1970, ICLEF's pre-tax profits virtually doubled every year. In 1971 they increased rather more slowly and rose by 'only' 36 per cent to £365,000. These results were achieved in a period when over-all ICL profits were also increasing rapidly, but not nearly as fast elsewhere as in South Africa. In the same five-year period ICL saw a profit increase of 30 per cent a year. In 1971, however, the rise was only 12 per cent.

South Africa is ICL's best sales area outside Europe. The Chairman of ICLEF, I. Q. Homes, in his report for the year ending September 1971, wrote: 'It is encouraging that ICL orders in South Africa during the year under reveiw have exceeded those of previous years notwithstanding a world-wide decline in order-taking in the computer industry.'

The ICL empire is a complex mixture of Government and private finance. In Britain the company arose from a merger in 1968 between International Computers and Tabulators and English Electric Computers with financial support from the Plessey Company and 13·5 million pounds from the British Government. ICL has an 84 per cent holding in International Computers (South Africa). The Company intends to increase the South African stake in its operations in the Republic to 30 per cent.

In the computer-management field one of the most interesting developments in 1971 was the joint American–South African venture between the Anglo American Corporation and the US Computer Sciences Corporation. The company, in which Anglo has 51 per cent control, aims to offer firms access to a world-wide time-sharing network so that they can get maximum computer usage at a lower cost than by installing their own machine. Known as Infoset, the project integrates two South African centres into a network of four centres in the United States, one in Canada and two in Australia.

This important international link-up was followed by a small but prestigious victory for South Africa a few months later. After waiting for five years, the Computer Society of South Africa was finally accepted into the International Federation for Information Processing (IFIP). The first attempt in 1966 failed because IFIP was not satisfied that membership of South Africa's Computer Society was multi-racial. The Society got round this by claiming that there was no legal barrier to membership against anyone of any race and that there was no request for an indication of race on the Society's application form.

The truth was that only a very small proportion of blacks works in the industry: in IBM South Africa, for example, in 1970 out of 750 employees only 40 were blacks. It was also a fact that a colour bar existed, for which IBM blames the South African Government. The company claims that it wanted to train black women to be computer operators but the Government forbade it.

In spite of this, IFIP extended its membership to South Africa. The *Financial Mail* wrote at the time that the decision 'represented a valuable step towards better interchange of technical information between South Africa and IFIP's 33 other national societies. . . . It may seem fairly unspectacular, but undoubtedly its greatest benefit will be to encourage "computer dialogue" with other countries.'[38]

6 The Patterns of the Past

> You should kill all you can, as it serves as a lesson
> to them when they talk things over at their fires at
> night – *Cecil Rhodes, quoted by William Plomer in his
> biography of Rhodes*
>
> I was brought up to regard Rhodes as a hero –
> *Harry Oppenheimer, in 'A Reassessment of Rhodes . . .'
> published in* Optima, *September 1970*

The South African gold-mining industry was called into
existence by the need of British capital to find profitable
outlets. Gold provided the basis on which the South African
economy grew up and it still provides the best illustration
of the nature and the closeness of the relationship between
South Africa and Britain.

In the last third of the nineteenth century Britain still
dominated the world economy, but the character of that
dominance was changing. Britain was no longer the world's
only industrial producer. Its chief rivals were the United
States, Germany, France and Belgium. As these countries
began to supply their own markets, and as their demand
for British goods contracted, Britain relied increasingly on
its trade with the 'underdeveloped' countries, in Asia,
Australasia, South America and Africa, with whom it could
still exchange manufactured goods for raw materials, and
whose economies were complementary to its own. Britain's
second line of action was to rely increasingly on 'invisible'
instead of 'visible' exports. As its share of world trade in
manufactures declined it needed new markets for its banking,
shipping, insurance and other commercial services, and
especially for its exports of capital. From being the industrial
workshop, Britain was becoming the money market of the
world.[1]

At the beginning of the period South Africa was poorly equipped to play any part in this changing world economy. The white population did provide a market for British manufactures but its needs were small and limited: the biggest import by far was textiles for clothing and furnishing; next came iron goods and leather goods, and imports of soap and candles, beer, vinegar and books were each worth more than imports of railway engines or machinery.[2] South Africa's staple export was wool, production of which grew slowly but steadily after 1850. In the 1860s there was a short-lived boom in the export of ostrich feathers for the fashionable ladies of mid-Victorian London. South Africa was not a very attractive proposition for the investment of British capital either. The Cape Government raised public loans on the London money market in the 1850s and 1860s, but in 1870 British holdings in the Cape and Natal were still estimated at less than sixteen million pounds.[3]

In 1867 diamonds were discovered at Kimberley. Diamond-mining got off to a slow start – up to about 1874 diamonds were mined by individual diggers who often had no more capital than their fare to Kimberley and enough to buy some rudimentary equipment. At first they were dug out of the river bed; then the 'pipes' which became the four great mines of Kimberley, De Beers, Dutoitspan and Bultfontein, were discovered. As the diggers quarried deeper into the diamond-bearing rock, rock falls and drainage problems made it essential for them to use more sophisticated equipment, and to invest more capital in the diggings.

By the mid-1870s an élite among the diamond diggers was emerging at Kimberley: men like Cecil Rhodes, Barney Barnato, George Albu, Joseph B. Robinson and Francis Baring-Gould. They began to look for ways of increasing their capital in order to buy out the smaller diggers and to borrow money on the local capital market. By the end of 1879 there were twelve companies with a total capital of £2,500,000. In 1880–81 there was a speculative boom in diamond shares and the number of new companies soared: by the end of 1881 there were seventy-one companies, among them Cecil Rhodes' De Beers. But the boom was almost entirely a local affair, with shares changing hands in Kimberley, or at farthest, in Cape Town, financed by diamond profits and by advances made by the Cape Town banks.

In the general collapse which followed the boom, the process of the amalgamation of the diamond companies began within an industry which now had an enormously expanded capital base. By the beginning of 1887, two companies stood out: De Beers, which had bought up most of the claims in the De Beers mine, and the Kimberley Central Company, founded by Barney Barnato, which owned the biggest single share in the Kimberley mine. To take over the Kimberley mine Rhodes needed a very large amount of capital, and to raise this, he looked, for the first time, outside the Cape Colony, to the financial centres of Europe. In August 1887 a syndicate formed by Rothschild & Sons in London advanced Rhodes £1,400,000. Rothschild's advance made diamond shares more respectable on the London market, but it did not mark the beginning of any large-scale capital inflow into the diamond mines. It was an exceptional advance to meet an exceptional situation: De Beers' once-and-for-all take-over of the Kimberley mines.

Diamond mining never did provide a big outlet for British or any other overseas capital. It was so fabulously profitable that it was able to finance itself from its own resources. In 1938 it was estimated that since the beginning the total foreign capital invested in the South African diamond industry was less than 20 million pounds, while the total value of diamonds mined since 1867 was over 320 million pounds.[4]

The major significance of the diamond-mining industry was the foundation it laid for the exploitation of gold. There was nothing fortuitous about the discovery of gold on the

Witwatersrand in 1885. Gold had been discovered in South
Africa as early as the 1850s, and in 1871 Edward Button, a
British immigrant, struck gold on his farm in the Eastern
Transvaal. But it could not be extracted until large-scale
capital was available to exploit it. By the 1880s British
investors were looking for profitable overseas outlets and
there was none better than the prospect opened up by the
biggest deposits of gold-bearing ore the world had ever
known.

In the first few years after the main gold reef was struck,
diamond diggers who had been bought out in the process of
amalgamation, diamond dealers who had links with the
international diamond firms of London, Amsterdam,
Hamburg, Berlin and Paris, and the successful diamond
magnates themselves, who had amassed huge fortunes at
Kimberley, moved to the Witwatersrand.

Cecil Rhodes, Barney Barnato, Alfred Beit, Julius Wernher,
Joseph B. Robinson, Francis Oates – these were men of
dissimilar origins who had little in common but their drive
to amass money and their ruthlessness as entrepreneurs.
Rhodes was the son of a Bishop's Stortford clergyman who
dreamed dreams about the supremacy of the British race.
He arrived in South Africa in 1870 to help his brother on
his cotton farm in Natal. Seven years later at Kimberley he
made a will which directed that the money he left should
be used for 'the establishment, promotion and development
of a Secret Society the aim and object whereof shall be the
extension of British rule throughout the world . . . and
especially the occupation by British settlers of the entire
continent of Africa, the Holy Land, the valley of the Euphra-
tes, the islands of Cyprus and Candia, the whole of South
America, the islands of the Pacific not heretofore possessed
by Great Britain, the whole of the Malay Archipelago, the
seaboard of China and Japan and the ultimate recovery of
the United States of America as an integral part of the
British Empire'. It has been written of Rhodes that the only

way in which his ideas changed in the whole of his adult life was that, towards the end of it, he expressed 'an un-hesitating readiness to accept the reunion of the race under the Stars and Stripes if it could not be obtained in any other way'.[5] On another occasion Rhodes expressed his philo-sophy more succinctly: 'I prefer land to niggers.'[6] Rhodes arrived on the Witwatersrand in 1887 and concentrated on buying up blocks in already proved and successful mines. Although his gold shares eventually made a substantial contribution to his income, which by the 1890s was over one million pounds a year, he never dominated the gold-mining industry as he dominated diamonds.

Barney Barnato was born Barnet Isaacs in Whitechapel, London, the son of an East End shopkeeper. He went to South Africa in 1873 with capital worth £30 and set himself up as a diamond buyer in Kimberley. He moved to Johannes-burg in 1888 and by the end of the year had acquired gold-mining interests on a large scale. It was Barnato who intro-duced diamond shares to the London stock market and as gold shares boomed he quickly became a power on the London Stock Exchange. He spent the rest of his life travel-ling on business between Johannesburg and the City of London. Towards the end of it he developed persecution mania and drowned himself from an ocean liner.

Alfred Beit was Rhodes' closest business associate. He came from a well-to-do family of Jewish merchants in Hamburg and learnt the diamond trade in Amsterdam. He was sent to Kimberley to buy diamonds by the Hamburg firm of D. Lippert & Co. in 1875. There he met Rhodes and became one of the four life-governors of De Beers. In 1890 in Johannesburg, with Julius Wernher, he formed the mining finance house of Wernher, Beit & Co., the firm which did most to give gold shares an internationally respectable image. Beit eventually acquired British citizenship, built himself a mansion in London's Park Lane and spent the last years of his life posing as an English gentleman.

113

Julius Wernher came from a merchant family in Darmstadt. At the age of twenty he was sent to London to learn banking. He travelled to Kimberley in 1870 as a diamond buyer for the Paris firm of Jules Porges and quickly made his fortune. He moved to London in the 1880s and managed the London end of the financing operations of Wernher, Beit & Co. He remained in London until his death in 1912, and never saw the Witwatersrand gold-mines in the period of their greatest development.

Joseph B. Robinson was born in Cape Colony and became a wool merchant. Quickly emerging as one of the leading diggers at Kimberley, he was the first to arrive on the Rand, buying up the Langlaagte Farm where the main reef was first struck.

Francis Oates was a Cornishman, sent by the Cornish miners to the first World Congress of Miners in Paris in 1867. He came to Kimberley as a mining engineer engaged by the Kimberley Mining Board in 1875 and became a Director and, after Rhodes' death, Chairman of De Beers. He was one of the first of a long line of British skilled workers who sold out their class interests in order to profit from race tyranny in South Africa.

These were some of the men who improvised methods of bringing capital from the London money market to the industry best able to absorb and multiply it, the gold-mining industry of the South African Witwatersrand.

For the first few years gold shares were sold in the offices of the diamond merchants along Hatton Garden and Holborn Viaduct. In those years many of the gold-mining companies were registered in London and the number of companies with London offices shot up from 145 to 315 in 1888. Consolidated Gold Fields, founded by Cecil Rhodes in 1887, was one of the earliest companies to be registered in London, and of its 125,000 shares, 100,000 were offered in London and 25,000 in South Africa. Towards the end of the 1889 boom, dealings in gold-mining shares were transferred to the London Stock Exchange and the discovery, after 1892, that it was possible to exploit the gold reef where it dipped, thousands of feet, to the 'deep levels' led to a second, bigger boom in gold shares in 1895. According to Frankel, the historian of South African mining capital, the links between the gold-mines and the London money market had grown so close by 1895 that the boom 'was due as much to financial conditions in London and Paris as to the potential development of deep-level mining on the Rand'.[7]

Technical and geological problems – and the fixed price of gold – have necessitated in gold-mining an industrial structure whose ownership was highly concentrated and which required large-scale investment of foreign capital. Under the 'group system', clusters of mining companies, which each operated one mine, were grouped together under larger 'mining finance' houses, which provided them with technical services and capital. The mining finance house could maintain overseas offices and develop contacts with international banks and financiers on a scale which individual mining companies, operating independently, did not have the resources to do. They also made mining shares more attractive to overseas investors by spreading the risks which investment in gold shares was bound to incur. Potential investors could choose between investing directly in individual mines, which might yield huge profits but which equally might fail and pay no dividends for years, and investing in a mining group within which losses in some mines would be counterbalanced by large yields in others, and which could guarantee a steady rate of return.

By the mid-nineties the hundreds of small gold-mining companies formed in the 1880s had been grouped into ten mining houses: by 1932 the ten had shrunk to six. Rand Mines, formed to exploit the 'deep levels' in 1893 as an offshoot of Wernher, Beit & Co., was the biggest and was the first of the mining finance houses to establish such a reputation for safety that its shares were bought by non-speculative investors on the London Stock Exchange. Consolidated Gold Fields, formed by Cecil Rhodes in 1887, was the group with the strongest British connections and remains a London-registered company today. Johannesburg Consolidated Investments (JCI) began its climb to preeminence in 1896 when its interests were merged with those of Barney Barnato. General Mining and Finance Company was formed by the German Dresdner Bank when it took over the firm of G. and L. Albu in 1895; later it became the main channel for the investment of Afrikaner capital in the gold-mines. A. Goerz & Company, which changed its name to Union Corporation after the First World War, was founded by Adolf Goerz in 1897: it began as a company whose registration was in London, but whose most influential shareholders were the German banks. The Anglo American Corporation, founded by Ernest Oppenheimer in 1917 with South African – and an extra injection of British and American – capital, is the only one of the six which does not have a continuous history stretching back to the formative years of the gold-mining industry in the 1890s. Anglo Transvaal, the seventh of the present-day mining finance houses, was formed in 1933.

The group finance system was the method by which the South African gold-mining industry obtained the first of its essential ingredients – huge amounts of overseas, mainly British, capital. Between 1887 and 1932, according to Frankel, the gold mines absorbed 200 million pounds of capital, of which 120 millions came from abroad. Most of this was invested before 1913. The effect of the capital requirements of the gold mines on the total amount of British capital invested in South Africa before the First World War can be seen in contemporary estimates: it was calculated that Britain had 34 million pounds invested in South Africa in 1884 and that this had jumped to 351 million pounds by 1911.[8]

The industry was also crucially dependent on large amounts of cheap labour. South Africa's gold-bearing ore is so low-grade that the mines could never have been opened up if their labour force had had to be paid 'European' rates. It is not just the rate of profit, but the very existence of the gold-mines as an outlet for British capital, that has always depended on the exploitation, at below subsistence wage rates, of black labour. Because of this the mining companies soon eliminated competition among themselves for black workers: they allowed an employers' organization, the Chamber of Mines, to establish a 'maximum average' for wages paid on each mine, and also established a monopoly of recruitment of workers through the Witwatersrand Native Labour Association. They were so successful that average monthly wages for black workers on the gold-mines fell from £3·04 in 1897 to £2·60 in 1913.[9] The mining companies have been able to keep wages so low that those paid to African workers today are, in real terms, at the same level as before the First World War.

The development of the gold mines created new economic forces and new class interests in South African politics. Into the pastoral community, created by the Boer farmers who had trekked north in the 1830s, came international capital and the interests which grew up around it, and an embryonic white working class. There was no automatic reason why international capital should use the profits produced by the gold-fields to foster development inside South Africa, and the Witwatersrand in the 1890s and 1900s was an enclave of wealth set in the middle of a scattered and poor farming community. As the money flowed out of the pockets of the City of London, was transformed into more money in the gold-mines and flowed back again, the Boer farmers looked on in envy. The methods by which they tried to obtain a share in the profits – monopolies on dynamite and railway building, and tariffs on imported goods – were clumsy ones. But essentially the struggle in the 1890s between the burgers of the Transvaal Republic and the mining magnates was a struggle by the burgers for a place in the sun.

This was the classic age of imperialism, when the British Government intervened to protect the interests of British capital. At the end of 1895, Jameson, a close friend and associate of Cecil Rhodes, with a small force of armed men, rode from Bechuanaland border into the Transvaal, in an attempt to spark off a rising inside in Johannesburg and replace the Boer Government with one dominated by the mining magnates. Joseph Chamberlain, who had become Colonial Secretary in 1895, knew of the plans for the raid and encouraged it. From 1899 to 1902 Britain fought the Boer War to establish political control over the Witwatersrand gold-fields.

The steps by which the Transvaal was first granted 'responsible government' in 1907 and then became part of the Union of South Africa, with Dominion status within the British Empire, in 1910, did not in themselves represent any resolution of the question of whether the Witwatersrand would continue to be an enclave whose profits flowed back to the metropolitan power or a source of wealth used to diversify South Africa's economy for the benefit of the Boer farmers. What it *did* represent was a revision of the framework in which the conflict was taking place, in which both sides traded advantages and disadvantages. The mining magnates wanted Union in order to bring an end to the inter-State squabbles over freight charges and tariffs which were dislocating South Africa's internal economy. In return they agreed to a change in the arena in which the struggle for political power would be played out. They abandoned direct British support and gambled on being able to retain political power inside the new Union Constitution.

There was one interest the mining magnates and the Afrikaner farmers shared – that cheap black labour should at all times be available, and that it be given no political voice. The Union Constitution provided for an all-white racial franchise in the Transvaal and Orange Free State, and a non-racial but heavily qualified franchise in Natal and the Cape. The only voice raised in favour of a black franchise was that of the Africans themselves – by the sending of a deputation to London before the Act of Union was passed, and by the formation of the African National Congress in 1912. Miners and farmers were in perfect agreement on the perpetuation of a coerced labour force. The 1911 Native Labour Regulation Act (which extended to the mines the criminal sanctions against contract-breaking or strikes already existing for other jobs) and the 1913 Land Act (which turned one-time African landowners into wage labourers or tenants forced to work for the owners of the land they occupied) attended to the labour needs of the two principal sectors of the economy at the time.

When the clash between white interest-groups over the status of Africans did come, it was a clash, not between white farmers and mining magnates, but between mining magnates and white workers. In the Rand strike of 1922 the mine-owners (faced with a falling rate of profit after World War I) fought to upgrade black workers at the expense of white. But far from being a first step by the mine owners along the path to racial equality, it was a class-based attempt to reduce the mines' total wage bill by employing black workers to do certain jobs previously done by whites at greatly reduced wage levels.

By 1918 South Africa had been drawn firmly into the world economy. But the part it played in that economy was a unique one: it was the world's major supplier of gold, and because of this its experiences in the 1920s and 1930s were quite untypical of those of the majority either of 'under-developed' or industrialized countries.

Between the wars the world economy contracted. The price of primary products fell and this meant that the 'under-developed' countries could only afford to buy smaller quantities of manufactured goods. So production of manufactured goods in the industrialized countries slumped, profits fell and the amount of new capital available for export shrank. In the 1920s there was still some new investment, though nothing like on the scale of the prewar period: in the 1930s new investment stopped and capital repayments to creditor countries exceeded new loans.

But the market for gold, as the basis of the world currency system, stayed firm. In the 1920s gold production continued to expand, though at a much slower rate than before the war. The gold-mines continued to absorb new capital, though on a much smaller scale. The amount of new investment fell from an estimated annual average of £4,628,000 in the years between 1887 and 1913 to £1,217,000 between 1913 and 1932.

Some of this investment still came from Britain. And some, for the first time, came from the USA. In 1917 Ernest Oppenheimer drew American interests, led by J. P. Morgan, into his Anglo American Corporation, and by 1929 total American investment in South Africa stood at more than 30 million pounds. But much of the new investment – a much higher proportion than before the war – came from inside South Africa itself. By the 1920s the mining finance houses had accumulated sufficient reserves of capital to be able to meet at least some of their capital needs from their own resources.

The 1920s was the great age of the Imperial banks. Britain's position, before the First World War, as the world's greatest imperialist power, was so strong that it was a long time in crumbling; and at the same time as the rate of increase in Britain's foreign investments was slowing down, British banks and insurance houses were entering the period of their greatest overseas expansion. In 1919 Lloyds took over the National Bank of New Zealand and Westminster took over the Royal Bank of Canada; and in 1925 Barclays, in a move described by the *Financial News*[10] as part of 'the real romance of Empire', took over the National Bank of

The Patterns of the Past

South Africa and consolidated its overseas holdings in a new subsidiary, Barclays Bank Dominion Colonial and Overseas (DCO). By 1925 the National Bank, formed under charter from President Kruger in 1891, had strengthened its position in the Cape by merging with the Bank of Africa and Barclays Bank DCO emerged from the takeover as South Africa's biggest bank.

The years 1929–32 were the time of the great slump: in 1931 Britain abandoned the gold standard, and in December 1932 South Africa followed. The price of gold rose – from 84s to 125s per ounce – and South Africa's gold-mining industry entered a new era.

The increase in the price of gold brought about the opening up of the Far West Rand gold-field and gave a new lease of life to the industry. From 1933 to 1936 mining development took place over an area nearly four times as large as the whole of the area covered in 1932. Against all the predictions of Jeremiahs who, as early as the 1920s, had been forecasting the exhaustion of South Africa's gold reserves, gold production increased steadily throughout the 1930s. The existence of the Far West Rand gold-field had been known before the rise in the gold price in 1932, but it was only the possibility of the greatly increased profits which the rise in the gold price brought about that enabled the mining finance companies to raise the capital to exploit it. Profits shot up from an average of 12·5 million pounds a year between 1913 and 1932 to an average of 32·5 millions between 1933 and 1939.[11] The role of Britain in this second period of expansion was quite different from the one it had played before the First World War, for whereas the initial development of the gold-mines was brought about by the search by British capital for outlets overseas, the development of the 1930s was triggered by a jump in profits which made it possible for the industry, against world trends, to attract new overseas capital in a period of capital scarcity.

Between 1933 and 1939 a total of 63 million pounds was

121

invested in the South African gold-mining industry: this represented an average of 9 million pounds a year.[12] Probably between one-third and one-half of this came from abroad.[13] The mining finance houses were now able to provide most of the capital expenditure incurred by the older mines from their own resources, and most of the new over-seas capital was used for the sinking and equipping of new mines. The trend for an increasing proportion of mining shares to be held inside South Africa continued, and by 1938 it was estimated that 40 per cent of shares were held by South Africans as against less than 15 per cent before the First World War.[14]

South Africa's gold exports gave it a special position as an importer of British goods. Alone among the primary producing countries, its earnings of foreign exchange did not fall in the inter-war years, and it was able to increase the level of its imports in a period when total world trade was contracting. The 1932 Ottawa Agreements, by which Britain and the Dominions exchanged preferences on each other's goods, enabled Britain temporarily to reverse South Africa's trend towards the diversification of its trade and to increase its share of the South African market: Britain's share in South Africa's imports, which had fallen from nearly 57 per cent in 1913 to 43 per cent in 1929, rose to 46 per cent in 1936.

Meanwhile, South Africa was building an industrial base. The most rapid periods of industrial development came about as a result of external stimuli provided by two world wars. But between the wars, too, the South African Government took deliberate steps to build up manufacturing industry. In 1925 it established protective duties for key industries, and at the same time tried to solve the problem of the poor whites by establishing black:white labour ratios for protected industries. In 1928, against opposition from the British steel firms, Stewart and Lloyd and Dorman Long, the South African Government established ISCOR, the

Government-controlled Iron and Steel Corporation which today produces 80 per cent of South Africa's steel.

Significantly, it was the Nationalist–Labour coalition that came to power in 1924 that made industrialization a major plank of its platform, and its measures were passed in the face of bitter opposition from the Unionist (later United) Party. The Nationalists and the Labour Party represented those national South African groups which wanted to retain part of the profits of the mining industry inside South Africa and use them to diversify the South African economy. The Unionists represented the interests of the mine owners and international capital, which feared competition from industry for labour and other resources. The struggle to use South Africa's resources to develop the South African economy was the same struggle as that between Boer farmers and mining magnates in the 1890s, but instead of the sale of state monopolies, the new weapons were aid to agriculture, protected industries and the use of state capital to build state corporations.

It was against the protests of mining capital that the South African Government used tax revenues (skimmed from the profits of the mining companies) to create ISCOR. After ISCOR, the state-run Industrial Development Corporation (founded in 1940) was used to stimulate other industrial growth points, and then came SASOL, to produce oil from coal and lay the basis for petrochemicals, and FOSKOR, to produce fertilizers.

But during the 1930s a new form of capital, one Afrikaner and agriculturally based, began to be mobilized: Afrikaner nationalists began to organize the use of Afrikaner savings for commerce and industry. When the Nationalist Party became the Government in 1948 it used State power to assist this new group of entrepreneurs and gradually this capital began to increase its proportional share of the economy at the expense of foreign capital.

Because it was not in the interests of British and other

overseas capital to invest in industries which would compete for resources with its investment in the gold mines, the early stages of South Africa's industrialization were almost wholly financed by South African capital. The small amount of overseas capital invested in industry before the Second World War came from the great semi-monopolies that dominated British, American and German industry in the 1920s. Nobel's Industries, which merged with three other companies to form ICI in 1926, took over control of the British South African Explosives Company in 1914.[15] Lever Brothers, which merged with the Dutch Margarine Union to form Unilever in 1929, pioneered a modern advertising technique in South Africa as early as the 1890s, by painting 'Sunlight Soap' on the pavements of Main Street, Port Elizabeth; in 1911 the company built a modern, large-scale factory to manufacture soap at Maydon Wharf in Durban.[16] Dunlop opened its first South African tyre factory in Durban in 1936. The American car firms, Ford and General Motors, established assembly plants in Port Elizabeth in the 1920s. Siemens set up a separate South African subsidiary in 1897: it built one of the first power stations on the Witwatersrand in the 1890s and began to manufacture power-station equipment in Johannesburg in 1926.[17]

Since the Second World War the South African economy has undergone a second revolution, comparable only to the period of the development of the gold and diamond mines between 1867 and 1913. From an 'underdeveloped' economy, dependent on the export of one raw material, gold, to pay for the purchase of the manufactures it needs from abroad and providing a relatively low standard of living, even for its white population, it has been transformed into a modern industrial economy. Gross Domestic Product rose from 800 million pounds in 1946 to over 7,000 millions in 1970.[18] The annual rate of growth between 1946 and 1966 at current prices was over 8 per cent and it rose to well over 9 per cent between 1967 and 1970.[19] Real *per capita* income increased at a rate of nearly 3 per cent between 1946 and 1966.[20] In 1936 manufacturing output constituted less than 15 per cent of total GDP: for 1970 it has been estimated that it stands at around 24 per cent.[21]

Overseas capital played an important role in this second revolution. Between 1946 and 1955 it has been estimated that 700 million pounds was invested in South Africa from abroad, 500 millions (or two-thirds) of it from Britain.[22] Between 1956, when official figures first become available, and 1969, a further 1,000 million pounds was invested.[23] The amount of overseas capital invested in South Africa since the Second World War is, in monetary terms, more than three times the 500 million pounds which Frankel estimated was the cumulative total of overseas investment in the whole of the period before the war.

In the immediate postwar period, overseas capital played a more important role in South Africa than it did in countries like Australia and New Zealand, whose dependence on British capital before the war had been equal to South Africa's. Australia and New Zealand were far better able to provide for their own capital needs after the war than they had been before it: the capital inflow into Australia between 1946 and 1955 has been estimated at 600 million pounds, less than the cumulative total of 800 million pounds of foreign capital invested in Australia before the war. Overseas capital represented about 23 per cent of total capital formation in South Africa in the ten years between 1946 and 1955, as against 9 per cent in Australia and 5 per cent in New Zealand.[24]

Foreign investors continued to put their money into gold. By 1955 the development of the Orange Free State mines had cost 200 million pounds. Anglo American Corporation alone raised 23,250,000 pounds in London between 1946 and 1953 for its South African mines and a further 8,600,000 on the Continent. In his 1955 statement, the Chairman,

Sir Ernest Oppenheimer, reported to shareholders on a 4 million pound loan negotiated with the Union Bank of Switzerland. But he stressed the continuing importance of Britain: 'I do want to emphasize, however, that the London money market has been – and still is – the main overseas source of funds for the development of the South African mining industry: and in view of the strong financial support the industry has had from that quarter over all these years, we, as a corporation, would not seek to attract new money from other centres by offering terms or concessions we would not equally offer to financial interests in England.'[25]

But the typical form which overseas investment has taken in South Africa since the Second World War has been direct investment in manufacturing industry by the major British, American, and to a lesser extent, Western European, corporations. Where before the war nearly all overseas investment was in mining shares, by 1956 the amount of money invested direct by foreign corporations had over-taken shareholdings and formed nearly 58 per cent of total overseas investment.[26] By 1963 the number of British firms with subsidiaries in South Africa was 394: by 1938 the number had risen to 485, and today it stands at 512.[27]

The new pattern of investment after the war was partly the result of developments within the economies of Britain and other investing countries. Since 1945, a much higher proportion of total overseas investment by all the major capitalist industrialized economies had gone to relatively developed economies and into manufacturing industry. Most of this investment has come direct from large corporations which have set up subsidiaries not just in South Africa but, in the case of Britain, in Canada, Australia, the USA and Europe, and in the case of the USA, in Europe, Canada and South America.[28] The change has also reflected the achievement of South African national interests, which succeeded, in the 1940s and 1950s, in building up a fully fledged industrial economy under South African control.

Although it was not in the interests of overseas capital to initiate industrialization, once this was under way, fostered by Government expenditure on basic industries and infra-structure, industry became an attractive outlet. At the same time the mining finance houses began to diversify.

In the postwar debate over the role which foreign capital should be allowed to play, Nationalist politicians carried attitudes developed in earlier years into a radically changed situation. Many of them regarded it with deep suspicion. But the Government itself showed a greater understanding: in 1960, Dr Haak, a former Minister of Economic Affairs, spelt out the role which the Government expected foreign capital to play, saying that overseas capital could operate most advantageously in South Africa if it took South African capital as a fully fledged partner, and that South African residents should acquire more voice, by share ownership, in determining policy in regard to production and distribution in the private sector. The Government, Dr Haak said, would not introduce compulsory measures to achieve this, but foreign companies should understand that these objectives enjoyed widespread and growing public support, and in their own long-term interests they should not ignore them.[29] Because of their new identity of interests, foreign companies have found no difficulty in accepting the role that the Government has laid down for them.

7   South Africa's Other Friends

> Naturally this growth habit of ours has attracted
> foreign investment. Britain, the USA, France,
> Switzerland, Germany and Japan have 2,875
> million pounds sterling planted in South Africa right
> now. And it's growing for them in a climate of
> stability and progress. . . . Plant it in South Africa
> and watch it grow – *South African Government advertise-*
> *ment in the* Financial Times *of 22 June 1970*

THE UNITED STATES

Shortly before delivering his 'State of the World' message in
1970 President Nixon received Sir Francis de Guingand, the
President of the pro-South Africa lobby group, the South
Africa Foundation. Sir Francis reported later that the meeting took place at a time 'when the Administration was re-
evaluating United States policy towards South Africa. The
occasion was taken to bring to the President's notice some
points which have received too little attention in the past. It
would be hard to overestimate the importance to South
Africa of this discussion.'[1]

Even allowing for a little boasting on Sir Francis' part, the
meeting was clearly important. When the State of the World
message came out in February 1970 the South African
Government found it 'realistic' and 'refreshing'. It included
the assessment, 'The 1960s have shown us – Africa and her
friends also – that the racial problems in the Southern half of
this continent will not be solved quickly. These tensions are
deeply rooted in the history of the region and thus in the
psychology of both black and white'.

Mr Nixon, in short, was arguing for caution. South Africa
was, in the current White House jargon, an 'area of low
priority'. As far as the United States was concerned,

128

Southern Africa was a region where Britain had played the major political role, and had its fingers frequently burnt in the process. As long as American business could preserve and expand its economic interests in Africa, both north and south of the Zambesi, there was no point in taking dramatic political initiatives.

A year later, in his 1971 State of the World message, Mr Nixon emphasized the new policy more strongly. 'The United States believes that the outside world can and should use its contacts with Southern Africa to promote and speed change. We do not therefore believe that the isolation of the white regimes serves African interests, *or our own* [authors' italics], or that of ultimate justice. A combination of contact and moral pressure serves all three . . .' American policy was now clear: political statements and gestures which identified the USA too closely with the white South might prejudice the American stake in independent Africa and might antagonize black American voters still further from the Administration. In 1970, when the British Government announced its intention to resume sales of arms to the regime, the White House was quick to suggest through back-ground briefings to the press that it was 'unhappy' about the decision. On the other hand, American policy was firm in opposing any move that might threaten the white South. It played a consistent role at the UN in opposing tough measures against South Africa. At the same time, from this deliberately chosen back seat, American policy sought every opportunity to minimize the importance of the confrontation between South Africa and the freedom-fighters. In discussions and decisions it made its wishes known by gentle hints. As the British Foreign Secretary, Sir Alec Douglas-Home, met Mr Ian Smith to find a Rhodesian 'settlement', Mr Nixon quietly signalled his impatience for an end to the quarrel by signing legislation permitting America to import Rhodesian chrome in violation of the UN sanctions.

Earlier the Administration had shown its support for the

Portuguese buffer States to the north of South Africa when the Secretary of State Mr William Rogers said in his 1970 policy statement on Africa, 'The declared Portuguese policy of racial toleration is an important factor. . . . We think this holds genuine hope for the future.' Mr Nixon underlined his tacit support for Portuguese colonial policy when in December 1971 he promised the Government an astonishing aid agreement worth up to 181 million pounds in return for air and naval bases in the Azores until 1974.

The development of this policy of support for the *status quo* in Southern Africa chimes with the growing American economic stake there. Between 1964 and 1969 Dollar Area investment in South Africa almost doubled from 238 million pounds to 435 millions. American companies were becoming involved in the rest of the white South. Gulf Oil is exploring the huge Cabinda oil field in Angola as well as being a significant investor in Mozambique. The American-owned Diamond Company of Western Angola has prospecting concessions all over Angola. American Metal Climax owns 29 per cent of Tsumeb, the largest mining complex in South-West Africa (which was racked at the end of 1971 by a prolonged and courageous strike by Africans protesting at the contract labour system, described by the International Commission of Jurists as 'akin to slavery').

In 1971, in a private memorandum, the State Department plainly revealed that the central objective of US policy was to preserve American economic interests in South Africa. The memorandum was written in response to the growing public pressure on American corporations to disengage from South Africa or at least support the Polaroid experiment. It began bluntly by stating 'the problem'. 'American firms have found that investment in South Africa is very profitable. Over 300 US firms there have a total of approximately 1 per cent of US direct private foreign investment abroad and collect about 1·6 per cent of the total world-wide profits. But the political ramifications of these investments have increasingly led to public relations difficulties for firms with interests in South Africa'. The memorandum went on to say that, with mounting pressure by trade unions, church groups, civil rights organizations, and college students 'many people predict that within a relatively short time (six months to two years) the issue will replace Vietnam as the issue of the day.'

The memorandum suggested that 'the best way to defend our economic interest in South Africa against attack' was to act towards non-whites 'as nearly as possible' as in the United States. It pointed out that many American firms paid Africans below the minimum subsistence level and advised them to make improvements: 'While the difference in some cases may be so large that to institute a full-subsistence minimum wage would incur substantial costs, the unusually high profits of American affiliates in South Africa suggest that being leaders in this area would not be an impossible burden.'

It has already been pointed out that the American stake in South Africa is barely a third of the British stake. The main wave of expansion came in the 1960s. Two years before Sharpeville, when the African nationalist movement was gathering strength, the American–South African Investment Corporation was formed as a way of attracting capital to the Republic at a period of great economic and psychological need for the white minority. The Corporation's founder was Charles Engelhard, at that time the Chairman of the huge US investment company, Engelhard Hanovia.

Mr Engelhard's career is a perfect example of the chameleon-like nature of international capitalism, ready to adjust to any political background provided economic interests are not jeopardized. It also demonstrates the fundamental coincidence of interest between American corporate liberalism and South African apartheid. A close friend of President Kennedy and President Johnson, Engelhard contributed generously to the Democratic Party. He represented the United States at the independence celebrations in Gabon, at the coronation of the Pope in 1963, and at the first anniversary of Algeria's independence. He served as United States representative to Zambia's independence ceremonies in 1964.

By many South Africans Engelhard is regarded as the saviour of the post-Sharpeville economy when, as capital flowed from the country he arranged a 12½ million pound loan with the United States. He sat on the board of the Witwatersrand Native Labour Association and the Native Recruiting Agency, two official agencies which bring in Africans from Mozambique and Rhodesia to work at below-subsistence wages in the mines of South Africa. As trustee of the South Africa Foundation, Engelhard's views were made unmistakably clear when he commented on Mr Vorster's selection as Prime Minister in 1966: 'The policy of South Africa as expressed by the new Prime Minister is as much in the interests of South Africa as anything I can think of or suggest. I am not a South African but there is nothing I would do better or differently.'[2]

The heart of Engelhard's portfolio was the Engelhard Minerals and Chemical Corporation, the world's largest refiner and fabricator of precious metals. Engelhard died in the spring of 1971, but by then he and his family had sold enough shares to give Anglo American a 51 per cent control of his company. Engelhard Hanovia's South African assets include Zululand Oil Exploration, South African Forest Investments, Boart and Hard Metal Products, Charter Consolidated Ltd (Anglo's London-based finance house), Rand Selection Trust, and Thomas Barlow & Sons. The Engelhard family has set up a new holding company, Engelhard Enterprises Inc., which has a South African subsidiary and this will control their interests in the continent. Through it they have acquired a share in an electronics company, Control Logic (Pty) Ltd, and in the Rand Mines consortium which is looking for off-shore oil.

The significance of these Engelhard dealings is that they show the complex interlocking system by which America and South Africa work in full co-operation. The spirit of Engelhard's important creation, the American–South African Investment Corporation, has ranged wide. Many other American corporations have gone into partnership with South African capital. Such joint ventures have the advantage for the recipient country of providing access to technical and managerial expertise. This factor has given American capital in South Africa a role far greater than its volume alone would justify. Even so, that volume is impressive: fifteen per cent of total foreign investment in 1969 came from the Dollar Area.

In the other territories of Southern Africa American capital has gone mainly into the extraction industries, prospecting for minerals and oil. In South Africa, as the Engelhard experience shows, American capital is still heavily engaged, in absolute terms, in minerals. Many of the household names of American mining operate in the Republic. Alcan Aluminium of South Africa is joining with Union Steel Corporation in a 6 million pound plant at Richards Bay. Kaiser Aluminium has built the largest productive aluminium hot line in South Africa. King Resources of Denver, Colorado controls the country's only titanium mine, situated in a border area near East London. Union Carbide's Chrome Corporation of South Africa produces 20 per cent of the country's chrome. US Steel has constructed a 6 million pound ferrochrome smelting plant in the Sekhukuniland border area in the Eastern Transvaal. With Newmont Mining and two South African companies, Anglovaal and De Beers, it is prospecting for copper and precious stones in Botswana and South-West Africa. Other strategic materials which the United States imports from Southern Africa, as the non-communist world's only supplier, are corundum, lithium and amosite asbestos.

In spite of the importance of South Africa's minerals, half

of American direct investment is now in manufacturing and one-fifth in oil as the table below shows:

UNITED STATES: VALUE OF PRIVATE DIRECT INVESTMENT BY INDUSTRY (IN PERCENTAGES)

	1959	1964	1968
Manufacturing	34	41	48
Petroleum*	—	—	21
Mining and Smelting	27	15	11
Trade	9	10	14
Other	30	34	5

*From 1959 data on the petroleum industry was included in 'other' industries.

Source: US Department of Commerce, *Survey of Current Business,* October 1968 and 1969.

The value to South Africa of these investments is at least threefold. In oil they help the country to fill the one gap in its otherwise extraordinary endowment of all the key industrial raw materials. In manufacturing they provide the country with the benefits of advanced American technology. As a symbol and a proof of American economic involvement they help to ensure that the United States is there at hand in case of a political emergency. South Africa depends on the West to a far greater extent than vice versa, yet the idea of Western withdrawal is at present unthinkable. South Africa is an important bastion of capitalism, policing the whole Southern part of the continent. In the early part of the century the United States relied on Britain to fulfil this function and create the climate of stability in which private capital could flourish. Now that Britain's role has diminshed, South Africa has taken it on. As American corporate interests see it, South Africa's job is to keep Southern Africa safe for investment.

FRANCE

France's main importance as a collaborator with South Africa has been in the military field. Although the French representative in the Security Council in 1963 said that his country 'would take all necessary measures to prevent the sale to South Africa of weapons that might be used for purposes of repression', in practice France has treated the embargo lightly. Panhard armoured cars are made in South Africa under French licence. Alouette and Super-Frelon helicopters have been sold regularly since 1963.

From 1964 until 1970, when the Conservative Government took office in Britain, France was the only country that tried to draw a distinction between arms 'that might be used for repression' and other military equipment. It supplied Mirage-III fighter-bombers and Mystères, and agreed to deliver three 'Daphne' submarines. A contract worth five million francs for the supply of radar equipment was signed in January 1967. In 1969 two French companies joined with the South African Council for Scientific and Industrial Research to develop an all-weather surface-to-air missile system, known as Cactus. A key factor in French willingness to supply arms throughout the 1960s, when other countries demurred, was the Gaullist policy of building up France's gold reserves as an alternative to relying on the dollar. Many of the arms deals were paid for in gold. Once again South Africa's privileged position as the main supplier of gold to the West gave her important leverage.

Less publicized than the arms deals, though almost as important in giving South Africa a chance to break new ground, has been the role of the French banks. Since 1965 several private and nationalized French banks have signed agreements with large South African organizations (ESCOM or ISCOR) either for the subscription of loans on the European currency market or for trading credits. The Credit Commercial de France led other French banks in backing the first loans by ESCOM.

In volume, France is still a comparatively small investor in South Africa. In 1966 it accounted for 5·2 per cent of foreign investment in South Africa, with a stake of 134 million pounds. But French capital is playing a large part in building the foundation for South Africa's development and in the exploration and refinement of oil, and French companies are joining in two of the biggest construction projects in South Africa, the building of the Henryk Verwoerd dam on the Orange River, and the tunnel under the Fish river.

The Compagnie Française des Petroles used to have complete control of Total South Africa (Pty) but in 1969 following the lead of other foreign corporations, it sold a block of shares in Total to a local South African group, the Afrikaner house, Volkskas. Total has also gone into partnership with South African State capital. At an estimated price of 9 million pounds Total took a 30 per cent interest in the State-owned oil refinery, Natref. Total operates the Total/Shell/BP/offshore-drilling consortium which is prospecting off the Cape Coast.

French trade with South Africa has been growing fast. In 1969 exports to South Africa rose by 40 per cent, and France became South Africa's fifth largest supplier. In the five years from 1965 to 1970, South Africa sales to France doubled. But France still sells more to South Africa than she imports. This chronic balance of trade in France's favour led to a new trade agreement making even easier the entry of South African products into France.

The special relationship between France and South Africa is founded on pragmatism: France's willingness to sell arms for gold has been exploited by the South African Government for the sake of two vital parts of the country's foreign policy – backdoor entrance into the Common Market, and 'dialogue' with independent Africa. When Mr Vorster paid his first visit to Europe in 1970, the only country he went to north of the Pyrenees was France, where he saw the French Prime Minister. French diplomats played a key role behind the scenes in bringing pressure to bear on President Houphouet-Boigny so that he became the first African head of State outside Southern Africa to welcome a 'dialogue' with South Africa.

At the United Nations France gives solid support to South Africa and to Portugal. French oil companies are prospecting in Angola and Mozambique. French firms are taking part in the building of the Cabora Bassa dam which has become a symbol of South Africa's determination to create a unified sphere of influence right up to the Zambezi.

WEST GERMANY

In 1969 the West German pavilion at the Rand Easter Show was opened by the Vice-President of the Bundestag, Herr Walter Scheel. Now Foreign Minister, and known mainly for his support for Herr Willy Brandt in West Germany's *'Ostpolitik'*, Herr Scheel showed by his high-level visit to South Africa that West Germany has a *'Südpolitik'* too. His presence in Johannesburg was a useful symbol of the extraordinarily rapid growth of trade between the two countries. West Germany is now South Africa's third largest trading partner.

In 1945 a devastated country, West Germany joined the postwar race for international markets and investment openings behind its Western allies and competitors. For many years its industrialists and bankers had their eyes only on expansion inside Germany, but as the economy developed, and the Deutschmark became one of the strongest currencies in the world, West Germany emerged as one of the most important capital-exporting countries. Its private direct investment abroad trebled between the end of 1963 and mid-1969, and though the bulk of this expansion took place in Western Europe, outside the continent West German capital expanded faster in South Africa than in the United States. Although the over-all figure in mid-1969 remained relatively low at 137 million DM, much other West German

E*

capital was channelled into South Africa through the banks of third countries. By 1970, 102 West German companies had subsidiaries in South Africa, including some of the famous names of German industry, like Farbwerke Hoechst, Krupp and Siemens.

The motives and attitudes of West German industrialists towards South Africa were like those of many other Western businessmen: South Africa provides an expanding market and is a useful springboard for trade with other countries, so why bother about its politics? The outlook was well summed up in a 200-word message written by the Economic Counsellor at the West German embassy in Pretoria for a survey on West Germany, published by the Johannesburg *Sunday Times* in 1971: 'Not only is two-way trade showing a satisfactory trend. There is a growing inclination on the part of German industry to invest in South Africa, especially in collaboration with South African firms. Exports are the lifeblood of a nation. The Germans look on South Africa as a stable land of golden opportunity because of the increasing purchasing power of all her races, and her growing role as an exporter. Some West German manufacturers are already using their South African subsidiaries as an extra workshop for supplying world markets. I can see this happening more and more.'[3]

West Germany is openly and deliberately following the path mapped out by British investors, the pioneers in South Africa: willingly going into partnership with South African firms, and using South Africa with its low wage costs as a 'workshop' for making products which can then be sold in third markets. The integration of South Africa in the Western economic system is likely to increase as inflation raises wages in the main Western economies, and as South Africa's own industrial potential expands. Although white wages in South Africa are showing inflationary tendencies similar to those of Western Europe, the wages of the black majority are safely pegged.

A good example of this 'workshop' process can be seen in the arrangement made by the Demag Corporation of Duisburg to use its South African subsidiary, Cranes South Africa (Pty) Ltd, to supply equipment for a steel works being built in Mexico. The company also supplies cranes for Angola, Mozambique and Rhodesia. As a manufacturer of machinery for feeding fresh air into the mines, Demag typifies another significant aspect of West German capital in South Africa – its importance as a supplier of high-quality machinery in key sectors of the economy. Chapter 2 has discussed the role of foreign capital in giving South Africa access to advanced machinery and technology. Much of West Germany's exports to South Africa consist of sophisticated equipment, especially electrical machinery supplied by Siemens and AEG.

Siemens boasts proudly that it produced the telephone used by President Kruger. After seventy-six years in South Africa, it is hardly surprising that the company operates no differently from any local company. It has provided advanced signalling equipment for South African Railways, the sixty motors needed for the largest heavy mill in South Africa, run by ISCOR, and two hydraulic turbines at the Henryk Verwoerd dam. It is collaborating in the South African Government's control of Namibia (South-West Africa) by providing the low-tension switchgear at the Swakop dam. It is supplying the control drives for a sugar mill in Mozambique.

Through Siemens, West Germany is also heavily involved in South Africa's nuclear programme. In return for uranium West Germany has shared its nuclear knowledge with South Africa. Siemens and Krupp have helped to develop the experimental nuclear reactor at Pelindaba, near Johannesburg, and Siemens is providing equipment for the Cabora Bassa dam in Mozambique. This was one of the projects which President Kaunda tried to have stopped when he visited Herr Brandt in Bonn in 1970 and asked him to with-

draw the West German Government's 38 million pound guarantees to firms involved in the strategic dam. The German Chancellor refused. He did say, however, that in future West Germany would consider the effect of similar projects on its relations with the rest of Africa, and one result of that was the decision in January 1971 by the West German firm, Urangesellschaft, to opt out of its eight-million pound share in exploiting uranium deposits at Rossing in Nambibia in collaboration with Rio Tinto-Zinc, when the West German Government declined to give it backing.

In South Africa itself German firms have worked closely with local corporations, both private and State-owned ones. AEG Telefunken's subsidiary, AEG South Africa (Pty) is working with ESCOM on a switchboard for the town of Belville in the Cape; in partnership with the local firm of Fuchs Electrical Industries (Pty) Ltd, it supplied equipment for the new central railway station at Cape Town. German firms provide ISCOR with many of its furnaces, rolling-mill trains and other heavy equipment.

Although they are late-comers, West German corporations are closely linked with the production and marketing of South African minerals, particularly the specialized grades. West Germany buys much of South Africa's vanadium output. Kloeckner and Co, of Duisburg, has a majority share in South-West African Lithium Mines (Pty) Ltd and founded the National Materials Service Corporation (NAMASCOR) as a joint venture with the state-owned Union Steel Corporation of South Africa Ltd (USCO). The Norddeutsche Raffinerie of Hamburg has formed the South Africa Ore Corporation Ltd in conjunction with the local firm, Otavi Mining Company (Pty) Ltd to increase its supply of raw materials. The company is prospecting for copper on the territory of South Africa's neighbours.

A particular feature of West Germany's involvement in

South Africa has been the part played by the commercial banks. As long ago as 1958, when only one other foreign commercial bank (from Switzerland) had an office in Johannesburg, the Commerzbank A.G. of Dusseldorf opened up. In 1968 the Dresdner Bank, and in 1969 the Deutsche Bank, followed suit. These agencies are not directly concerned with banking but they deal with investment issues and keep in touch with the corresponding banks in West Germany. By means of loans, bonds and financial credit they have helped the flow of West German capital to South Africa, and have also been instrumental in finding South African firms who want to buy licences to manufacture West German goods locally, or to go into partnership with German companies. And at the other end of the process, West German banks backed loan issues put up by South African corporations in the European money market. The first foreign loan ever issued in the Federal Republic to which private buyers could subscribe by buying bonds on the stock exchange was a Deutsche Bank loan in 1958 of 50 million DM for the Anglo American Corporation. In January 1962, less than two years after Sharpeville, when South African credit was still low, the Deutsche Bank led a consortium guaranteeing a loan to the South African Government worth over 4 million pounds at 5·5 per cent over three years. In October 1968 the Dresdner Bank, in the name of an international consortium, put up an even larger loan of 11 million pounds for ESCOM.

The trade organization now known as the South African–German Chamber of Trade and Industry was formed soon after the war in 1949, three years before the two countries even re-established diplomatic relations. Since then trade has grown phenomenally. In 1950 South Africa exports to West Germany amounted to 13 million pounds; in 1969 they had shot up ten times to 131 million pounds. Imports rose more than twenty times over the same period from 9 million pounds to 190 millions. These figures do not cover all West

Germany's imports from South Africa as some reach the Federal Republic via Britain. Even so South Africa still has a heavy trade deficit with West Germany, some of which is financed by the sale to West German firms of shares in local South African companies. The pattern of trade is the familiar colonial one; South Africa exports fruit and raw materials, particularly minerals; West Germany exports finished products.

Finally, immigration: Germany is considered by the South African Government 'a country of origin', in which it makes particular efforts to recruit skilled white immigrants. It has recruiting offices in three German cities, Cologne, Hamburg and Munich, and their work has paid off, for by mid-1970 West Germany was the main single source of immigrants to South Africa after Britain. In the two years from 1968 to 1970 they were going out at the rate of 3,000 a year, or 8.1 per cent of the total number from the West. The high rate of British emigration to South Africa must be accounted for partly by the continuing stagnation in the British economy and the increasing rate of 'normal' unemployment, but West Germans were going out to South Africa during a continuing boom at home, and one of the main reasons must be the growing commercial and cultural links between the two countries.

JAPAN

In 1970 a leading South African economic journal estimated that by the end of the decade Japan would have overtaken Britain as South Africa's biggest export market.[4] The projection was based on the phenomenal growth of the country's trade with Japan which was rising between 1966 and 1970 at a rate of 26 per cent a year. By then Japan had already outstripped the United States as South Africa's second best customer.

This huge explosion of trade, and indeed the whole recent history of Japanese–South African relations, provided dramatic evidence of the way economic interests can alter and re-direct foreign policy. At the end of the Second World War Japan and South Africa both stood some way outside the mainstream of capitalist development, but as they have both become integrated into the Western system – South Africa as a key supplier of minerals and a base for industrial expansion in Africa, and Japan as a main link in the United States' Pacific chain – it was natural that the two countries should draw closer together. Japan's massive industrial expansion has made it an avid importer of raw materials, which South Africa is well able to supply; on its part, South Africa is a promising outlet for the products of Japan's light industry, for its textiles and consumer goods.

Strategic considerations are also pushing the two countries together. Japan's position as a world power is bound to make it look closely at South Africa's role as the policeman of the Southern part of the continent, and a key source of strategic minerals. For South Africa's policy-makers Japan is an up-and-coming country to which it is worth building bridges. The decision to grant Japanese visitors the status of 'honorary whites' was a shrewd political calculation. However, South Africa does not yet allow them to settle permanently in the country, or to marry whites; the one concession is that the authorities do not prosecute, under the Immorality Act, Japanese who live with whites. South Africans who marry Japanese are now allowed to visit their homeland, though they may not live there permanently.

Visas for businessmen, tourists and journalists have been speeded up. Occasionally, there are blunders: early in 1970, for example, a visa was at first refused to the champion Japanese jockey, Sueo Matsuzawa. but the decision was quickly reversed after protests from Japan.

On the Japanese side official policy is slowly swinging away from solidarity with the Africans and Asians and drawing closer to the West. Japan still bans arms sales to South Africa; it officially condemns apartheid; it maintains its diplomatic

143

relations at the level of consulates-general, but all this is increasingly a matter of formality and appearance as trade and economic links grow stronger.

South Africa has lifted the embargo on Japanese invest-ment, but Japan still prohibits permanent investment in South Africa in accordance with the United Nations ban, which also forbids the provision of technical assistance. But what are such bans worth when both the Nissan Motor Corporation and Toyota, for example, sell and assemble cars in South Africa? In the first half of 1971 the Datsun-1600, designed by Nissan, was the third most popular car sold there.

Japan conveniently fails to define 'investment', and the history of Datsun–Nissan in South Africa shows how the UN ban can be evaded. It began in 1958 with the flotation of Datsun Motor Vehicle Distributors (Pty) to market commercial vehicles made by Nissan of Japan. Until 1961 these were imported, fully assembled. Then the decision was taken to assemble them locally, and the work was done under contract by a firm in Durban. But the South African Government's programme of making car assemblers use a minimum of parts with 'local content', i.e. made in South Africa, led to the creation of a holding company known as the Datsun–Nissan Investment Company. This company built a factory at Rosslyn near Pretoria, to take advantage of the specially cheap labour available in a border area. It is wholly owned by South Africans to comply with the Japanese Government's 'ban'. Instead the Nissan Motor Corporation makes a profit from the sale of components to the flourishing South African outlet, which in turn, after a bad patch in 1969 and 1970, made pre-tax profits of almost 2 million pounds in 1971 and gained 13 per cent of the South African commercial vehicle market and 6 per cent of the passenger market. The Nissan Motor Corporation admits that it provides technical assistance to the South African company.

The Toyota company is also successful in South Africa.

Its cars are assembled by a wholly owned subsidiary of Wesco Investments Ltd. Motor-car and truck components are by far and away the largest item Japan exports to South Africa, – one-third of total sales in 1969.

The Japanese car-manufacturers' device of setting up plants inside South Africa in order to ensure a larger share of the market has been used by other Japanese industries. Since 1968 four of the largest Japanese conglomerates, Mitsubishi Heavy Industries, the Mitsui Mining Company, Nissho Iwai, and C. Itoh have established branches there. As South African pressure for foreign companies to allow greater local participation and control grows, Japan's 'restriction' on Japanese ownership is being turned to advantage: she can claim to have pioneered the acceptance of South African control.

For South Africa, Japan's economic importance stems from its huge demand for imported minerals. Its political importance is in the fact that, of all the countries of Asia and Africa, it is the first country with which South Africa has begun a dialogue as a way of lessening the threat of isolation; it has a place in South Africa's grand design for an alliance stretching across the Southern hemisphere from Argentina to Australia. As a gesture of faith in this growing friendship, the South African Government decided in 1971 to go ahead with its most ambitious construction project so far: a scheme to lay 500 miles of electrified railway from the Sishen Iron Ore mines in the Northern Cape to the coast, and to build a new harbour at Saldanha Bay, north of Cape Town, particularly for shipments to Japan. The project has been planned and financed by the State-owned Iron and Steel Corporation. Ore deliveries will not start until 1975 but in the meantime South Africa has won contracts to export to Japan vast quantities of coking coal, expected to reach three million tons a year by 1976. Coal exports are a particularly good prospect for South Africa because of the very low labour costs involved. What has delayed South African expansion here so far has been transport bottlenecks and generally inadequate rail and harbour facilities.

Japan is already a good customer for South African manganese, and now for increasing amounts of uranium, since it plans to increase generation of nuclear power three-fold between 1975 and 1985. Already one big client, the Tohuku Electric Power Company, is buying natural uranium from the State-owned South African NUFCOR. As an exporter, Japan competes with leading Western firms for the advanced technology contracts for building South Africa's industrial infrastructure: for instance, Japanese firms have provided the micro-wave communication equipment for the Durban–Sasolburg oil pipeline, hydro-electric turbines for the Henryk Verwoerd dam, an oxygen plant for ISCOR's Vanderbijlpark works, and transformers for ESCOM.

It is ironic that, as Japan itself develops into a major exporter of capital and of capital goods, its main role in the Western market as a supplier of cheap electronic products and light consumer goods may be taken over by South Africa. The cliché about Japanese radio transistors being available all over the world may go out of date: the first South African transistors have already been sold in Japan. Rising wages there are already beginning to price some light goods out of the international market. This is a chance which South Africa, with wages at poverty-level for an oppressed labour force, is waiting for. It is preparing to offer Japan tools and motor components. This sets the pattern for the future, but today's trade is already high in volume: South Africa is Japan's main supplier of ferrous alloys and pig-iron, its second largest supplier of maize, its third largest of wool and sugar. By the late 1960s Japan took twelve per cent of South Africa's exports, and supplied eight per cent of its imports. The prediction that it may be South Africa's best customer by 1980 is not entirely fanciful.

8 The Companies: Image and Reality

> If you start moralizing about whom you'll trade with
> and whom you won't, where do you stop? – *Lord
> Nelson, Chairman of the General Electric Company, in* The
> Director *April/May 1971*
>
> General Motors South Africa does not discriminate
> between the races as to wages – except for a
> difference in starting rates which are higher for
> whites than for Coloured or native employees –
> *James Roche, Chairman of General Motors* [1]

Nowadays every major international firm has its 'philosophy'.
As the economic, and hence the political power of these huge
corporations increases, boards of directors and public relations departments have been doing some thinking, in order
to find answers for the minority of shareholders, journalists,
politicians, trade unionists and other busybodies who occasionally ask them irksome questions about 'corporate responsibility'. What is being done to lessen the shock of sudden
redundancy for long-service employees? What about pollu-
tion? How do you justify your involvement in South Africa?

The questions are more probing and more insistent than
they used to be, and none of them is more of a nuisance to
companies than the one about South Africa. Even so,
answers have to be given, and investigators who have
approached corporations on this subject have now learned
enough about company psychology to be able to make a
few generalizations.

Most firms will tend to make little of their role in South
Africa, but to make the most of the wages they claim to be
paying their African workers. In all cases they will say that
they are paying higher wages than other firms in the same

147

field. In most cases they will throw up their hands at suggestions that they are paying less than the poverty line. In almost no case will they give details of their actual wage figures. When they do, it is a rare sign of honesty.

Most firms will argue that it is not their role to interfere in South African Government policy. although they will claim that, behind the scenes, they are doing their bit to improve things. Most firms will say that they cannot break the law, but boast of 'bending the rules' as far as they can in order to hire more Africans. Few firms will admit that hiring more Africans at lower wages is good business. All firms argue that their involvement in South Africa does not imply approval of apartheid. One almost universally valid conclusion is that as the issue of South Africa has grown in prominence, companies have become more and more willing to express their 'philosophy' but less willing to produce the facts to back up their case. The *Financial Mail*[2] correctly forecast the development when it commented in 1971 on the campaign to reveal foreign business links with South Africa: 'One defence open to those trading with this corner of the world is that of secrecy, and this may be expected to increase from now on.'

Our experience fully bears this out. Many firms declined our request for interviews and were reluctant to supply information. Usually the refusals were polite and diplomatic. Occasionally the replies seemed to indicate a siege mentality: General Motors South Africa (Pty) Ltd, for example, declined on the grounds that past experience had shown that any information made available 'was immediately relayed to Black Power movements in the United States'. Yet even Mr W. E. Luke, the Chairman of the pro-South African UKSATA, told a group of senior industrialists at the annual council luncheon in London on 22 November 1971 that they should not try to cover up.[3] 'What we are asked to do,' he said, 'is to improve the wages, training facilities and conditions of work generally of the under-privileged people we employ in South Africa, and even to devote funds towards their self-help and educational projects. The moral aspect of our involvement is constantly raised; I believe we should accept the challenge, proclaim our belief in the morality of our operations and at the same time show by our record there that we have nothing to be ashamed of. Certain outside pressures are legitimate; others are not. Pressures to improve wages and working conditions are surely among the former.'

In the United States, Congressman Charles Diggs, who visited South Africa in 1971, and has campaigned vigorously for 'American firms to push beyond the limits of the permissible and end their racist practices', is urging the American Government to set up the appropriate machinery to investigate the way US firms operate in South Africa. In the long run secrecy will be no solution for corporations.

It is no solution in the short run, either. Although very few firms took up Mr Luke's suggestion of showing 'by our record that we have nothing to be ashamed of', enough is known about the wage policies and over-all involvement of a cross-section of companies for a clear picture to emerge. Later in this chapter there are a number of case studies of key foreign firms operating in South Africa, but the first point to deal with is their 'philosophy'.

Few firms fail to emphasize that they disapprove of apartheid. Verbal condemnation of apartheid is, of course, a *sine qua non* of any respectable discussion of South Africa – at least outside South Africa, but attitudes expressed in a company's head office in London or New York are not always put into practice in South Africa.

In July 1969 a commercial consultancy firm, Market Research Africa (Pty) Ltd, compiled 'a study of the attitudes of American and Canadian businessmen based in South Africa towards selected issues regarding the South African economy, business and politics'.[4] Out of 106 replies to the questionnaire (a third of those approached) an astonishing 77 per cent felt that South Africa's racial policies represented an 'approach that is, under the circumstances at least, an attempt to develop a solution'. Less than one in ten companies felt that the approach was 'altogether incorrect'. As many as 31 per cent said that they would vote Nationalist if they were eligible to vote, 32 per cent would support the United Party and 20 per cent the Progressive Party. This means that 63 per cent supported parties openly espousing white supremacy and the general system of apartheid.

In a series of interviews in South Africa conducted on behalf of the United Church of Christ in the USA, Mr Timothy H. Smith, a researcher for the Church's Council for Christian Social Action put together more data about company attitudes. He reported that there seemed to be little difference between American subsidiaries, whether they had South Africans or Americans as top management or not, 'in their conduct in South Africa and the reports fed back to the parent company about the economic and social conditions of South Africa'.[5]

In his report he wrote: 'The social relations of American businessmen in South Africa may be a partial indicator of their attitudes. When top management were asked whether they had any friends or acquaintances in the African, Asian, or Cape Coloured communities, to a man the answer was no. One of the more sensitive men admitted that the closest contact he had made with Africans was at the US Embassy July the Fourth function. Echoing the situation of all interviewed he explained that inter-racial contact for American businessmen in South Africa is tremendously difficult unless a person made extreme efforts. The grossest reaction came in July 1970 from the managing director of the Ford Motor Company in South Africa who simply stated 'I don't mix with them in the States; I don't mix with them here, and if I went back to the States, I wouldn't mix with them there either.'

Smith went on, 'The only close contact top businessmen had with non-whites was with their servants; yet many talked as though they were experts on the customs, culture, superstitions and problems of non-whites.' Many used the word 'Bantu' instead of African, which was symbolic of 'their insensitivity to African feelings since many Africans find the term highly offensive . . . Such executives will use what power they have both in the macrocosm of South African society and in the microcosm of their plant to perpetuate a *status quo* that rests on white superiority, denies black workers political rights, a living and just wage, and the right to organize. . . . At best the American and South African manager reflects a warm paternalism, concerned from afar with "these people's needs", at worst an impersonal desire to bring "these uncivilized savages" into a technical age and work them hard for the American factory's profit.' Finally he concluded: 'The vast majority of those interviewed stated that life for non-whites in South Africa had improved substantially over the past ten years as the economy boomed and as the standard of living increased. . . . The cross-section of those businessmen had very little knowledge of non-whites maltreatment, suffering or inconvenience. Very few knew of the massive removals of Africans being carried out by the Government, for instance.'

From the evidence we have about the attitudes of executives of British companies, there is no reason to believe that they differ from those of their American and Canadian colleagues. Denis Herbstein, when he conducted the series of interviews for the London *Sunday Times*,[6] found the same use of the word 'Bantu' and the same lack of contact. In London, businessmen show a similar range of attitudes, once they have made the statutory condemnation of apartheid. Some show sympathy for 'the Afrikaner mentality': 'They've got nowhere else to go to.' Others speak of 'Bantu' or 'natives'. Sir Val Duncan, Chairman of Rio Tinto–Zinc shows a powerful streak of paternalism. At the company's annual general meeting in 1971 he said that it was his conviction that 'all mankind is the same but different peoples are at different stages of development. It is our privilege to better the lot of everyone who works with us.'[7] Questioned in an interview with one of the authors about his attitude to investment in Namibia (South-West Africa) he said, 'I once asked a super-Liberal "What particular people there are going to get up from under a banana-tree or wherever it is and run the country?" If they're well-paid and become gradually middle-class and settled, then they will help the country in the long run. At the moment we're faced by a vacuum.' At the annual general meeting Sir Val said it was not the job of firms such as RTZ to determine the 'right answers' to the South African situation.

At Dunlop senior management took a relaxed attitude towards apartheid. Mr M. Bexon, a director of both the parent board and of Dunlop South Africa explained that things could not be 'that intolerable' in South Africa because, he said, it was not difficult to get executives from Britain to go out to work in the Dunlop plant there but it was very hard to get them out to Zambia.

Companies have two other main justifications for continuing in South Africa. One, of course, is that by fostering economic growth they are incidentally working for racial change. Chapter 3 has shown the fallacy of the notion that Africans are becoming better off. Do the companies believe it themselves? It is not impossible that some do. To a casual observer, returning to South Africa's white areas at intervals of two or three years, there is evidence of change. There are more blacks in the cities, and many of them are doing jobs which a few years ago only whites would have done. What is true in general is equally likely to be true in the particular companies which British or American businessmen work in or visit. The mistake is to interpret this as proof of progress rather than, as Chapter 4 has argued, as a 'floating upward' of the colour bar. The illusion of significant change tends to be propagated in the English-speaking South African business community particularly, among just the group with whom visiting foreign businessmen have most contact. The Johannesburg *Sunday Times* is the main press voice of the United Party which claims to speak for the businessman. It carried a huge front-page story in January 1971[8] under the startling headline 'Dramatic decade of massive economic integration'. 'Apartheid collapses'. it went on, 'dependence on non-white labour is absolute.' To back this point, the paper declared that 'seventy-two per cent of the nation's workers are now non-whites; South Africa is now absolutely and irrevocably dependent on non-white labour for economic survival; the integration of non-whites into the South African economy is so far-reaching and so deep-rooted that it can never be reversed or eliminated; job reservation scarcely exists.' This mirrors the view held by many businessmen, and in its context in the Johannesburg *Sunday Times*, it was a good piece of party political propaganda, setting up an Aunt Sally version of apartheid, as though the Nationalists intended to make the economy an all-white one. In fact the paper was merely drawing attention to the well-known increase in the size of the black labour force, an entirely predictable feature of the expanding economy. What the paper did not point out is that the wage-rate normally falls for Africans who take over white jobs, and that Africans are still barred from being promoted above whites.

Individual employers like to echo the point about 'apartheid collapsing. They claim to be undermining job reservation behind the scenes, and very often they are: 'You'd be surprised to find what jobs Africans are doing in our plant', said an executive of one British firm. Like representatives of most of the firms which are doing the same thing, he insisted on anonymity, for fear the Government or the white trade unions might step in.

At the same time employers are aware of the two points the Johannesburg *Sunday Times* did not mention in its 'splash' item – the falling wage-rate and the bar to promotion for Africans. The executive in England who spoke about job

reservation was asked whether this meant that Africans were
being paid less for the same work? 'Yes, but it's like England
where we try to get a job that is done by a fitter reclassified
so that it can be done by a fitter's mate. If you get the job
moved to a non-union chap it would be done for less. I
don't think the drive for non-whites to do work for less is
any less fair than what is done here in a European context.'
As for promoting Africans over whites: T. B. Higgins, an
English director of Unilever, told Denis Herbstein of the
London *Sunday Times* that is was a 'silly question' when he
asked if whites worked under blacks: 'The laws and customs
are such that it never happens.'[9] An executive of one of the
ten leading British companies in South Africa made the same
point to the authors: 'You can't put a black man in charge
of a white. For commercial reasons you can't employ a black
man to sell to a white. That doesn't leave much scope, I
admit. Having said that, we do try to treat people on their
merits.'

The second justification which firms generally give for
their presence in South Africa is that they provide work.
Sometimes this point is put in the negative: 'IBM believes
that the destruction of jobs of both blacks and whites by
withdrawal from South Africa would be morally untenable.'[10]
In its bald form the argument is irrelevant since the issue
in South Africa is not one of creating employment. By defini-
tion employers provide jobs: Victorian colliery owners provided work for children. The question is: what are the wages
for the job and what are the conditions of work.

The evidence here shows that foreign firms are little better
than South African ones. Although some of them claim to
be bringing higher standards to bear, and indeed use this
'civilizing role' as a further justification for continued involvement, most firms are indistinguishable from their South
African counterparts. The pioneer firms have been South
African, as the US State Department memorandum on
American firms pointed out. 'US subsidiaries and affiliates

have not been conspicuously different from other firms in South Africa. Many have treated their non-white workers better than many South African firms but as a group their record has not been outstanding. Rather, certain South African firms have been the leaders in the labour relations field. Local managers often adopt South African attitudes, and even when they do not they are understandably unwilling to sacrifice profits or risk public and governmental criticism without clear guidance from company headquarters.'

Similar comments were made by a fifteen-man study team representing six American churches which visited South Africa in November 1971. They said they could not leave the country 'without indicating our distress at the general lack of initiative by US corporations up to now to upgrade the total conditions of the black workers in this country.'[11] The group determined to ask the corporations' head offices in the US 'Why they had not helped to establish black trade unions, why they had not raised wages and benefits to give blacks parity with whites, why they had not set up effective job-training schemes to allow blacks upward mobility, and why they had not provided housing, transport and education for black employees and their families who barely eked out an existence under intolerable conditions'?

Timothy Smith in his survey of American firms reported that 'Workers were not paid with any consideration given to their worth or to their needs (to stay alive). They were paid within the customary norms set by the South African business community.'[12] He notes that Union Acceptances Ltd, a Johannesburg-based firm which produces a handbook of comparative wages and benefits for employees for the use of corporations who want to remain competitive, had recently included only 4 pages (out of 334) on black wages. Until then, he says, comparative statistics were of little interest to employers who merely paid what they chose.

In his survey, Denis Herbstein quoted Louis Nelson, an Indian member of the executive of the Trade Union Council of South Africa, who said 'British industrialists could set the pace, because they are intelligent and sophisticated. Instead they perpetuate the low wage policy and job reservation.' Herbstein's own researches bore out this comment: the ten British companies he investigated, Afrox (a subsidiary of British Oxygen), British Leyland, Dunlop, Guest Keen and Nettlefolds, ICI, Premier Milling (a subsidiary of Associated British Foods), Pilkington, Robert Hudson, Unilever, and White's Portland Cement (a subsidiary of Associated Portland Cement) all started Africans below the Association of Chambers of Commerce poverty line. White's Portland Cement was unwilling to give him wage figures, but the *Rand Daily Mail* reported six months later than the company's minimum rate at its Lichtenburg plant was £2·47 a week[13] – one of the lowest wage-rates for industrial workers in the whole of South Africa.

In the provision of pensions for Africans, British companies appeared to do a little better than local firms. Apart from Premier Milling and Leyland, each of the companies Herbstein investigated did have a scheme though it was rarely as generous as the one for whites. There is nothing in South African law to prevent companies making improvements here. One South African company, South African Breweries, is unusual in having a pension scheme that is claimed to offer benefits comparable to those of whites.[14] It argues for the scheme on straight commercial lines, in that it reduces labour turnover and increases employees' identification with the company.

As for medical aid schemes for Africans, the record of foreign companies is poor. Caltex has no scheme, and nor do any of the companies in Herbstein's survey. Afrox, which does have a scheme for whites, says that one for Africans is unnecessary because they can all get free medicine from the Government health service. W. R. Stephens, Managing Director of ICI South Africa told Herbstein: 'It is the sort of thing we would like to do but it is very difficult to administer. If a single black girl who has been working for you for twenty years has five children, what do you do?' Dunlop South Africa, whose Personnel Manager, Aubrey Getaz, has served as President of the Natal Employers' Association, pressed the association to allow Africans to join the Natal Industries Medical Aid Scheme. In its own factory in Durban in the spring of 1971 Dunlop was operating a scheme only for whites, Coloureds and Indians. Like I C I, it argues that, in the case of Africans, the extended family creates 'a problem'.[15]

It would be unrealistic to expect companies to welcome the formation of African trade unions, and, sure enough, few see the absence of registered unions of African workers as a disadvantage. Their complacency was typified by the President of the South Africa–Britain Trade Association, by W. R. Stephens, when he came to London in October 1971 as head of a mission organized by the Association. Asked at a press conference whether it was true that Africans had no right to strike, Mr Stephens seemed to have forgotten; he said he thought it was so but that he would refer the question to the white trade-union leader in the mission for confirmation. Commenting on the same issue in July 1971, the *Financial Mail* wrote: 'Everyone knows that although African workers are legally allowed to form trade unions, these unions are denied recognition under the Industrial Conciliation Act. That means Africans cannot participate directly in collective bargaining over how much they should be paid, how many hours they should work, what their working conditions should be, whether they should enjoy fringe benefits like pensions, canteens, and so on. Instead their needs and aspirations are supposed to be formulated, interpreted and then represented at Industrial Council meetings and Wage Board hearings by Government officials. Those officials have to be whites in terms of the Bantu Labour (Settlement of Disputes) Act which seeks in this way to compensate Africans for being denied the right of normal collective bargaining.'[16]

Thirty or forty years ago African trade unions were slowly tackling employers on wages and conditions, but since then they have been systematically broken by a combination of industrial and political repression (a further example of the way business and politics mix). The historical facts did not, however, prevent Brian Inglis of GKN telling Herbstein that the majority of the 'natives' were not 'ready for unionism'. Jimmy Sutherland, the Managing Director of African Oxygen, told him that Africans 'are uneducated and led by agitators into pitfalls'.

The one form of inadequate quasi-union activity which is officially allowed for Africans is that under Section 7 of the Bantu Labour (Settlement of Disputes) Act 'works committees' can be set up and registered in any factory or plant employing more than 20 Africans. In 1969, the Minister of Labour, Marais Viljoen, said that there were 24 statutory committees in existence plus 52 non-statutory ones. This represents less than 1 per cent of the number of registered factories in South Africa. After investigating the situation, Muriel Horrell of the South African Institute of Race Relations discovered that only 13 of the 24 were functioning together with another 11 which the Minister had omitted.[17] Some of these appeared to exist in name only. At Robert Hudson & Sons, Dick Wardrup, the Managing Director, told Herbstein that the company had 'no objections to African unions, of course not. It simplifies communication and discipline. As to the political implications this is the risk you take.' A few months later the *Financial Mail* reported[18] that although Robert Hudson & Sons in Benoni had a registered works committee, the acting Personnel Manager in charge of Africans said he did not know if it was still operating. Asked why he did not know, he replied he was to busy to take an interest in such things.

The *Financial Mail* has argued that firms should make more use of these works committees: 'There is an urgent need for employers to take the initiative on behalf of their otherwise voiceless black workers. This machinery may be a poor substitute for direct trade-union participation. But it is all there is, and there is no excuse for not ensuring the best use is made of it.' Some companies have informal and non-statutory committees. At the Dunlop plant in Durban, where two committees were formed in 1960 they represent 1,358 blue-collar and clerical workers. They meet management regularly and are said to be free to consider all working conditions, including wages, and 'are sure of a sympathetic hearing', the *Financial Mail* reports.[19] At Dunlop's head office in London, management says the committees 'operate like trade unions as far as we're concerned. We see the trade union situation changing, and unions coming.' Dunlop is an exception. Most companies have no such committees.

In the field of social policy, few firms have taken up the Polaroid corporation's idea of giving almost a third of their South African profits towards African education. RTZ is planning a scheme at the Palabora copper mine but no sum has yet been announced. Most companies have in-service training arrangements for their staff but these obviously have a bearing potentially on performance and profits. M. L. Bexon, a director of Dunlop, says that the problem with welfare schemes is 'Where do you stop? If you operate internationally there's something to do in every country. You could very well say that British industry should be helping old-age pensioners in this country. To run a welfare scheme all round the world would be very expensive.'

In spite of their pretended 'neutrality' towards South Africa's racial policies, and their reluctance to make a contribution towards African education or other welfare projects, many companies readily give money to the South Africa Foundation, an avowed lobby group 'whose *raison d'être*', as a US State Department memo puts it, 'is to justify South Africa and South African society'. Yet, as Timothy Smith discovered in his interviews, many of the same companies felt that contributions to the Institute of Race Relations or the Christian Institute of South Africa, both of which oppose apartheid, would be 'political acts'.[20]

Companies show a similar 'neutrality' if they are challenged on the issues of segregation, or discriminatory wage policies. One exception is Barclays, which says it is 'a commercial bank whose aim is to make its facilities available to all without discrimination on grounds of race or colour'.[21] Yet a recent annual report of Barclays Bank DCO shows a photograph of a Barclays branch with separate white and black entrances. Most firms make no pretence at all. Their constant refrain is that they have no choice but to accept the position. According to ICI, for example, 'the policies of the governments of certain countries with whom we trade may be unattractive but of necessity the companies that we operate throughout the world must be subject to the laws of the country in which they are located'.[22] Esso says: 'As a guest corporation in South Africa we are required to operate within the law of the country as indeed we are obliged to conform to the laws enacted by the sovereign government of any country in which we operate.'[23] Deere & Company, a large American manufacturer of agricultural equipment put it this way: 'Naturally as corporate citizens Deere & Company and its affiliates expect to obey the laws of the land in which they operate.'[24]

The role of the obedient guest tends to be adopted when it is convenient. Deere is an interesting case. From 1967, because it was not South African policy to boycott Rhodeisa, Deere South Africa continued to export farm implements to Rhodesia, despite the United Nations sanctions. As a company registered in South Africa, though American-owned, it played the polite guest. In the same year the South African Government put pressure on Deere South Africa to increase the local content of the products it marketed in South Africa. This time, however, in a report to the Government, Deere complained, saying that an increase in the local content would be detrimental to the buyer and to the South African economy. The Government gave in.[25]

The increased pressure which a few shareholders have started to bring, the occasional disruption at an annual general meeting, or the threat that this or that institution – university, trade union, or church – may withdraw its funds have made most firms worry more about their image than the reality of apartheid. After surveying attitudes in South Africa in December 1969, the *Wall Street Journal* reached the following conclusion,[26] and it could equally well apply to British business: 'Discussions with executives of US firms in South Africa reveal that the question of condemnation at home is not much more than a public-relations problem to them. Most are sincere in believing their presence in a land committed to the policies of apartheid is ambivalent at worst, and at best greatly beneficial to the blacks of South Africa'.

Within the bland over-all view, of course, some individual differences of opinion arise. Some businessmen are utterly defiant, like Don Ryder, the Chairman of the Reed Corporation, who said of his critics, '. . . I'll be ready for them when they start trying to disrupt Reed meetings. What South Africa needs for a better overseas understanding of its problems is for more and more companies to have plants here.'[27] Others express apparently agonizing doubts. Sir Raymond Brookes, the Chairman of GKN, was asked about apartheid at the annual general meeting in May 1971, and had this to say: 'It is not for me to enter into the vexed question of apartheid or South Africa and that kind of thing. It is sufficient to say that some of us who may be presumed to be unmindful of these things are not unmindful. We see, we have our feelings of terrible reservations and, perhaps unobtrusively, we seek to make a contribution to the solution of the problem.'[28] Sympathetic words – but Sir Raymond ruled the question out of order. For most businessmen, whether they are doubting or defiant, apartheid is still either an irrelevant issue or one which they are unwilling to confront.

NINE CASE STUDIES

We now look in more detail at seven British companies and two American ones, all with a close involvement in South Africa. Seven have subsidiaries there. One manages a company in which it has a substantial minority interest. One is a nationalized corporation.

They were selected mainly because they represent a cross-section of the areas where foreign companies are most active: two car companies, one tyre manufacturer, an oil company, a mining company, a chemical combine, a heavy engineering firm, an electrical company and a steel corporation. An additional factor in their selection was that, with the exception of the General Electric Company (and the British Steel Corporation, which was not approached on this point) they were all prepared to provide information on their wages either to the authors or other researchers. It can probably be safely assumed that those companies which refused to co-operate are paying even lower wages. In Appendix 1 there is a list of all the British companies with subsidiaries or associates in South Africa, complete as far as the authors know; most of the companies we approached were unwilling to give wage figures or other detailed information.

The following companies, then, are probably those with above-average wage-rates.

THE RIO TINTO–ZINC CORPORATION

By any standards, the Rio Tinto–Zinc Corporation is one of the most successful multi-national mining and mining finance companies in the world. In 1954 it sold a two-thirds' share in its unprofitable Rio Tinto pyrite mines in Spain to a consortium of Spanish banks and found itself with 8 million pounds available for investment. From that seed it has created a world-wide corporation which in 1970 had a turnover of 496 million pounds and an operating profit before tax of over 80·7 millions.

Two mergers have helped in the company's phenomenal growth. In 1962 the Rio Tinto Company, whose principal interests by then were in copper and uranium, joined forces with the Consolidated Zinc Corporation which mined lead, zinc and aluminium. Six years later R T Z joined with Borax (Holdings) Ltd. The group now mines most of the major minerals as well as manufacturing explosives, chemicals, and industrial plastics.

R T Z's Chairman, Sir Val Duncan, prides himself and his company on long-term thinking. R T Z has largely confined itself to what he calls 'the more mature democracies'.[29] 'There was not a lot of cunning behind it but when we had done it we realized how right we were,' he adds. Included in the 'mature democracies', with Britain, the United States, Canada and Australia, is South Africa. Of all the R T Z's interests, its South African associated company, the Palabora Mining Company Ltd, is the most successful. In 1970 only 7·7 per cent of R T Z's assets were in South Africa but 42 per cent of the group's profits came from Palabora, a giant copper mine in the north-east Transvaal, on the edge of the Kruger National Park.

In 1971 there was a sharp drop in the world price for copper and Palabora's profits fell by almost one-third. Nevertheless, the mine's basic strength is assured. As Sir Val told the annual general meeting in 1968, 'As far as Palabora is concerned, it is one of the cheapest copper producers in the world. This means that there is no foreseeable price for copper which would make it an unremunerative operation.'[30]

Two factors provide the key to R T Z's successful performance. One is its technical skill. Most of its mines are huge, opencast operations run by highly capital-intensive methods. Instead of complex and expensive underground pits, R T Z operates giant excavating and haulage equipment – vast diggers and 100-ton trucks. This allows it, for example, at Palabora, to make a profit out of the lowest grade ore mined

163

anywhere in the world, some of it with a copper content of only 0·2 per cent.

Low wages undoubtedly help too. RTZ says its African workers earned on average only £33·92 a month in August 1971,[31] adding that 'quite a number of African employees earn over £51 a month. Haulage-truck drivers earn approximately £66·67 a month.' The company does not disclose what is the minimum wage it pays. Although the earnings quoted are above the nation-wide South African wage for African copper-miners, the company maintains different gradings for African and white workers. The original plans for the mine were made on the assumption that, even if it employed all European labour, it would be profitable. If this was correct, the company could afford to give equal pay for equal work regardless of race, but it prefers to take advantage of lower African wages. Whites have 27 days' paid holiday a year after three years; Africans have 15 days.

Palabora employs 846 Europeans and 2,272 Africans. RTZ boasts that it does not use the contract-labour system which is the foundation of most South African mining, with married men, on one-year or two-year contracts, living as 'bachelors' in dormitories. Instead, its African workers live in a specially built segregated township, Namakgale, which was developed by the Department of Bantu Administration. The absence of artificial 'bachelor' quarters is certainly an advantage, and one which the company claims it was able to achieve in spite of initial opposition from the Government.[32] But Palabora is a designated 'border area', with a Government-sponsored phosphate mine and a developing white town, both able to benefit from the existence of plentiful cheap labour in an African reserve nearby. The miners' wives make useful domestic servants in the white homes. So, there is no need to bring in Africans under a contract-labour system to live as 'bachelors'. Expansion at Phalaborwa, as the white town is called, fits in well with the Government's 'separate development' plan for creating decentralized growth points to which industrialists will eventually come.

Besides its technical expertise, RTZ's other hallmark is its willingness to diversify the ownership of its operations. Its interest in Palabora is only 38·9 per cent although it manages the mine. Another third of the company approximately is owned by the US Newmont Mining Corporation, Selection Trust, and the Union Corporation, while South African institutions and individual shareholders own the rest. The State of South Africa *Yearbook* for 1971, a Government-supported economic handbook, comments that 'About two-thirds of Palabora's capital comes from overseas sources – a healthy sign of confidence in the Republic.'[33]

An even more encouraging 'sign of confidence' for Pretoria is RTZ's decision to go ahead with opening a huge uranium mine at Rossing in Namibia (South-West Africa). Because South Africa's occupation of Namibia has been repeatedly condemned by the United Nations and declared illegal by the International Court of Justice in the Hague, at least one Western company has bowed to pressure and refrained from investing in the territory. The German company, Urangesellschaft which was also prospecting for uranium retreated when the West German Government refused to provide financial guarantees for the scheme. Not so RTZ, nor indeed the British Government which not only made no attempt to dissuade British companies, but even approved a contract whereby RTZ's mine will supply uranium to the United Kingdom Atomic Energy Authority: the contract was first passed by Anthony Wedgwood-Benn, Minister of Technology in the last Labour Government. At Rossing RTZ is in partnership with the General Mining and Finance Corporation Ltd, the Afrikaner-dominated finance group, and with the State-supported Industrial Development Corporation. The mine's capital cost is 50 million pounds.

RTZ has a 99 per cent interest in Rio Tinto (Rhodesia), which operated four gold-mines in Rhodesia at the time of the illegal Declaration of Independence. While sanctions were still in operation, Rio Tinto (Rhodesia) opened a new nickel mine. The company's after-tax profits in 1969 were £860,000, three times higher than the figure for 1968. Sir Val Duncan was one of the first senior businessmen to visit Rhodesia within days of the drawing up of the settlement proposals in November 1971. The company has also been prospecting for diamonds in Lesotho.

This diversity of interest is matched by that of the controlling interests on the RTZ parent board, a classic example of interlocking directorships, giving RTZ links with the boards of many of Britain's main banking, insurance, and industrial institutions. Sir Val himself is on the board of the Bank of England. His Deputy-Chairman, Sir Mark Turner, is also a Deputy-Chairman of the merchant bankers, Kleinwort & Benson, on whose board Mr Reginald Maudling used to sit until the 1970 General Election. Sir Mark is also a director of the Commercial Union Assurance Co., of Midland and International Banks Ltd, of British Home Stores and of the National Cash Register Company. Lord Clitheroe, another RTZ director, is chairman of the Mercantile Investment Trust Ltd, a deputy-chairman of Tube Investments and of the National Westminster Bank, and sits on the boards of Coutts & Co., of Union Minière, and of the Benguela Railway Company, which operates in Portuguese-controlled Angola.

Through D. R. Colville and Gerald Coke, RTZ has links with the boards of the merchant banks, N. M. Rothschild & Sons Ltd, and S. G. Warburg & Co. Another director is Baron Guy de Rothschild, President of the Banque Rothschild. S. Spiro is Managing Director of Charter Consolidated and Deputy-Chairman of Cape Asbestos. Irish and Australian banks are represented by Sir Basil Goulding, a director of the Bank of Ireland, and E. L. Baillieu, a director of the Australian and New Zealand Bank Ltd. Mark Littman is Deputy-Chairman of the British Steel Corporation.

The board of Palabora is a similar cross-section of leading South African and international industrialists and bankers, including C. B. Andrews, Managing Director of the Union Corporation and Chairman of five of its gold-mines, G. A. Macmillan, General Manager of the I D C and a director of the S A S O L Marketing Company, C. S. Barlow, executive director of Thomas Barlow & Sons, Deputy-Chairman of the Standard Bank of South Africa, a director of South African Breweries and South African Eagle Insurance, M. D. Banghart, Chairman of the O'Kiep Copper Company and a director of the American–South African Investment Co., and P. Malozemoff, President of Newmont Mining Corporation,

With an area of interest like this, it is not surprising that Sir Val Duncan and R T Z are prepared to work within the *status quo* in South Africa. The way to bring about change is as he sees it, to raise the standard of living through economic development. Although he told us he has never found a conflict between morality and business so far, he believes that in some circumstances he *could* see non-economic considerations overriding questions of profit. In Nazi Germany? 'Yes, I could see that in any country that was unwise enough to have submitted to Adolf Hitler and the horrors he perpetrated on the Jewish community we might well have had great difficulties in continuing.'[34] But, Sir Val added, it is not fair to say that South Africa is comparable with Nazi Germany. Is there anywhere in today's world where R T Z would not invest for moral reasons? 'Yes,' Sir Val replied after some thought, 'Chile. They have stolen a whole copper industry from the Americans without compensation. We are not jackals. I would not go in there now and operate mines which have been stolen.'

BRITISH LEYLAND

In 1970 the profit made by Leyland Motor Corporation of South Africa exceeded the total world profit of the Leyland Group. Leyland South Africa's profits rose 17 per cent to a record 4·8 million pounds; the profits of the whole Leyland Group slumped from 40 million pounds to 4 millions.[35] There could be no more striking illustration of the part played by investment in South Africa in the operations of British big business than the importance of its South African subsidiary to Britain's eighth largest industrial company.

There are other indications of the importance Leyland attaches to its South African operations. When its overseas activities were reorganized in a new holding company, British Leyland International Ltd, at the end of 1970, the job of Managing Director went to J. H. Plane, Chairman of Leyland South Africa. Most of Leyland's 125 million pounds of over-seas investment has gone to South Africa and Australia and J. H. Plane has gone on record as saying that South Africa is one of the most promising countries in the world.[36]

Leyland South Africa ranks tenth among the hundred leading industrial companies in South Africa. It is the country's sixth biggest motor-vehicle manufacturer and prob-ably produces the biggest range of vehicles, from the Jaguar XJ6, which it has manufactured in South Africa since 1969 to its very successful 'Eland' heavy trucks; from its Landrover 10-seater bus to its hydraulic excavators. It holds 7 per cent of the South African car market and a resounding 30 per cent of the truck market. It specializes in heavy vehicles and has nearly 100 per cent of the four-wheel-drive market and 95 per cent of the market for heavy trucks and buses.

Leyland's Managing Director, Neville Organ, like most of the company's top management, is a South African and is anxious to stress that Leyland is a South African company. Unlike General Motors and Ford, which are wholly-owned subsidiaries of their US parent corporations, Leyland South Africa has offered its shares on the local market. British Leyland Motor Corporation holds a controlling 56·7 per cent but Leyland's shares are quoted on the Johannesburg Stock Exchange and Sanlam, the large Afrikaans insurance house is a major investor. Local participation in the share capital of the South African subsidiaries of overseas companies is something the South African Government wants to see increased and from its point of view, Leyland is a trail-blazer.

This may be one reason why South Africa's Government-controlled corporations have smiled on Leyland in the bestowal of orders and contracts. In its biggest-ever single order last year, Leyland supplied 380 heavy trucks to South African Railways and Leyland South Africa's Chairman told shareholders that the largest increase in the company's turn over had come from 'the capture of a far greater proportion of business from the Government sector than we had in the past'.[37]

Until recently Leyland had another link with the Government through its shareholding in PUTCO (Public Utility Transport Corporation). PUTCO is one of the main operators of bus services to the African townships in the Witwatersrand area and outside Pretoria and Durban. The company has two Government-appointed directors on its Board and receives a Government subsidy. Transport facilities provided for Africans are in general notoriously over-crowded and expensive, and the accident rate is high. For many years Leyland held a 47.54 per cent investment in PUTCO. It was forced to sell its holding in August 1971 because of a Government ruling that, as a vehicle supplier, it was irregular for it to own shares in a vehicle-operating company.

Leyland has expanded very rapidly. It opened its Black-heath plant near Cape Town in 1956 and since then has opened up works in Natal and the Transvaal. The key to this expansion has been the Government's 'forced industrialization' policy. Since 1961 South Africa has used import-control restrictions to induce vehicle manufacturers to increase the local content of their models. In the early stages of this 'local content' programme, manufacturers had to guarantee that their models would reach 55 per cent South African content by weight within three and a half years of their signing a 'declaration of intent'. What this meant for Leyland was that, instead of importing engines from its British factory, it had to manufacture them inside South Africa. Its plant at Blackheath was expanded and in 1967 the company set in motion its programme for the manufacture of diesel engines at Elandsfontein.

Leyland's plans to meet the third and latest phase of the Government's local content programme, introduced on 1 January 1971, are the biggest announced by any of South Africa's main motor vehicle manufacturers. In the next four years, according to J. H. Plane, it will double its investment from 14 million pounds to 39 millions.[38] By the beginning of 1976 five Leyland car models will be at least 66 per cent South-African-manufactured.

Increasing regional integration between Leyland's South African and Australian operations should also help Leyland to expand. The parent group has plans for Leyland South Africa to exchange components with the parent company's Australian subsidiary. The South African operation will exchange exhaust systems, fuel tanks and generators for Australian-made electrical systems, steering assemblies, dashboards, gauges and speedometers.

Most of the new expansion will take place at the Blackheath plant where the company employs more than 2,000, mostly Coloured, workers. In the last few years Leyland has been forced to make a *volte face* over its attitude towards unionization at Blackheath. When the Coloured Western Province Motor Assembly Workers' Union started trying to recruit there ten years ago, the company would not allow officials on the premises and called the police to prevent them from talking to workers outside. Jack Heeger, now the Secretary of the Union, has told how, in the mid-sixties, a mass meeting of almost 2,000 men, which he helped to organize, was broken up by the police at the management's request.[39] Since 1966 the company has recognized the Union and has negotiated a series of wage agreements.

The small number of whites employed at Blackheath all have supervisory jobs; no white man does any work on the cars being produced there. Work on the assembly line is all done by Coloureds, but their most senior job is that of charge-hand inspector. Over the years the Union has repeatedly asked the firm to appoint Coloured foremen, but Leyland has always refused; there has been no 'upgrading' of Coloureds into 'white' jobs at Blackheath and the racial pattern of job allotment remains exactly the same as it was ten years ago. This has happened in spite of the fact that Blackheath is excluded from the job reservation determination made for the motor vehicle industry. The only provision in the determination which applies to Blackheath is one which prevents the replacement of Coloured workers by Africans.

Unskilled labourers at Blackheath were paid £7·22 for a 44-hour week in January 1971. Semi-skilled workers started at £8·26 a week and could earn £10·54 after five years. (The starting rate for semi-skilled workers at Ford and General Motors plants at Port Elizabeth was £8·97 a week.) A small number of skilled Coloured workers could earn £13·76 a week but they were few. Skills were learnt on the job and there were no apprenticeship schemes for Coloured workers, although the Union pressed the company to give its workers better training.[40] Coloured women were employed as canteen assistants and cooks, beginning at £6·97 for a 44-hour week and were £7·67, respectively.

Most of these wage rates are less than the £11 a week which the Motor Assembly Workers' Union says represents 'an effective minimum level'.[41] They are around the £7 a week which a survey, quoted in the Union's report, reckoned to cover only food, clothing, rent, fuel, transport, cleaning and tax. In January 1972 average wages for African and Coloured unskilled and semi-skilled workers in all Leyland's South African plants were £30·29 a month.

One of the main grievances of Coloured workers at Blackheath is the rising cost of transport to and from the factory. Blackheath is well outside Cape Town and workers have to travel from Athlone, Cape Town's Coloured suburb, and from the surrounding towns. The minimum return fare from Bonteheuwel, where many workers live, is 17p a day and some workers pay as much as £1 a week in fares.[43]

The fringe benefits Leyland provides for its Coloured workers are few and far between. There is no pension scheme for Coloureds although there is one for whites. There is a whites-only medical aid scheme and an inferior sick fund for Coloureds: under this, lower-paid workers can pay 7p a week and get £4 per week in benefit for the first 13 weeks and then £2 a week until the twenty-sixth week; benefit does not extend to the workers' families. Leyland's white and Coloured workers are equal only in death, when their families are all entitled to receive £25 from the Nuffield Trust.[44]

Leyland is one of the few British companies in South Africa which, because it employs mostly Coloured labour, has had to face strong union pressure over the pay and conditions of black workers. It has rejected the workers' main demands.

Leyland South Africa's total labour force is about 4,500 and at its Durban and Elandsfontein plant it employs large numbers of Africans. They are subject to all the usual restrictions on African workers and Leyland's management is unwilling to disclose information about their wages and working conditions.

IMPERIAL CHEMICAL INDUSTRIES

Although ICI (South Africa) is a very small part of the world-wide ICI operation, it is one of the most profitable. While the group's over-all pre-tax profits dropped in 1970 by 19·5 per cent, ICI (SA)'s rose by 13 per cent. ICI is a first-class example of a company which, because of a falling profit rate at home, is planning to expand more and more abroad. In March 1971 it announced plans to cut its investment in the United Kingdom by 25 per cent over the next three years while doubling its overseas investment in one year.

A month later the company's new Chairman, Mr Jack Callard, said that ICI was 'profit-hungry'.[45] There were very great prospects for growth: 'We look at it all with a pretty ruthless eye,' he said, and confirmed that although 65 per cent of the company's assets were in Britain, more and more growth would come from abroad. Most of this will come from investment going into the United States and Europe, but South Africa is not excluded.

In 1970 ICI(SA) had pre-tax profits of £3,641,000. Its interests there comprise three subsidiaries, ICI Pharmaceuticals, Optilon Africa, and ICI(Angola), and a large minority holding in two other companies – 37½ per cent in South Africa Nylon Spinners, and 42½ per cent in African Explosives and Chemical Industries Ltd. In addition ICI (SA) distributes and markets the imported chemicals, resins, dyestuffs and plastics that cannot be manufactured economically in South Africa by AE & CI. This is one of the most profitable activities for the company, and it produced an astonishing 45 per cent increase in trading profit in 1970. That percentage only represents the profit increase attributable to ICI(SA). Much of the profit on these exports to South Africa is earned by the parent company in Britain. South Africa is now ICI's second largest export market after the United States. With such success it was only to be expected that ICI(SA) would plan to expand. In July 1971 a £1·5 million pound expansion scheme was announced. The company hoped to increase its local turnover by 10 per cent within the year.

The origins of ICI's investment in South Africa go back to the end of the last century. Nobel's Explosives Company, which started there in the late 1890s, was later absorbed by Nobel's Industries Ltd, one of the constituent companies which went into ICI when it was formed in 1926. Through Nobel, ICI acquired its interest in African Explosives and Chemical Industries Ltd.

ICI's share in AE & CI illustrates the way British and South African capital frequently interlock. ICI's share in AE & CI is 42½ per cent, and ICI's Chairman is a Deputy-Chairman of AE & CI. Another 42½ per cent is held by De Beers Consolidated Mines Ltd and 15 per cent by the South African public. AE & CI employs just over 15,000 people, had annual sales of 77 million pounds in 1930, and produces industrial explosives, chemicals, paint and fertilizers.

Through AE & CI, ICI has links with Mozambique, and with the building of the Cabora Bassa dam, one of the biggest strategic projects in the white South. In partnership with two Portugueses firms, AE & CI is setting up an explosives factory in Lourenço Marques which will supply equipment to the dam. Before the factory was put in hand, AE & CI was already supplying the dam from South Africa.[46]

AE & CI has a wholly owned subsidiary in Rhodesia which expanded fast in the late 1960s in spite of sanctions; in 1969 sales were up by 13·8 per cent; in 1970 they rose by 8·7 per cent. The company started extending its plant in 1969 to ensure that its 100 per cent monopoly of Rhodesia's requirements for phosphate fertilizer should continue 'for some years to come'.[47]

ICI's links with South African Nylon Spinners also provide an interesting illustration of the partnership between British and South African capital, this time with the admixture of Government capital through the State-run Industrial Development Corporation. ICI's share in SA Nylon Spinners which spins 'Terylene' and nylon from imported raw materials is 37½ per centl De Beers has another 37½ per cent, AE & CI has 15 per cent and the IDC 10 per cent.

ICI and AE & CI have collaborated closely with the South African Government in its plans for South Africa's continued industrialization. Chapter 2 discussed AE & CI's agreement to construct and operate munitions factories for the Government. The money for the plant came from the

State, and AE & CI received a fee. In 1951 when the IDC decided to encourage the local production of textiles as part of its drive for fast industrialization and self-sufficiency for South Africa, it set up with Courtaulds and SNIA Viscosa of Italy the South African Industrial Cellulose Corporation (SAICCOR) to produce rayon pulp. AE & CI was asked to build a chlorine plant for it. In the following year, when South Africa began to produce uranium, AE & CI helped in the development of seventeen uranium extraction plants.[48] In 1971 AE & CI was given leave by the Government to build a new ammonia plant at Modderfontein.[49]

AE & CI is now one of the lynch-pins of the South African economy. It operates the two largest commercial explosives factories in the world. It supplies 70 per cent of the South African market for ammonia. It pioneered the local production of plastics, and now supplies the whole of the market for PVC. The group has been growing at a fantastic rate: in the 1960s its pre-tax profits rose three-fold from just under 5 million pounds in 1960 to 15 million in 1970. Much of the growth has come in the period 1969–71. In 1969 pre-tax profits were up by 30 per cent; in 1970 they were up by 25 per cent.

Compared with AE & CI, ICI(SA), the wholly owned subsidiary of ICI is a smaller operation. It has three factories – two zip-fastener plants at Port Elizabeth and Durban, and a pharmaceutical processing plant at Alberton near Johannesburg. The board has two British directors and four South African (three of whom used to be British). The company was incorporated in 1935 but did not begin trading until 1950.

In March 1971, when Denis Herbstein interviewed the company's Managing Director, W. R. Stephens, and three of his colleagues, the total staff consisted of 471 whites and 560 blacks. The blacks included 12 Indians, 188 Coloured women at the Port Elizabeth plant, 95 Coloured men and 265 Africans.

The lowest wage was paid to about 50 African cleaners, who started at £7·38 a week. They received annual increments, reaching £12·51 after 11 years.[50] There have been across-the-board wage increases on 1 January for the last four years. The authors were told by the company that in January 1972 the minimum annual salary was £505, a weekly rate of £9·71.[51] African packers in March 1971 were being paid a starting rate of £8·30, rising after 11 years to £13·55. The highest African rate went to some handyman painters and printing shop operators, who could earn up to £22·41 a week. On the issue of wages lower than the poverty datum line set by the Association of Chambers of Commerce of £33·77 a month for a family of five in Johannesburg, company officials said that virtually everyone earning less would be unmarried or have fewer than three children; the average man with three children and reasonable service would be earning more. The lowest paid white workers started at £768 a year.[52]

Low though these wages are, they are probably some way above the average for the industry. However, like most firms, ICI(SA) is not yet paying the rate for the job. It employs some Africans as punch-card operators. They start at £10 a week and can rise to £30. But a white girl in the same job would get £30 when she starts. The company argues that what it saves on wages it loses on productivity: officials complained that Africans had not been a success. Wages apart, the main issue in ICI's South African involvement is its contribution to AE & CI, and to strengthening the white-dominated economy.

BRITISH STEEL CORPORATION

The British Steel Corporation's interest in South African industry is one of the most significant examples of the growing inter-relation between foreign capital, private domestic capital and South African State capital. In the case of the BSC, the mixture has the added refinement that the foreign capital comes from the British State-owned sector instead of from British private industry.

At the time of nationalization in 1967, the British Steel Corporation acquired a job lot of South African subsidiaries and minority shareholdings in South African companies which had belonged to the fourteen major UK steel companies from which it was formed. Among them was a 100 per cent holding in Baldwins, the second largest steel stockholder in South Africa; a 49 per cent holding in Stewarts and Lloyds, the biggest South African manufacturer of tubes and pipes and the country's nineteenth largest industrial company; and a 43 per cent interest in Dorman Long (Africa), South Africa's biggest structural engineering company and thirty-sixth in the list of its largest companies. These interests alone gave the Corporation a very substantial stake in the South African steel and heavy engineering industry. In addition, it acquired a large number of smaller holdings: its total stake in South Africa has been estimated at approximately 25 million pounds.

Its newly acquired South African interests brought the British Steel Corporation into partnership with South African private capital and especially with the industrial interests of mining finance houses. Anglo American owned 35 per cent of Stewarts and Lloyds, and Stewarts and Lloyds and Dorman Long were both quoted on the Johannesburg Stock Exchange and were part-owned by South African shareholders.

In the summer of 1970, shortly after the Conservative Government came to power, the BSC agreed to a reorganization of its South African interests in such a way that it not only went into partnership with South African State capital, but effectively handed over control of the companies in which it had interests to the South African State-owned steel giant ISCOR. In a complicated series of mergers the BSC ceded Baldwins to Stewarts and Lloyds and the South African Government handed over Tube and Pipe Industries, Stewarts and Lloyds' major competitor. The Corporation then exchanged its holdings in Stewarts and Lloyds and Dorman Long for a 35 per cent holding in a new company, International Pipe and Steel Investments South Africa (IPSA), in which ISCOR holds 50 per cent of the stock. The remaining 15 per cent of IPSA is held by Anglo American. The new holding company owns a controlling share in Stewarts and Lloyds, Dorman Long and in Vanderbijl Engineering (VANENCO), a State-owned firm which was ISCOR's contribution to the partnership.

The significance of the change-over lies not in its effect on wages and working conditions, which will probably remain much the same as before, but in the increased control it will give the South African Government over the commanding heights of the economy.[53] ISCOR has been an instrument of State policy ever since its formation in 1928; one of its most important functions has been to agree with the Government the prices of steel products – South African steel did not rise significantly in price for eighteen years before July 1970, when ISCOR introduced a price rise of 15 per cent. The system has meant that South African industry has had access to low-cost raw materials and can also be used to contain inflation and to regulate South Africa's balance of payments. The Government has also been able to use ISCOR as an instrument of economic power, forcing the economies of other African countries to become more and more dependent on South Africa. In 1970, for example, ISCOR contracted to supply Malawi with steel products at 15 per cent below their domestic prices at a time when there was a great shortage of steel within South Africa. BSC's handing over of control of the three companies in which it had the largest single interest will give ISCOR more power and greater flexibility to manipulate the South African economy.

Since the Conservative Government took office in 1970, the BSC has been strengthening its South African links in other ways. In January 1971, in the face of growing unemployment in Britain, it awarded a 5·9 million pound contract for the supply of sophisticated steel production equipment to four South African companies, among them its associate company, Dorman Long. The Corporation has also been looking into the economics of purchasing some of its iron ore from South Africa and in June 1971 it received a shipment of 18,000 tons of ore for testing, sent by ISCOR from South Africa's newly discovered Sishen ore deposits in the northern Cape. W. N. Menzies-Wilson, the BSC director responsible for raw material purchases, is a former Chairman of Stewarts and Lloyds South Africa, and a former director of another South African metallurgical company, AMCOR. At the end of 1971 it was reported that the BSC was to adopt a policy of building steel plants near iron ore deposits and that South Africa and also Australia were under consideration as possible sites. South Africa was later rejected as a site.

Ever since its formation, the British Steel Corporation has pursued policies which have brought it closer into line with South Africa's economic needs and with the Nationalist Government's policies. In their relations with South Africa there is little to choose between British nationalized industry and private big business.

DUNLOP HOLDINGS

The beginning of Chapter 1 quoted Reginald Maudling's comment that 'South African trade and industry is just as much based on apartheid as cricket is.' He spoke with knowledge: at the time he was on the board of Dunlop Holdings Ltd, which owns a 70 per cent controlling interest in Dunlop South Africa.

The South African company is well integrated into the local apartheid system. Dunlop opened its first tyre depot in South Africa in 1896, and the company was the first to set up a tyre factory there in 1935. Dunlop South Africa pays different rates for African and white workers. It accepts contracts from the South African Government. It is building a plant in a 'border area' in line with the Nationalist Government's scheme for siting industry in accordance with the policy of separate development. For this it receives generous Government help worth 3·85 million pounds.

The importance of these operations to Dunlop's over-all strength can be gauged from the fact that in 1970, although Africa as a whole provides only 9 per cent of the company's turnover, while Britain provided 43 per cent, Africa produced exactly as much profit before tax and interest. Operations in Britain and in Africa each accounted for 17 per cent of the group's total profits. Of the over-all African profit, Dunlop South Africa with 3·47 million pounds produced more than half. The company's return on capital employed was 20·1 per cent.

Dunlop South Africa's group profits doubled between 1965 and 1969. The 1970 figure was, in fact a decrease, and in 1971 profits fell by another thid. The main reasons were rising costs of raw materials, the effects of the South African Government's anti-inflationary policies which reduced the demand for cars, and increased imports of foreign tyres.

But these were expected to be only temporary setbacks. Dunlop showed its confidence in the long-term possibilities of continued expansion when, at the end of 1970, it announced that it was to spend 3 million pounds on modernizing its tyre plant at Durban and 6 million pounds on the new border-area plant at Ladysmith. The choice of a border area was significant and meant that Dunlop was eligible for one of the loans which the State-sponsored IDC is prepared to give companies which cooperate with its plans to decentralize and halt the influx of Africans into 'white' areas. Dunlop's director of tyre operations, George Sandison, told the *Financial Mail*: 'Ladysmith has virtually everything a tyre factory needs. It is convenient to the country's main tyre markets; has coal, water, and electricity; is in the middle of the Tugela basin, potentially South Africa's most active industrial growth point; and has an ample supply of African labour. This last point is of importance to Dunlop.'[54]

At Dunlop's head office in London, company officials reject the argument that going into a border area assists apartheid. Mr M. Bexon, a director of both the parent board and of Dunlop South Africa says: 'If I were Prime Minister of South Africa I would still be talking about the dispersal of industry even if there were no apartheid. It makes sense not to have this enormous congestion in the cities. It's rather like all the inducements you get in this country, to go to South Wales for example, so that you don't get all the indigenous Welsh coming into the major conurbations.'[55]

The Ladysmith plant will come into operation by 1973, and by the end of 1975 all car-tyre manufacturing will be switched from Durban to the new plant. This expansion programme was planned to be so rapid that the company was forced to look for extra finance in Europe on the Eurodollar market. In 1971 it floated a 3 million pound loan in Europe. This was in addition to 2 million pounds worth of loans negotiated in 1969. In both cases the company needed to keep on good terms with the South African Government as exchange approval had to be obtained.

Part of Dunlop's high profitability is undoubtedly accounted for by low African wages. On this point Dunlop was the most forthcoming and co-operative of any company the authors approached. Unlike almost all other companies, which either had no details of South African wage figures in their London office, or said they had none, or refused to divulge them, Dunlop *did* have figures and were prepared to show some of them. Denis Herbstein was also given full details of wages when he approached Hugh Archibald, the Managing Director of Dunlop South Africa.

Dunlop told the authors that the South African company has worked out a 'philosophy' on 'non-white' employment and is moving towards equal pay for equal work, although

181

it claimed that this is not an issue yet because of the differences in skill-levels between whites and Africans. The company says that average African wages in 1969 were £440 a year (which is just about equivalent to the poverty line) and that this was an increase of 24 per cent since 1965, whereas white wages remained virtually static. In 1969, in the Durban factory, average African wages were £510 a year, average Coloured wages £897 a year and average white wages £1,431 a year.

The lowest wage paid was for an unskilled labourer at the Durban plant, who was getting between £5·65 and £8·15 a week. This is substantially below the poverty line. The maximum African rate was for a senior charge-hand whose scale ranged from £8·65 to £11·54. At Dunlop Semtex, the flooring subsidiary, the maximum for a senior African charge-hand was £17·30 a week, an increase of a third. At Dunlop Industrial Products the maximum was £75·90 a month.

Dunlop South Africa employs about 5,000 people. At Durban the factory has approximately 2,400 people, of whom 1,430 are Africans. Like other firms, Dunlop reserves certain categories of job for Africans, others for Coloureds and Indians, and still others for whites. Its African workers in Durban, its largest plant, live in two townships, Umlazi and Kwa Mashu, 10 miles away.

Low though Dunlop's wages are, they are above average in that most of the staff are at least on or just above the poverty datum line. Dunlop claims that it pays Africans at approximately double the statutory minimum laid down in the agreements for the rubber industry. Dunlop plan eventually to employ 1,140 people in a border area plant. In these areas, as we have seen, the normal industrial council and other wage agreements do not apply.

GUEST KEEN & NETTLEFOLDS

'We have interests in South Africa which have grown up

over the years and we must safeguard shareholders' interests. We can only do that by taking advantage of conditions as they are,' said Brian Inglis, Managing Director of Guest Keen & Nettlefolds South Africa, the holding company which controls GKN's interests in Southern Africa.[56]

As Britain's biggest manufacturer of steel products and one of the world's largest engineering groups, GKN was well placed to penetrate the South African market in the boom years after the Second World War. It started operations in 1948 and rapidly diversified from the manufacture of nuts and bolts into the design and construction of steel reinforcement systems, scaffolding, steel flooring and steel furniture and office equipment, and from automotive components into presswork for commercial vehicle cabs and general presswork for the motor industry and for domestic appliances. Today GKN's South African operation is concentrated in the supply of equipment to the building and construction industry, where Southern Africa accounts for nearly 14 per cent of GKN's world sales and in the manufacture of steel consumer products. where Southern Africa accounts for over 9 per cent of world sales. GKN Mills manufactures a range of heavy construction equipment including cement shutters for dams and tunnels; GKN Sankey makes office furniture, partitioning and shelving – in 1970 it launched itself into the large store-shelving market; GKN Twisteel manufactures steel flooring. Two smaller subsidiaries, GKN Walter and Deane of Pinetown, Natal and Combined Reinforcing Services supply general engineering equipment and steel reinforcement systems.

GKN has also bought its way into the leading automotive component and the biggest nuts and bolts manufacturer in South Africa – it has a 20 per cent interest in Borg-Warner South Africa, a 25 per cent interest in Birfield Ruberowen, a 50 per cent interest in Guest Keen Anglovaal Automotive Components which it owns jointly with Anglovaal, one of South Africa's seven largest mining finance houses and a 12·5 per cent trade investment in National Bolts and Rivets.

On 2 January 1971 GKN South Africa employed 3,529 people. Of these nearly 900 (655 blacks and 217 whites) were employed by GKN Mills at its factory six miles west of Johannesburg, the largest of its kind in Southern Africa. Most of the blacks employed at the factory were Africans but a few were Coloured or Indian. Of the Africans 544 were unskilled yard-labourers who started at £5·50 for a 45-hour week and earned an average of 14p an hour. 98 were semi-skilled and erected scaffolding under white supervision: they were paid an average of 32p an hour. The highest-paid Africans were truck drivers and GKN claims that they could earn up to £23 a week. The lowest white wage was a £23·30 minimum for welders.[57]

GKN Mills operated a medical assistance scheme which excluded all blacks, and a provident fund, which was open to whites and Coloureds earning a minimum of 24p an hour, but which excluded Africans.

There was no recognized black union at any of GKN's South African factories. Brian Inglis says that most Africans are 'not ready' to form trades unions and that he would only be in favour of the setting up of black unions 'if it was going to be helpful to the industry'.[58] According to the company, the works manager at GKN Mills 'keeps in touch with senior Africans'; he acts as 'godfather' to black employees and 'receives and acts on complaints'. But GKN is unable to give practical examples of how this works. There is no works committee operating in the company (see p. 158), even though these committees operate as management tools in other companies.

Some of the fields in which GKN operates – construction equipment for large-scale engineering projects, automotive components – are the kinds of products which South African industry regards as natural leaders in its attempts to expand its markets northwards. GKN's exports to Zambia and Rhodesia are already substantial and it is rapidly expanding exports to Mozambique. GKN South Africa also controls a network of GKN plants in Rhodesia, Mozambique and Zambia. In Rhodesia GKN Mills makes construction equipment and the group's Zambian subsidiary, Bolt Manufacturers Africa, has plants in Bulawayo and Salisbury. In Zambia, Bolt Manufacturers, in which GKN South Africa has a 51 per cent holding, operates at Kitwe and Lusaka. Early in 1970, GKN announced plans for the setting up of a new plant at Machava, a fast-growing industrial area outside Lourenço Marques in Mozambique. The plant will be operated by a new company, GKN Mills (Mozambique), formed in partnership with a Mozambique firm, Lohmann & Co., and will manufacture formwork for scaffolding systems and other equipment for the construction industry. GKN South Africa denies that it is 'directly' involved in Cabora Bassa, Mozambique's giant hydro-electric project, against which there has been an international campaign.

As a manufacturer of intermediate products – automotive components and steel parts for machinery – GKN is not a 'natural exporter' and the bulk of its operations – 84 per cent of turnover in 1970 – still takes place in the United Kingdom. Southern Africa accounts for 3 per cent – 13 million pounds in 1970 – of GKN's total turnover and GKN South Africa's trading surplus is 1·2 million pounds. Europe also accounts for 3 per cent of total turnover. Southern Africa is GKN's third largest sphere of operations overseas after India, which accounts for 5 per cent of total turnover, and Australasia, which accounts for 4 per cent.

But the company, like other UK industrial giants, is looking increasingly to expansion overseas to make up for the slowing-down of its rate of expansion at home. In 1970 GKN's before-tax profits-to-assets ratio was 17·7 per cent overseas and only 13·6 per cent at home. In his 1970 report to share-holders Sir Raymond Brookes, GKN's Chairman, made his attitude on this question clear. He said: 'The chronic and persisting lack of effective growth in United

Kingdom productivity has at its roots years of unrewarding
obsession with outdated political prejudices and discredited
economic theories, enforced adherence to restrictive practices,
confusion of liberty with licence, excessive tax disincentives,
diminishing cash flows and depleted investment confidence.
. . . In these circumstances confrontation between Government and extremists who, without regard to the real wishes
and best interests of the majority, seek to maintain disruptive
power and privilege outside the law was and is inevitable. . . .
Accordingly for the United Kingdom economy as a whole it
is prudent to assume modest growth, continuing but diminishing inflation, and in the short term a high level of intentionally
inspired industrial unrest.'

Sir Raymond's conclusion was that 'foreign operations
have the potential to contribute an increasing proportion of
Group activity and earnings.' In the face of his analysis of
falling profit ratios in Britain, it seems likely that South
Africa will rate high in GKN's plans for future expansion.

GENERAL ELECTRIC COMPANY

The General Electric Company is highly intolerant of inquiries
about its economic involvement in South Africa. One share-
holder asked the Chairman Lord Nelson at the annual general
meeting in September 1971 for more information about the
company's role there, and about the products of subsidiaries
and their relationship to apartheid. Lord Nelson replied with
the bland generalization that trade did not imply political
approval, and that 'if we took the view that everybody we
disliked in the world we would not trade with, we would
then be faced with, I am sure, great protests about the lack
of growth on the one hand or the lack of employment on the
other or the creation of redundancies.'[59]

When the share-holder argued that the answer was 'a red
herring and you know it', GEC's Managing Director, Sir
Arnold Weinstock (who had until then left the answering

to the Chairman) called out: 'Shut up, you have had your say.' The official transcript of the meeting then continues:

Share-holder: You have to consider——
Sir Arnold Weinstock: Shut up. Shut up.
Share-holder: Don't tell me to shut up.
Sir A. W.: I'm telling you to shut up.
Share-holder: The share-holders are supposed to have a voice.
Sir A. W.: At the proper time.

Lord Nelson then went on answering questions.

The authors' own approach to the company for an interview with Sir Arnold, and for information about GEC's dealings in South Africa, was equally unproductive; some months before, when Denis Herbstein went to South Africa and requested an interview with the company there, he was told from head office in London that they refused permission; no reason was given in either case.

The authors make no apology, therefore, for relying on wage information supplied by the General Secretary and the Assistant General Secretary of the South African Electrical Workers Association. They report that they, too, find GEC one of the hardest companies to deal with.[60]

GEC is the biggest British electrical concern in South Africa, and one of the largest firms in the electrical field. It employs some 4,000 people. It has a turnover of 25 million pounds a year with five operating companies: GEC–AEI of South Africa (Pty) Ltd, which makes general products ranging from domestic appliances to light electrical goods; GEC–English Electric of South Africa (Pty) Ltd, which has two plants at Benoni and Germiston, and a foundry at Springs, and produces industrial electrical equipment; AEI Henley Africa (Pty) Ltd, an important telecommunications business; GEC–Elliott Automation (Pty) Ltd which provides technical information on automation; and Endean Manufacturing Co (Pty) Ltd, makers of switchgear and other equipment for the mining industry. The over-all holding company, GEC South Africa Ltd, is not quoted on the Johannesburg Stock Exchange and keeps its profits a close secret.

In addition, Marconi South Africa, which has assembled and supplied closed-circuit television to the South African Defence Forces,[61] is a subsidiary of GEC Marconi Electronics Ltd. The company also has minority holdings in a number of associated companies, like African Cables and Telephone Manufacturers of South Africa (Pty) Ltd. Through its subsidiaries and associates the company does a great deal of business with the South African Government and its State corporations. In 1971 alone it won contracts to supply 10 million pounds' worth of equipment for 100 new locomotives for South African Railways, and 5·5 million pounds' worth of electronic control machinery to the Electricity Supply Commission.

On wages, in many cases, GEC South Africa pays the minimum rates laid down for the electrical industry in the Industrial Council agreements, with a small increment for length of service and sometimes a production bonus. The lowest grade of pay for Africans doing general labouring, scrap recovery, or sealing ends, as laid down in June 1970 was 10·7p an hour. The top rate for Africans – in GEC only very few reach it – was 21·5p an hour.[62] For an average 45-hour week this produces a pay-range from £4·81 to 9·67; both figures are below ASSCOM's poverty line. The company has two life- and provident-funds, one for people above the maximum rate for Africans, i.e., only for whites, Coloureds and Indians, and a second fund for Africans. The distinction between the funds is therefore purely economic: it so happens that the dividing point exactly matches the wages-ceiling for Africans, and so Africans are in a different fund from everyone else.[63]

GENERAL MOTORS

It is a General Motors' boast, much-advertised, that the firm has made a major contribution to the growth and development of South Africa.[64]

General Motors South Africa employs 5,500 workers, 3,500 of whom are black. The company pays 1,500 workers on a salary basis and 4,000 on an hourly basis. The racial composition of the hourly labour force has changed considerably in recent years, shifting from almost entirely white employees to about 65 per cent blacks, but all the top hourly positions are reserved for whites.

According to the Chairman of the Board, J. M. Roche, General Motors South Africa does not discriminate between the races in wages – 'except for a difference in starting rates which are higher for Whites than for Coloured or Native [sic] employees'. The starting wage for Africans and Coloureds at the GM engine plant in Port Elizabeth is 19p an hour or £27·69 a month. A semi-skilled worker, usually a Coloured receives between 26p and 36p an hour. Machine setters and changers are mostly whites, earning between 51p and 72p an hour. A skilled artisan, invariably white, receives over £1·28 an hour.

General Motors gives as one reason for the discrepancy between black and white starting rates the General Motors' compensatory hospital benefit scheme and the fact that blacks pay lower rents and lower transportation costs.[65] (These, it should be said, are a consequence of Government-enforced residential and other segregation measures under apartheid which afford Africans, not benefits, but gross deprivation.)

Since the suspension of job reservation in the motor industry in 1968, the company has negotiated with the whites-only trade union on the job categories to be reserved for whites. On the whole the white union has been adamant that white employees must be safeguarded against the encroachment of blacks into their preserves; however, union and company have recently negotiated job arrangements on a week-to-week basis, depending on the state of the labour market. Company and union thus operate an agreement which gives the white union the final say on the types of jobs blacks may perform.

While trying to get the white union to agree to the filtering of blacks into jobs vacated by whites, the company has actively encouraged skilled white labour to emigrate from Europe and Latin America to meet the need for skilled labour. Supervisory and control positions remain a monopoly of the white workers. As a company plant manager in South Africa said: 'We are dependent on the skilled white man to keep us in business and on the Coloured man to keep us running.'[66]

For forty-two years General Motors operated without a union. Then it established a house committee to discuss wages on an informal basis. Previously this committee was all-white but Coloured union representatives were admitted recently, and now about half the Coloured workers are represented on it.

General Motors provides workers with a canteen, with a pre-employment medical examination, a chest x-ray annually and an emergency medical service. The company has a medical aid plan for all employees and dependents, sickness and accident insurance, group life insurance and a retirement plan.

Many of the notions expressed by company spokesmen have familiar South African racial overtones. For instance, to the Chairman of the Board, J. M. Roche, Africans are 'natives', a term strongly resented by Africans. One of the plant managers said about Africans: 'I wouldn't say these people don't have any reasoning power, but what they do have is very limited.'[67]

More diplomatic but equally paternalistic was the statement by the Managing Director, William P. Slocum: 'I feel that companies such as ours are really performing a very useful service. . . . Our non-white peoples here in South

Africa can work their way into the economy to come out of their rural and tribal existence out in the country where they can actually participate in a civilised industrial life and this is pretty much the story of the development of the US.' (*Sic.*)[68]

General Motors takes pains to explain that it is non-political. The Managing Director has said 'I don't consider it appropriate to work publicly for changes in laws.'[69] The company's argument for neutrality falls to the ground, however, for General Motors is a member of the South African Foundation which works hard to defend apartheid from criticism.

CALTEX

Caltex Petroleum Corporation (jointly owned by Standard Oil of California and Texaco) admits only too readily that 'We have a healthy working relationship with the Government'.[70] The company explains in justification that this is because Government officials feel that oil is too significant to be left to the oil man.

Caltex, Mobil and Esso between them refine and transport just under half of South Africa's oil imports. True to oil-company belief that Government calls the tune, these companies adjust themselves with ease to official policy and practice on labour and wages.

Caltex employs 1,700 workers in South Africa. Of these 550 are blacks, occupying most of the unskilled and semi-skilled positions. The company claims to pay the same rate to whites and blacks who perform the same job; however, a company official admitted: 'Mind you, there are different grades. The black salesmen who sell paraffin heat are doing a different job than the white suppliers to petrol stations.'[71]

There are eight grades of employees: blacks generally in the lower grades (1 to 5), and whites dominating grades 6 to 8. Thus, the majority of black workers are floor sweepers, kitchen-hands, messengers and charge-hands and the whites are operators, clerical assistants, truck drivers and sales representatives. Wages for the three lowest grades range from £6·66 a week to £8·15 a week; in the two top grades wages range from £12·31 to £29·74 a week. The company's scale for weekly wages shows that the minimum pay for an unskilled black worker is £3·22 whereas the minimum for a white worker is £16·86 a week.

Corporation policy and executive attitudes both blend well into the South African scene. R. D. Wrigley, Junior, formerly the American manager of Caltex South Africa, is a member of the South Africa Foundation; Caltex regularly runs advertisement campaigns in South African newspapers and magazines. Recognizing South Africa's anxious search for self-sufficiency in oil, one ran as follows: 'Ahead of Caltex lies many years of research and perhaps disappointment – or the discovery which will free South Africa for all time from dependence on outside oil supplies.'

9 Experiments and Failures

> We must remember that reform is true conservatism – *Harry Oppenheimer*

As pressure on foreign businesses to stop exploiting black workers in South Africa has mounted, some response has been made: in the face of the demand 'to get on or get out', anxious industrialists have been casting round for ways of making changes that will placate those pressing for total withdrawal. The old claim that business has nothing to do with politics was exposed as an evasion when companies were challenged to pay decent wages to their own employees at least, even if they said that they could not or would not oppose South Africa's racial system outright. The best publicized of these efforts to deal with critical pressure was the so-called Polaroid experiment.

POLAROID

It dates back to the autumn of 1970, when a group called the Polaroid Revolutionary Workers Movement (PRWM) was formed in Cambridge, Massachusetts. The group produced posters and leaflets with the message 'Polaroid imprisons blacks in just 60 seconds.' This was a reference to Polaroid's photographic identity-card system, used in South Africa to produce the passes by which the Government controls the African population.

In the United States, Polaroid has a 'liberal' image. It employs blacks and it encourages its executives to sit on local community boards. Its President, Edwin Land, is a trustee of the Ford Foundation and a member of the President's Foreign Intelligence Advisory Board.

G   193

The issue of Polaroid's involvement in South Africa had first been raised six years earlier but came to nothing. The 1970 campaign was more effectively organized. On 6 October the company declared that Polaroid had not sold its equipment to the South African Government but only to its local distributors, Frank and Hirsch.[1] It admitted that the identification system was being sold to the South African army and air force, but it claimed that Polaroid was 'unique in South Africa in its adoption of full equal employment practices for blacks'. The claim surprised a director of Frank & Hirsch, Mr O. J. Berman, who was later reported[2] as saying: 'I do not know where they could have obtained such a statement. We are governed by the laws of the country. Would they allow the existence of such a policy? It is not possible.'

On 8 October 1970, the PRWM presented the Corporation with the following demands: It should disengage completely from South Africa, and stop doing business there, directly or indirectly; it should make a public statement condemning apartheid, to be published in the United States and in South Africa; it should turn over some of its profits to the liberation movements in Southern Africa. The company rejected the demands. On 27 October the movement then called for a world-wide boycott of all Polaroid products. There were mass demonstrations in Boston. At the end of the year the company decided to send a four-man study team to South Africa. In a massive send-off the company explained why it was concerned about South Africa in an advertisement in the Boston newspapers, and took credit for being a pioneer:

Why was Polaroid chosen to be the first company to face pressure about business in South Africa? Perhaps because the revolutionaries thought we would take the subject seriously. They were right. We do. We have built a company on the principle that people should be recognised as individuals. We abhor apartheid. . . . We feel South Africa is a question that other companies will try to answer in the future. We seem to be the first. Our answer may not be right for other companies. But we intend to take the time and effort and thought to be sure it is right for us.[3]

The first thing the Polaroid team discovered in South Africa was that Polaroid instant cameras were being used to photograph Africans applying for pass-books. After ten days the four men returned with their recommendations:

(1) Polaroid should stay in South Africa and set up an experimental programme for a year.

(2) It should discontinue its sales to the South African Government.

(3) The company's distributors, Frank & Hirsch, should 'improve dramatically' the salaries and other benefits of its black staff.

(4) Polaroid should set up a 'well-defined' programme to train black employees for important jobs in the company.

(5) A portion of the company's profits should go towards expanding educational opportunities for Africans.

The Polaroid Corporation accepted all the recommendations, and placed another advertisement in the newspapers to announce the fact. It also donated £8,300 to the Black United Front, a Boston community fund. The almost universal first reaction was that it was a public relations exercise, likely to have little impact on apartheid. The PRWM rejected the company's decision and repeated its call for total disengagement; the South African Ambassador to the United States, Harold Taswell, attacked the decision bitterly, saying: 'We in South Africa are used to the "holier than thou" approach. We know there are those who like to confess South Africa's "sins" in public and who hope thereby to save their own souls.'

The *Financial Mail*[4] analyzed what the company's decision would mean at bottom. Frank & Hirsch employed a few Coloureds and Indians, and 155 Africans. Of these, 37 were classified as unskilled and received a minimum wage of

£35 a month. This, the *Mail* commented, was £6–£8 more than the statutory minimum in the distributive trade, but £1·80 less than the subsistence minimum calculated by the Johannesburg municipality for a family of five in the African township, Soweto, and £24 a month less than the minimum effective level (MEL) calculated by the Institute of Race Relations. This is based on the argument that, to be realistic, budget calculations must include the cost of household utensils, furniture and bedding, plus medical bills, education costs and other expenses such as postage, entertainment, gifts and taxation.

In September 1971, the *Wall Street Journal*[5] followed up the experiment and was told by Mr Hirsch that, since the beginning of the year, blacks in the company had received average pay increases of 22 per cent. The minimum wage had been raised to £41 per month, and the company had increased the number of its black supervisors from two to eight, earning between £88 and £120 a month (about the same as a white junior typist).

In spite of these promotions, Africans could not rise higher than the rank of supervisor, or go on the board, as the *Financial Mail* pointed out. The South African Government has made it clear that as a general principle it will not allow whites to work under blacks.

In the matter of education, the paper commented that the experiment looked more promising. Polaroid was said to be giving about £6,000 to the African-controlled Association for Education and Cultural Advancement. It had also promised to pay for the education of about 500 black students, at a cost estimated by the *Financial Mail* of about £34,000 a year out of a total South African profit of between £88,000 and £120,000 a year. (These figures were estimated by the *Financial Mail*, since the company does not disclose them.)

For a company to give a third of its profits to African education was clearly an unusual advance. Its political impact, however, was not likely to be dramatic, a point made clear in a penetrating analysis by John Miller, Cape Town correspondent of the *Daily Telegraph*, who wrote that 'the Nationalists have never stood in the way of these educational schemes, or of grants by overseas companies to organizations specializing in improving African education. In fact, it could be said they positively welcome such investment because it aids the grand but little-financed blueprint of separate development.'[6] Miller also reported that 'on salaries the Government has no objection to individual firms paying non-whites vastly better rates.' To suggest that Polaroid's much-publicized decision was a devastating blow to Mr Vorster was '. . . as unrealistic as so much thinking on South Africa. Polaroid had no intention of changing South Africa's labour laws. Thus Africans employed by its distributor will continue to work segregated from whites. They will not be allowed to give an order to a white man, or to a white secretary.' Miller concluded that Polaroid was 'a long, long way from ushering in a socio-economic, let alone a political revolution'. And in spite of the first sharp reaction by the South African Ambassador to Washington, Mr Vorster was reported to be unworried by the Polaroid decision. The Economics Minister, Mr Lourens Muller, went on record as having no objections to it.[7]

What, then, caused the great Polaroid splash? The main reason was that it was the first public response by a major international corporation to anti-apartheid pressure. Polaroid had conceded the propriety of that pressure, and had made a public declaration of intent, saying that businessmen could do better. Until then, both actions had been taboo in the business community. When it became clear that it was little more than a public relations exercise ('What they lost on the swings in South Africa, they thought they would pick up in prestige on the roundabouts in the States', as the chairman of another large corporation put it), other firms stopped disapproving of it. As a way of moderating or delaying pressure for complete withdrawal from South

Africa it seemed a harmless device. However, although some corporations showed momentary interest, few rushed to follow the example, for fear of starting a landslide.

In its follow-up article in September 1971, the *Wall Street Journal* reported, in exaggerated terms, as it turned out, that the Polaroid campaign was 'proving to be a catalyst in the drive to upgrade non-white workers'. At least a dozen American firms had contacted Polaroid, its South African distributors or Africans connected with its educational programmes, for information, including Warner Brothers, the Coca-Cola Corporation, the Chase Manhattan Bank, and J. R. Watkins Company, a Minnesota cosmetics firm.

Several other American firms approached the South African Institute of Race Relations for suggestions on how to improve conditions for African staff. In May 1971 the Institute prepared a memorandum which was distributed privately to foundations, private individuals and some businessmen. The memorandum's argument (which was attributed only to the author, Dudley Horner, and not to the Institute) rejected disengagement from South Africa as impractical, without the help of UN military action, and urged instead a solution best described as 'Polaroid minus'. It was that companies should provide better pay and conditions for Africans, develop the border areas, and give money for African education but without Polaroid's key proviso: after a year the company would reassess progress and reconsider withdrawal then.

Five months later, when Dudley Horner and John Kane-Berman, analyzed for the Institute the over-all changes since Polaroid's January announcement,[8] they found business had done little or nothing. They reported, first, that it was extremely difficult to assess the impact of the Polaroid experiment on other companies because they are 'usually unwilling to reveal information about wage levels and employment practices'; caution and secrecy were even the watchwords for many firms approaching the Institute for information – they made anonymous telephone calls to ask about its first memorandum. Less than 10 per cent of the 300 American companies operating in South Africa contacted the Institute openly, Horner and Kane-Berman reported. Those who did included Kellogg, Chrysler, Ford, General Motors, Sperry Rand, Union Carbide, American Metal Climax, Gillette, Rank Xerox, IBM and McGraw-Hill World News. Only 4 of the 500 British companies did, directly or through subsidiaries: they were ICI, Berkshire International (SA) Ltd, Bestobell Ltd, and Harold Marthinsen and Co. Ltd (part of the Delta Metal Holdings Group).

This distinction between British and American companies provided an interesting sidelight on the two countries' different approaches to public demands for corporate responsibility. In the United States the Polaroid issue created a great stir. Mr Ramsey Clark, a former Attorney-General, said Polaroid should have no more than a year of grace to prove itself or to withdraw.[9] Senator Edward Kennedy, less decisively, said the experiment should only last for 'a restricted trial period'.[10] Congressman Diggs held a series of hearings in Washington and sent out a questionnaire to every major corporation investing in or trading with South Africa. Several leading American churchmen visited South Africa and endorsed the experiment. It became official United States Government policy when the American Consul-General in Johannesburg issued 'guidelines' to American subsidiaries advising them to 'transplant American standards entirely' to the Republic except when South African law made this impossible. He made six concrete suggestions: introduce equal hiring terms; maintain equal prospects and terms of promotion: apply equal pay for equal work; set up scholarships for workers or their dependants; let black workers join pension and medical aid funds; contribute to the South African Government's National Bursaries Fund with money earmarked for black students.

While all this activity was going on, not one MP in Britain
made a sustained public campaign on the issue. The British
Government began the year by announcing the resumption
of arms sales to South Africa and ended it with the proposed
settlement with the minority régime in Rhodesia. In the end
the distinction between British and American responses
may simply be accounted for by the American flair for public
relations. The results of the Polaroid experiment in concrete
terms were virtually nil. At the end of the experimental
year, on 30 December 1971, although Polaroid announced
that it would continue the programme rather than withdraw,
it conceded that 'the visible effects on other companies of
our experiment have been limited', but it also claimed that
the programme had shown what could be done: 'In this
respect the experiment has exceeded the expectations of
many.' The Institute of Race Relations was blunter. In its
November 1971 survey, it concluded that every one of the
seventeen companies which consented to disclose their wage
rates was still paying Africans below the minimum effective
level of £59, and thirteen were paying some Africans below
the poverty line. The thirteen were: AE & CI, African
Oxygen (a subsidiary of British Oxygen), Premier Milling
(a subsidiary of Associated British Foods), Unilever, South
African Breweries, Teal Holdings, Russell Holdings, South
African Associated Newspapers, Lawson's Motors Group,
Protea Holdings, OK Bazaars, Unsgaard and Samson
Holdings, and the United States National Aeronautics and
Space Administrattion (NASA). The Institute concluded:
'If the Polaroid experiment was intended significantly to
improve the wages and working conditions of black South
Africans in general, it must be regarded as a failure.'

BARCLAYS BANK: EQUAL PAY FOR EQUAL WORK?
If Polaroid has become a symbol for American involvement
in apartheid, then its counterpart in Britain is undoubtedly
Barclays. At its Annual General Meeting on 13 January

1971, Sir Frederic Seebohm, Chairman of the Bank's International division (then Barclays Bank DCO, but since 1 October 1971 Barclays Bank International), made no bones about this, launching an attack on all who called into question the company's involvement in South Africa.

His one concrete piece of information was that the company had recently obtained the Government's permission for the employment of Coloured girls outside Coloured areas. 'We believe we are the first bank to achieve this,' he said. And he may well have been right.

It was clearly a pioneering gesture, but it is relevant to ask why Barclays made it and what it is likely to achieve. Was it a recognition that some of the pressure brought by the Bank's 'revolutionary anarchist' critics, as Sir Frederic called them, was legitimate and well-applied? Was it to direct their attention to other, less 'progressive' banks? Was it because, earlier in the year President Kaunda, supported by Uganda, Tanzania and Guyana, told Barclays that he was looking at the Bank's over-all record and at its ties with the pro-South African trade lobby, the United Kingdom South Africa Trade Association, and would reconsider Barclay's future status and interests in Zambia?

There is no certain answer. When the authors approached Sir Frederic for an interview in November 1971, he declined on the grounds that this was '. . . not the appropriate moment for me to say any more. My views are well known.' Talking to the *Observer* in January 1971, he did at least speculate on why the South African Government had allowed it.[11] 'It happened partly because we were able to prove that it was not competitive with white labour, partly because they're a bit frightened of us.'

Unlike many other businessmen, Sir Frederic believes in doing things openly and boldly; while they claim they are 'doing their bit' behind the scenes', he asks what is the point of that? As a pioneer, Sir Frederic must take credit for that, too. He told the *Observer*: 'The other thing you can do is to ignore the law. Provided you do it discreetly, you can get away with it. But if you have a few girls working away in a back room, it doesn't do much good. I prefer to go bald-headed at it.'

Another good example of the 'bald-headed' approach came in September 1971 when Barclays, together with the Standard Bank, announced a policy of equal pay for equal work. Blacks and whites would, from that time, be paid on the same scales. Again the move was a pioneering one. Again, too, it is appropriate to ask why Barclays made it, and what it achieved.

Each bank employs about 200 blacks in clerical positions at branches throughout South Africa and Namibia. Black sub-accountants could now get a maximum of £240 a month.[12] However, most of them would still be working in 'non-white areas'. There was still no provision in Barclays pay-scale for black managers or assistant managers, and the majority of the bank's black employees were near the bottom of the pay-scale. As a Barclays spokesman put it, 'equal pay was partly designed as an incentive for non-white staff.' It did not bring a sudden large windfall to very many people; as the *Rand Daily Mail* commented: 'The actual increases are quite small.'[13]

As for the bank's motives, the *Rand Daily Mail* speculated that 'the banks presumably know the difference between a sound investment and an idealistic gesture, so it is significant that for some years they have had about the best record in South Africa for improving non-white wages. . . . It is bound to have a salutary effect on job motivation and productivity.'

A real breakthrough would have come if the bank had also been able to defy the apartheid laws successfully. Barclays' 'bald-headed' approach met with a resounding failure here, in a situation that was near farce. On the same day as it announced the equal pay scheme, Barclays employed a black bank clerk, Mr Johannes Noge, in its Sauer

Street, Johannesburg, branch. He was not appointed primarily in an integrationist spirit. A Barclays spokesman explained that the branch had many black customers and an extra clerk was needed to relieve pressure.[14] A white commissionaire was employed to direct black customers to Mr Noge, who also used separate toilet and washing facilities. Even so, Mr Noge's employment was enough of a breach of apartheid regulations for Mr Marais Viljoen, the Minister of Labour, to intervene. He proclaimed that the Government would not tolerate this type of 'shoulder-to-shoulder work integration', and demanded that a special cubicle be built round Mr Noge to separate him from the white bank staff, and that he only serve black customers. Barclays promptly complied.[15]

Ludicrous though this result was, and however obscure the bank's motives, it was at least a departure from traditional practice. Two months later the Institute of Race Relations reported that of forty-five companies whose wage-rates had been publicly disclosed, at least partially, the two banks and IBM were the only ones that paid all races on a single wage-scale.[16]

THE OPPENHEIMER PHENOMENON

I don't think that business has much power anywhere today, really – *Harry Oppenheimer*[17]

In the modern world political power has its base in economic power and strength – *Harry Oppenheimer*[18]

A satirist once remarked that Mr Harry Oppenheimer, Chairman of the Anglo American Corporation, South Africa's leading company, believes in multifacialism. As head of a vast mining and industrial complex with interests all over the world, Oppenheimer conforms to local conditions in Zambia as readily as in South Africa. A regular critic of apartheid, he has probably done more than anyone else to fuel the economic machine on which the strength of white supremacy depends. A supporter of the Progressive

Party, Oppenheimer has helped to run munitions factories for the Governments of Dr Verwoerd and Mr Vorster.

To many people, both inside South Africa and beyond its borders, Oppenheimer has become the symbol of the theory which the *Economist* once sympathetically called 'the richer, the lefter':[19] as South Africa becomes more prosperous, the absurdity of racial discrimination will be obvious to all, and the country will become more liberal. Time and time again critics of Western involvement in South Africa are referred to this or that speech by Harry Oppenheimer. Look, they are told, there is your refutation, a man who fearlessly attacks the Government, and not just any man but someone with a tremendous amount to lose. He is leading the business-men's onslaught on apartheid far more effectively than outside critics, and behind the scenes he is quietly but impressively improving conditions for Africans.

In this section we look at Oppenheimer's record, his vision of South Africa, and the way in which his statements match the practice of his companies. If the South African Government is 'a bit frightened' of Barclays Bank, as Sir Frederic Seebohm boasts, how much more frightened should they be of Oppenheimer, the largest employer in South Africa after the Government itself? If any man could defy the Government and confound the country's labour laws, it should be Oppenheimer.

There is no shortage of evidence that the Nationalists have mixed feelings about Oppenheimer. English-speaking, a Jew and a capitalist, he aroused many of the deepest resentments in people of fundamentalist, Christian farming stock: was he a new Judas, prepared to sell out the white race for money, the legendary Afrikaans villain, 'Hoggen-heimer'? But after twenty years of being in power, and two decades of fruitful collaboration between Afrikaans-speaking Government and English-speaking industry, the Nationalists have largely lost their suspicions. Oppenheimer has proved his loyalty. He was one of the first businessmen to go into partnership with Afrikaner capital. In 1965 he helped the Afrikaans Federale Mynbou to take over General Mining, one of the largest mining finance houses. He is linked with Dr Albert Wessels in Wesco Investments Ltd, the first Afrikaner to penetrate the motor industry. He is a firm supporter of Mr Vorster's 'outward-looking' policy of seeking close trade and investment links with independent Africa.

Occasionally, still, the old Afrikaner suspicion comes to the surface, and Oppenheimer's loyalty is questioned. But in the event Mr Vorster has taken Oppenheimer's side and not that of his critics. During the 1970 general election campaign, Dr Carel de Wet, the Minister of Planning and Mines, suddenly attacked Oppenheimer for 'sabotaging' the Government's apartheid programme, alleging that he did not want to participate in the border area programme. Unless he showed more willingness to respond to incentives to relocate industry near the reserves, Dr de Wet said, any applications by Anglo companies to expand in the urban areas would be scrutinized to see that regulations were not being evaded.

Oppenheimer was in Australia at the time, but he rushed home, and issued a statement to the press, denying the charge.[20] He did not oppose the Government, and was 'only too happy to establish industries in the border areas. . . . I have said innumerable times that a country cannot develop its full economic potential if it does not make the best use of its labour force. But this is quite a different thing from trying to sabotage your Government's policy by the way you run your company.' Mr Vorster made it clear which side he supported. He reprimanded Dr de Wet and at the first available opportunity demoted him.

In another situation, one that could have been far more damaging, Mr Vorster again defended Oppenheimer against the Nationalist right wing. This was over the Hoek Report, a study originally commissioned by Dr Verwoerd to examine the power of the Oppenheimer empire within the economy. The motives behind the Report, and the way in which it was compiled, owed much to the 'Hoggenheimer' myth, but when it was submitted to Mr Vorster, he refused to publish it, and was promptly attacked by his right wing for turning a blind eye to the Oppenheimer 'threat'.

As a typical example of Mr Vorster's faith in Oppenheimer, in 1971 the South African Government awarded Oppenheimer's African Explosives and Chemical Industries Ltd the victory in what the *Financial Mail* called 'one of the biggest politico-industrial gunfights we've seen for years'. The issue was over who would get permission to build the country's next ammonia plant, costing up to twenty million pounds. The other bidder might perhaps have been expected to have Mr Vorster's sympathy since it was a huge Afrikaner-dominated company, Federale Kunsmis, in which the Government had invested some of its own money through the IDC. Instead, the approval went to AE & CI. The deal hardly bore out the notion that Oppenheimer and the Government are permanently at daggers drawn.

It is ironic that, on the Oppenheimer issue, the extreme right wing of the Nationalists, the *'verkramptes'*, find themselves in alignment with the 'bridge-builders' outside South Africa, who claim that Oppenheimer is an implacable opponent of the Government and the present political system. Both groups tend to look at what Oppenheimer says rather than what he does. However, even his statements reveal that his differences with the Government are really narrow. What Oppenheimer criticizes are the Government's labour policies: as he said in answer to Dr de Wet, 'A country cannot develop its full economic potential if it does not make the best use of its labour force.' No word there about equal rights for Africans. No call for integrated education, for an end to segregation, for adult suffrage.

In 1970, Oppenheimer gave a lecture commemorating Cecil Rhodes, and in it he revealed something of the model he has for an ideal South Africa. Although the methods Rhodes employed 'certainly involved harshness, and perhaps even trickery', he was inspired by 'a great vision'.[21] It was of 'a great modern industrialized state in South Africa in which all civilized men could enjoy equal rights'. And, Oppenheimer said, this vision was still valid. It was 'the only way we will be able to remain safe and prosperous'. Inspiring words, except for that one phrase – 'all civilized men'.

The device of confining political power to the 'civilized' is almost as old as the first white settler in South Africa. As long as a minority arrogates to itself the right to define who is 'civilized' and who is not, it is nothing more than a technique for perpetuating minority control. What Oppenheimer seems to have in mind is a meritocracy, in which racial differences will carry less weight than educational, property or class differences. This is the goal of the Progressive Party which Oppenheimer supports. In time, and little by little, the vote will be given to a few more Africans who manage to break through the barrier of an inferior, segregated educational system and achieve middle-class status. The idea is neither bold nor original: on his shining white horse Oppenheimer has ridden up with nothing more to offer than Mr Ian Smith's majority rule but not in my lifetime'. And that is thoroughly appropriate since one result of Rhodes' vision is Rhodesia.

Oppenheimer's criticisms of the Government's labour policies are no more courageous or original. As long ago as 1958 a lobby of Afrikaans- and English-speaking businessmen was formed under the title 'the Bantu Wage and Productivity Association' (recently renamed the Productivity and Wage Association). Its members were farsighted enough to see that they could get improved results out of their African workers if they were better paid: at the crudest level, people on starvation wages are not physically fit enough to do a hard day's work. The more sophisticated version of the argument is that South Africa needs more skilled labour if its growth rate is to be maintained. Since white labour is scarce, that must mean 'raising the quality of black labour.'

In its thirteen years of operation the Association has gathered a wide range of support among industrialists. Its approach is well illustrated by the slogan put forward at its annual general meeting in 1970 by the then president, Mr C. G. Corbett. The Bantu, he said, should not be looked at as 'the non-European problem': 'The Bantu are our (*sic*) national asset.' As an employers' organization, the PWA claims to be strictly separate from politics. This gives its aims a welcome frankness and bluntness, and frees them from 'liberal' hypocrisies.

On the subject of wages the PWA says that its purpose is '... to expand steadily the purchasing power of our employees. We suggested in 1958 the humble target of increasing the purchasing power of Bantu workers in commerce and industry by £150,000,000.' To raise productivity, it argues for 'labour stability, increased production, and higher efficiency'. Another good reason for higher wages, apparently, is that 'plans must be made to pay high enough wages to each and every employee so that they can have the satisfaction of covering their own cost of housing, services and transport, etc., so that these costs are no longer a tax burden on commerce and industry.'

There is no room here for sentimental nonsense about low wages: poverty is bad propaganda. As Article 4 of the PWA Summary of Purposes puts it: 'Moreover, the very existence of a substantial sub-economic population section in South Africa affords great opportunities for destructive propaganda and exploitation by forces inimical to the system of the private ownership of capital'. Raising productivity comes before ending starvation: 'In addition to efforts to promote payment of increased wages in consideration of increased productivity,' says Article 15, 'the Association will also make representations for the increase of statutory minimum wage-rates for unskilled workers with the object of increasing such wages to a reasonable subsistence level as rapidly as is economically possible.'

The only difference between Oppenheimer's sentiments and those of the PWA is in point of style: Oppenheimer's is much less ponderous.

Clearly there are distinctions between the vision of society held by the PWA and industrialists like Oppenheimer, and that held by the Nationalist Party, but they are more apparent than real. Oppenheimer envisages a meritocracy, led by the white population. Mr Vorster believes in separate development. The difference is that between one social system shaped like a pyramid with the whites at the top, and another system shaped like a cross-section of two steps, a taller white step next to a lower black one. The proponents of separate development see the safeguard for the whites in separation, politically and economically, if not physically and geographically. The 'meritocrats' see it in the creation of an African middle-class which will identify with the white group above it in the hierarchy rather than with the oppressed masses at the bottom. Both theories are based on white control, in the first case through the law and the constitution, in the second case through the fact that the whites start with all the privileges of wealth, education and control of the economic system.

The reality in all Southern Africa is a mixture of the two systems. In South Africa itself the emphasis in theory is on separation, but the fact is that the social structure is already developing meritocratic features. In Rhodesia, after the settlement with Britain, the emphasis was to have been on a meritocracy, though the reality would contain plenty of racial separation. In as much as apartheid is equivalent to white supremacy, the term applies equally in both countries.

Oppenheimer's vision is not concerned with a democratic South Africa, but with economic growth. Does it offer at least the chance of some short-term improvement for Africans, and a greater share in the country's wealth? Chapter 4 concluded that it does not. A section of the black urban population may be narrowing the gap between it and the whites immediately above, and it may be better off than a decade ago. But over-all, as the population increases and the reserves are left undeveloped, the last ten years have only brought a widening of the pay gap, and a fall in average incomes for Africans.

The argument for Oppenheimer makes its last stand on the point that enlightened entrepreneurs are doing what they can in their own fields to improve wages and conditions for Africans. Here one must look at Oppenheimer's record. There is no dispute about his charitable benefactions: he has given substantial sums to charities for blacks in South Africa and in the neighbouring territories; he pays for regular flights to take South Africa's leading surgeons to perform operations at his expense in hospitals in Swaziland. But his real power lies not in what he can do through private charity but through his control of the largest group of mines in the country and his position as South Africa's second largest employer. The Anglo American Corporation's gold-mines use 110,000 Africans. It likes to claim that it is the best employer among the mine-owners: a press statement put out in August 1971 boasted that over the last ten years the group's mines had increased the gold-mine worker's average pay by 87 per cent.

Put into real terms, the rise looks less impressive. In August 1971 Oppenheimer was paying an average wage of £12·84 a month.[22] Employers are quick to point out that every worker receives free food, housing and medical services, claimed altogether to be worth an additional £14·70 a month. This still leaves the African with an average wage of £27·54 a month, and that is well below the ASSCOM poverty line. Average white earnings in August 1971, without food and housing, were £210 a month.

The average African wage figures also conceal a discrepancy between semi-skilled and unskilled workers. The earnings of African team leaders in the Anglo American mines rose by 26 per cent between July and August 1971, from £22·60 to £28·44, but labourers' pay went up only 19 per cent from £6·42 to £7·64 a month. 'Novices' had a mere 5 per cent increase: in August their pay rose to the astonishing height of £6·40 a month.

Over a quarter of Oppenheimer's gold-miners, some 27,500 men, are 'novices'. This large proportion of people, paid conveniently at the lowest rate on the scale, is a result of the contract labour system. Every year the mines bring in a new batch of workers. Separated from their families, they live in compounds on the mines, and sleep in barracks on concrete bunks, at least a dozen men to a hut. It is a poor reward for one of the hardest and most dangerous jobs in the world. In spite of safety precautions, approximately a hundred Africans die every year in Oppenheimer's gold-mines. After visiting his deepest gold-mine in 1963, he told the press: 'It's quite amusing but I wouldn't like to work there.'[23]

Oppenheimer's repeated calls to the Government for a more settled African labour force have to be seen against the requirements of industry. The cost in terms of money and time of training Africans for skilled jobs is becoming too great. When it comes to unskilled jobs in the mines there is little sign that Oppenheimer is opposed to the contract labour system. Over the years the pay gap between average white and average African earnings in the mines has widened. In 1936 the ratio of white to black earnings was 10·7:1. By 1966 it had risen to 17·5 : 1, and by mid-1970 to 20·3 : 1.[24] Against this background Oppenheimer naturally caused a stir with his announcement in September 1971 at the annual conference of the Trade Union Council of South Africa (TUCSA) that equal pay for equal work for all employees regardless of race was the ultimate aim of the Anglo American

Corporation. The promise was widely reported around the world, and Oppenheimer's stock as a liberal rose a few notches. A day or so later, in a small report on an inside page of the *Rand Daily Mail*,[25] Oppenheimer explained his clarion call. 'The Anglo American Corporation is not a one-man show but as far as I am concerned as Chairman this is the policy I would like to see. But I wouldn't like to suggest that something dramatic is going to happen because it simply wouldn't be true and it is not possible. . . . I would as far as I can accelerate it in any business I was concerned with and I would strive to follow the policy within the limits which are set – firstly by the law and secondly by conventions which if broken could land a person in trouble. I know this sounds perhaps rather feeble but there are limitations which apply to anybody who has got the practical job of running businesses.' The remarks did not receive world-wide publicity.

There is nothing, in fact, in South African law or convention to prevent a dramatic increase in African wages. Nor is there anything in the Anglo American Corporation's profit figures to prevent it. The group's after-tax profits in 1970 were 22·9 million pounds. In the gold-mines dividends of 42 million pounds were paid out. Oppenheimer's practical achievements show him to be as orthodox as any other industrialist operating in the Republic. Where he differs from most businessmen is in his skilful use of public relations and in his advocacy of a 'civilized' meritocracy for South Africa. Oppenheimer is far-sighted enough to realize that a capitalist economic system can best be maintained in the Republic by strengthening its economic, political and military links with the rest of the capitalist world, and by the gradual award of privileges to the tiny African middle class. If this middle class can be made an elite, identifying more with the white minority than with the African masses, it may as it grows provide a useful buffer for white supremacy. As far as apartheid is a flexible system for preserving white control, this policy is apartheid's best long-term defence.

10 Business Plays Politics

The South Africa Foundation seems to have chosen
the British Government – *an unnamed M P commenting
on Mr Heath's Cabinet, quoted with approval in the
Foundation's Annual Report for 1970*

South Africa is well supplied with powerful British friends. At
every level of British industry and in most quarters of the
Conservative Party particularly there is a ready acceptance
of the *status quo* in the whole of Southern Africa. No less than
eight members of the present Conservative Cabinet sat on the
boards of companies with subsidiaries there until they were
required to give up their posts temporarily while they serve
as Ministers.

On the Conservative back benches, 23 M Ps still have
directorships in groups with subsidiaries in South Africa,
and many more are with companies that trade there. It has
been calculated that of the 490 British companies with South
African interests in 1969 161 made donations to the Conservative Party and its allies.[1] The party itself received
£358,790; a further £178,725 went to British United
Industrialists which has been described as virtually a
Conservative Party collecting agency; and another £78,212
went to right-wing groups like the Economic League.

The tendency to equate British interests glibly with
business interests and in particular with the interests of
companies that deal with South Africa comes naturally to a
political party with these background connections. But
important though these individual links between M Ps and
industry are, the over-all influence of commercial interests on
British foreign policy is both wider and more insidious. The
experience of six years of Labour rule helps to make the point.

Only four Labour M Ps have directorships in companies with South African subsidiaries. In addition, one or two Cabinet Ministers have had direct connections with South Africa before or since they held office. Douglas Jay, for example, a former President of the Board of Trade, was a director of Courtaulds. Lord George Brown works for Courtaulds now. However, in spite of Labour's few formal links with companies directly benefiting from trade and investment with South Africa, Labour's record on apartheid was different only in detail from that of the present Conservative Government. Labour asked for a cricket tour to be cancelled. It upheld the United Nations arms embargo (although it continued to honour contracts made by the Conservatives before it took office). But, far more importantly from the South African point of view, it encouraged the unconditional continuation and expansion of British trade and investment with the Republic. Indeed, on both the occasions of friction – the cricket tour and the arms embargo – the Labour Government hastened to undo any damage that might have been done to British economic links with South Africa. Soon after the 1967 arms embargo row, when Labour, after much hesitation, decided to maintain the ban, John Davies, then Director-General of the Confederation of British Industry, went out to South Africa to soothe industrialists there; Anthony Crosland, President of the Board of Trade, took the opportunity of sending him a sympathetic letter to use in his discussions. The letter was perhaps the clearest statement of Labour policy on South Africa in its whole term of office, and it repays extensive quotation. 'In 1967', Crosland wrote

we sent goods worth nearly 260 million pounds to South Africa, or 5 per cent of our total exports. It is now one of our biggest markets after the United States. Our investment in South Africa has been estimated to be of the order of 1,000 million pounds by the Reserve Bank of South Africa; we estimate that about one-tenth of UK overseas direct investment is in South Africa. We are also very conscious of the importance attached by South Africa to her exports to the U K; these continue to represent about one-third of South Africa's total exports. We have firmly resisted political pressure to terminate the preferential access enjoyed by South African products.

Our concern to see this valuable trade develop and to avoid any economic confrontation with South Africa has been repeatedly made clear in Parliament and the U N. Though it has been the policy of the Government to implement the U N resolution on arms, the Government has made it clear that it does not consider that political differences between independent states can be resolved by resorting to general trade sanctions and we have made very clear in the United Nations and elsewhere our view that sanctions which have had to be applied in the special case of Southern Rhodesia must not be allowed to spread.[2]

After the cancellation of the Springbok cricket tour to Britain in May 1970, the Labour Government told its trade officials to reassure South Africans that this must not affect trade. In an interview with the *Rand Daily Mail*, Mr Robin Farquharson, Britain's consul-general and director of trade development in South Africa said that no comparison should be drawn between the cancellation of the cricket tour and trade relations between the two countries.[3] Two months earlier, Sir Leslie O'Brien, the Governor of the Bank of England, was in South Africa with his wife on a visit which included a courtesy call on Mr Vorster. He warned British political activists to remember Britain's 'important' trading and financial links with the Republic and cautioned people against 'thinking only in political terms'. The *Rand Daily Mail* commented, 'He and Lady O'Brien have not come to South Africa as trading envoys from Britain as such, but better representatives could hardly be found.'[4]

Of course no British Cabinet Minister, and few industrialists ever rise to their feet for a speech on Southern Africa in general without making the ritual proclamation of abhorrence for apartheid. But that abhorrence soon lessens at the prospect of expanding British trade with South Africa, and of enlarging Britain's investment stake. Successive British governments, Labour as well as Conservative, have made it their business to maintain the best possible economic relationship with South Africa. Faced with a choice between opposing apartheid and increasing trade, the decision has been easy: the Department of Trade and Industry's pamphlet, *Hints to Businessmen: South Africa* (which came out under Labour) makes it clear that the Government's philosophy is, in effect, 'Shut up'. The pamphlet puts it more long-windedly:

The two main political parties (in South Africa) do not disagree about the principle of separate treatment for those of European and non-European descent. The difference between them lies principally in the way in which they think this principle should be applied. The visitor will find that these problems tend to figure prominently in discussion. When engaged in business dealings visitors would be well advised not to become involved in controversy on political and social matters that arouse deep feeling in South Africa.

Against this background of bi-partisan support for maintaining the economic *status quo* with South Africa, perhaps the remarkable thing is that events like the arms ban, or the cancellation of the cricket tour took place at all. Occasionally popular pressure and demonstrations on a wide scale at home, or diplomatic pressure at the United Nations bring about changes. But on the whole South Africa has had things all her own way.

THE UNITED KINGDOM–SOUTH AFRICA TRADE ASSOCIATION

Still, in the last few years, as Britain's economic role in South Africa has come increasingly under scrutiny, white South Africa's friends have had to play a more organized role. In 1965, a year after Labour came to power and imposed the arms ban, the United Kingdom–South African Trade Association (UKSATA) was set up. A wide range of British companies contribute to it. Its Council includes the chairmen or directors of most of the major corporations from BOAC to

Guest, Keen and Nettlefolds, from Plessey to Associated Portland Cement, from Barclays Bank International to Whitbread. It has a sister organization in the Republic, the South Africa–Britain Trade Association (SABRITA), which in turn is supported by most of the biggest companies in the Republic, including the South Africa-based subsidiaries of British companies.

Five years before UKSATA, an equally powerful business propaganda group was set up. Called the South Africa Foundation, its scope was wider than merely trade and investment. Although it was formed by and subscribed to almost entirely by industrialists (and although it naturally made the usual claim of being 'non-political'), it aims to propagate 'the strategic, political and economic importance of South Africa for the non-communist world'. It began a few months before Sharpeville and announced its specific intention of 'stemming the tide of ignorance, criticism and misrepresentation against the Republic'.

The main lobby group for trade and investment is UKSATA. Appropriately enough, it shares offices in London with the Confederation of British Industry. The CBI's Deputy Director-General, Mr J. R. Whitehorn, is a member of UKSATA's Council. UKSATA's Chairman, Mr W. E. Luke (who is also Chairman of Lindustries Ltd, a company with substantial interests in South Africa) is on the Council of the CBI. Mr Luke was also Chairman of the British National Export Council's Southern Africa Committee from 1965-8 and on its Council until the Conservative Government decided to replace the BNEC by a high-powered Export Board in 1971.

At the head of UKSATA are three other men who illustrate the immense power of the organization. Its President is Sir Nicholas Cayzer, the Chairman of the British and Commonwealth Shipping Company and of Union Castle Steamship Company which own a large slice of Safmarine, the South African shipping line, and a Vice-

President of the South Africa Foundation. UKSATA's Director is George Mason, a former head of the Africa Department of ICI, who has publicly protested against sanctions on Rhodesia. Its Vice-President is Lord Cole, the Chairman of Rolls-Royce.

With this backing, and supported when it started by 55 companies (the number had risen by March 1971 to 227 companies) it was not surprising that UKSATA gained immediate access to Whitehall. At the annual general meeting in June 1967 the Chairman said:

Continuous contact has been maintained with the Government and Opposition at the highest level. The President and Chairman have briefed the Prime Minister, the President of the Board of Trade and the Leader and Deputy Leader of the Opposition both verbally and in writing of the extent of the British stake in South Africa and the effects on the British economy and people of any confrontation with the Republic. The Prime Minister has said in the House of Commons and in writing to the President that the quarrel with Rhodesia must not be allowed to develop into a confrontation whether economic or military involving the whole of Southern Africa. The President and Chairman have also discussed all the problems affecting two-way trade with Mr Heath and Sir Alec Douglas-Home.

UKSATA's Chairman made it clear that the organization was not sitting idly by in the campaign that was beginning to be mounted for the Government to lift the arms embargo on South Africa: 'Your Executive Committee has been concerned with the effects of the arms embargo on our trade with South Africa, and it is hoped that there may be a possibility of some successful influence being exerted.'

How nearly that influence succeeded was revealed by Mr Luke at the A.G.M. in the following year: 'The President and I have been in direct touch with the Prime Minister, the President of the Board of Trade, the Foreign Office, the Leader of the Opposition and Sir Alec on the arms embargo issue, and on other matters affecting our trade with the Republic. It may also not be appreciated that very effective pressures are continually exerted through the CBI and the BNEC, on both of whose Councils I serve. I believe that the battle on the decision on the supply of arms was within an ace of being won, and that the four Cabinet Ministers mainly concerned were, in fact, all on our side.'

In the end the decision went against UKSATA and South Africa. But the Association recovered quickly and started exerting its influence at top level, this time in South Africa, to minimize the effect of the arms row on its members' profits. As Mr Luke told the A.G.M. in 1968: 'Our friends in SABRITA have continuously advocated moderation in South Africa despite unpopular political decisions and I think they have achieved some success. I was able to see the Minister of External Affairs and the Ministers of Finance and Economic Affairs while I was in the Republic and have reason to believe that the South African Government will delay placing contracts for naval craft and accessories and airborne weapons with other countries as long as possible in the hopes of a change of Government here or a change of heart by the Socialist Government.'

When the change of Government did occur in 1970, UKSATA was of, course, pleased. But in an aside in his statement at the A.G.M. in 1971 Mr Luke paid touching tribute to Mr Wilson's record on South Africa: 'Speaking for myself, I am convinced that the new Conservative Government will be much more realistic and less emotional about the issues at stake than the Labour Government was and I hope that in saying this I am not revealing any political bias save on this particular point. The United Kingdom South Africa Trade Association is not allied to any political party and it is only fair to say that Mr Wilson and the previous Government encouraged industrialists to trade with South Africa. Indeed I was appointed to the post as Chairman of the British National Export Council's Southern Africa Committee by the Labour Government and held office for the normal period of three years.'

The political and industrial pull which UKSATA can exert is well illustrated by the guests it attracts at its annual council luncheon. In the place of honour at its October 1970 lunch was the South African Ambassador to Britain, Dr H. G. Luttig. Chief guest was Earl Jellicoe, a member of the incoming Conservative Government, and Leader of the House of Lords; before the 1970 election, he was a director of Smiths Industries, which provides electronic instruments for the Hawker Siddeley Buccaneer, the plane the South African Government wanted to buy once the arms embargo was lifted.

Other guests included four leading civil servants, the permanent secretaries at the Treasury and the Department of Trade and Industry, and the permanent under-secretaries at the Foreign Office and the Department of Employment and Productivity, the Director-General of the Central Office of Information, the President of the CBI and Lord Thomson the Chairman of the Thomson Organization, which controls *The Times* among other newspapers.

UKSATA would not be the efficient organization that it is if it had failed to take the opportunity of spreading its propaganda in front of its distinguished guests. Sir Nicholas Cayzer asked what right Britain 'or indeed any other nation had to create moralistic barriers to the natural process of evolution in South Africa'.[6] The extraordinary expansion of the South African economy 'to which we are contributing with British investment and know-how has produced a situation which I for one am convinced is going to have a profound effect on the development of human relations in South Africa'. The 'inexorable pressures of economic life' and the demand for skilled labour would undermine apartheid. A similar line was taken by Mr Luke who told the guests that 'South Africa is very useful as a whipping-boy for self-righteous left-wingers and for cynical protesters who believe they can gain moral capital without any personal risk and from a safe distance. . . . If the screwball idealists

had their way South Africa's civilization would be destroyed
and this would be a disaster not only to all sections of the
community in South Africa but also to the Western world.'

Mr Luke's imaginative turn of phrase also took in the
'principles-before-profit brigade' as he warned that 'the
pressures from the anti-South African lobby who object to
the South African Government's social and political policies
are growing stronger as the months go by'. But then he
reassured his audience: 'Without the encouragement of
most of Britain's leading companies who are members of
UKSATA our task would have been even more difficult
than it has been.'

Lord Jellicoe put the Government point of view. An
expansion of trade between Britain and South Africa was
not only 'in our interest but in the interests of a freer world'.
We in Britain should beware of 'cutting off our export nose
in order to placate our political critics abroad'. Having
abandoned the arduous role of world policeman, Britain
should eschew 'the more self-righteous role of inter-continen-
tal nag or nanny'.

Most of the arguments expressed at that lunch belong to
the two main lines of UKSATA's thought. The first line
is 'Hands off South Africa' with its two subsidiary themes:
(a) South Africa's problems are 'complex', and are not
therefore susceptible of 'simplistic solutions' imposed by
outsiders; and (b) Britain's economic stake in South Africa
is so vast and profitable that she must not risk antagonizing
the Republic for fear of damaging it. The second line is the
increasingly popular one, that economic development is
undermining apartheid.

THE SOUTH AFRICA FOUNDATION

Both arguments are broadly similar to those put forward
by the South Africa Foundation. It is no surprise to find
that Mr Luke and Sir Nicholas Cayzer are both trustees
of the Foundation although its role is wider than that of

UKSATA and its membership is mainly South African. Formed in the crisis of the early 1960s, when some foreign capital started to leave the country, the Afrikaners and English-speaking South Africans who set up the Foundation intended to forestall the country's isolation. Their aim was 'to present to the world a true picture of South Africa, the historical and natural forces which have shaped the destinies of her peoples and the contribution which they have made to the wealth, security and happiness of the African continent and the world as a whole'.

The Foundation deserves close study. Where the South African Government attempts to justify the policy of separate development, the South Africa Foundation concentrates on selling the image of the country as a prosperous, stable haven for investment, where foreign businessmen can earn good profits. The Foundation is the voice of the business community in South Africa, the public relations arm of those who make money out of the present system.

Needless to say, its members do not oppose white supremacy. What they want, they say, is greater flexibility in the apartheid system so as to make more productive use of cheap black labour. But the main object is to maintain foreign investment and to oppose any threats of trade boycotts and to 'play our part in establishing South African leadership in Africa'.

In the eleven years in which it has operated the Foundation has proved itself to be one of the most effective propaganda organizations in the Western world. In a sense its job has not been difficult. Few Western industrialists are inclined to question the propriety of investment and trade with South Africa, so that in arguing against boycott the Foundation is pushing at an open door. But in the space of a decade the Foundation has successfully removed most of what scepticism there was in the business community after Sharpeville, and has even turned some doubters into active supporters of the South African system.

A glance at the Foundation's letter-head is enough to show the weight and prestige of its trustees in the industrial community. They include an executive committee of twenty-six men, plus a President and Deputy-President. They represent the chairmen and managing directors of some of the largest companies in South Africa. Many of these are subsidiaries of British and American corporations.

The President is Major-General Sir Francis de Guingand, a former *aide-de-camp* to Field Marshal Montgomery. He settled in South Africa in 1947 and was by 1970 a director of Rothmans of Pall Mall Ltd, of Canadian Breweries Ltd, of Associated Manganese Mines of South Africa Ltd, and of some seven other companies. His deputy, Dr Etienne Rousseau, is one of the leading Afrikaner industrialists, the Chairman of Sasol, of Gascor, of Natref (the giant oil and gas combines), and a director of Dunlop South Africa and Dorman Long (Africa) Ltd. The executive committee consists of men like F. H. Y. Bamford, the Chairman of South African Manganese Ltd, and a director of the Armaments Development and Production Corporation of South Africa; C. S. Barlow, Managing Director of the American–South African Investment Company, and Chairman of Thomas Barlow & Sons Ltd; C. L. F. Borckenhagen, Chairman of Honeywell Computers South Africa (Pty) Ltd, and a director of African Oxygen Ltd, a subsidiary of British Oxygen; C. S. Corder, a director of the Goodyear Tyre and Rubber Company (South Africa) (Pty) Ltd; D. P. de Villiers, a committee member of the United States–South African Leadership Exchange Programme; Dr J. E. Holloway, a former Ambassador to Washington and now a director of International Computers (South Africa) (Pty) Ltd; and Dr F. Mayer, a director of the Trust Bank and of Massey-Ferguson (South Africa) Ltd.

The Foundation claims to be non-political, and makes much of the fact that no politician is allowed to be a trustee. It is true that it takes no sides in current South African party

223

politics, and has representatives of both the Afrikaans and English-speaking business communities. This undoubtedly helps to give it extra standing in the outside world. Since both the United Party and the Nationalists agree on basic points, supporters of both can happily support the Foundation too.

But it is as political as any public relations organization is bound to be which has no black members, and which was set up specifically 'to present to the world a true picture of South Africa'.

The Foundation has an annual budget of £258,000 from its corporation membership. It has offices in London, Paris, Bonn and Washington. It used to put out a glossy periodical called *Perspective*, not unlike the South African Government's own publication, *Panorama*. In 1970 it changed to a more subtle quarterly called *South Africa International*. This has the look of an academic journal, contains articles by university professors, diplomats and senior businessmen, and contains no illustrations.

The most effective of the Foundation's techniques are its lavish invitations to influential foreign politicians and industrialists to come to South Africa 'to see for themselves'. Known within the Foundation as 'the treatment', these generous junketings have produced some of the very best propaganda for South Africa. In the last few years, the British Foreign Secretary Sir Alec Douglas-Home, the Chancellor of the Exchequer, Mr Anthony Barber and the Speaker, Mr Selwyn Lloyd, have all been out to South Africa as Foundation guests. Recently the Foundation has been expanding into Western Europe and North America. In 1971 it invited M. Pierre Sudreau, a former Gaullist Minister who was at one time tipped as a future contender for the French Presidency and General Kruls, the Dutch Editor-in-Chief of the official NATO publication, *Fifteen Nations*. In March 1971 it organized a five-day seminar in Johannesburg, under the aegis of the American Management Association, at which industrialists from the United States, Canada, Britain and Western Europe were invited 'to make a first-hand assessment of business opportunities in South Africa'.

These visits rarely fail to pay off. After his tour Mr Selwyn Lloyd wrote an article entitled South Africa: Time for Reappraisal in the *Reader's Digest* of 11 September 1970. (*Reader's Digest* itself made a pre-tax profit of £200,000 from its South African operations in 1970.)[7]

General Kruls gave his impressions in *South Africa International* for July 1971. After a preamble in which he 'greatly hesitates after such a short time to express an opinion', the NATO official says outright that 'the principle of separate development which is the main foundation of the apartheid policy could lead to an acceptable solution, especially for the Bantu.' The General continued: 'It is not South Africa which has to go on its knees to ask for ships and weapons and support, but the countries of NATO that must ask South Africa to do its utmost to maintain its position of the African continent and to assist the countries of Western Europe and North America not only to keep the sea lanes open but to prevent further penetration into African countries. This is a tremendous burden for South Africa and therefore she has to be supported.' As Major-General Sir Francis de Guingand put it in his presidential address in Durban on 24 March 1971, 'Our policy of inviting to this country opinion-makers of high stature has proved most successful and paid valuable dividends.'

The South Africa Foundation's role in relation to the South African Government has been described as comparable to that of German industry in relation to Hitler's régime in the late 1930s.[8] It was significant that the Foundation changed to an 'outward-looking' posture soon after Mr Vorster's Government decided to adopt this policy itself. The basis of the policy is the promotion of the idea of 'dialogue' between South Africa and the rest of the world, but especially black Africa to the north, and the boosting of particular Government-appointed black leaders as spokesmen for the country's Africans.

In 1970 the Foundation began to sponsor visits by Southern Africans to Europe. It sent selected Africans from Lesotho and the other former High Commission territories, and it also paid for two Coloured educationalists from South Africa, invited to Britain by the Foreign Office, to go to the Continent afterwards.

Clearly the value of this form of 'tokenism' was not lost on the sophisticated operators in the Foundation. Blacks who get permission to travel out of South Africa are so rare that many people in Europe or North America who meet them are bound to be tempted to accept them as representative, especially if they criticize the Government on minor issues. It was left to Major-General de Guingand to explain the thinking behind the Foundation's policy in his revealing Presidential address in 1971. Calling for more contact 'at top level' between the different communities in South Africa he said, 'If it is done at the top, openly, confidently, for all the world to see, our international reputation could change dramatically.' But in case this notion might worry his audience, the Foundation's President quickly set their minds at rest: 'There is of course an old fear that social contacts lead to integration. What I am talking about is some form of contact between representative *leaders* [italics in original] of our various communities. This would be a beginning, and a beginning in safety, towards friendly dialogue between our own black and brown and white nations while beginning to talk with those beyond our borders at the same time.'

After the meeting, the Foundation began to put the idea into practice. It invited Chief Gatsha Buthelezi, the Chief Executive Officer of the Zululand Bantustan, and other black leaders to a banquet and they have since agreed on some form of continuing association. But the Foundation drew the line at inviting blacks to join it as full members.

The Foundation now boasts that between seventy and eighty per cent of the main business companies operating in South Africa subscribe to it. These include the biggest foreign companies. Among the American members there are John Deere, Caterpillar, Mobil Oil, Caltex, International Harvester, Union Carbide, Chrysler, General Motors and Barlow-Weyerhauser. Several British companies or their subsidiaries have directors who are Executive Trustees of the Foundation – Dunlop, Davy Ashmore, Eagle Star Insurance, Barclays Bank International, Cadbury–Schweppes, Rothmans, Raleigh Cycles, Metal Box and Consolidated Gold Fields. Their interest in an organization whose aim is to 'stem the tide of ignorance, criticism and misrepresentation against the Republic' is obvious. They are well aware that the role of foreign companies in South Africa is coming increasingly under attack. The South African Foundation is the most powerful organization available for spreading the propaganda that contact and dialogue with South Africa are the best tools for bringing about change.

Every issue of *South Africa International* concludes with a progress report from each of the Foundation's overseas offices on the success of this line. In July 1971 the Foundation's London director reported that there had been 'further attempts to put pressure on British firms and businessmen with South African connections' and to 'shame them before public opinion at home'. But he added, 'British business appears to be tough enough to take it.' The director of the office in the United States reported that some editorials in American newspapers welcomed the move towards dialogue between the Ivory Coast and South Africa and expressed the hope that in the United States 'with patient diplomacy the quiet voices of reason and goodwill may yet prevail.'

A good example of this 'patient diplomacy' is the Foundation's increasing willingness to approach journalists with offers of help in preparing articles about South Africa. The lavish hospitality bestowed on visiting industrialists is offered to journalists too. In 1969 the Foundation's Annual Report boasted: 'Particularly noteworthy in the economic sphere were a highly enthusiastic feature in *Business Week* and a series of articles in the *Wall Street Journal*. Both writers had been assisted by the Foundation.'

The value of 'non-political' propaganda of all kind was openly expressed during hearings conducted by the US Senate Foreign Relations Committee in March 1963. The Committee Chairman, Senator J. William Fulbright, produced a letter in evidence, dated 22 November 1961, from the head of an American public relations firm to South Africa's Director of State Information, who had employed him. The letter said at one point, 'What much of this work proves – beyond doubt – is the value of positive non-political propaganda to create an effect essentially political. Political propaganda as such would have been largely ineffective. But institutional publicity – touching on South Africa's general life, economic, cultural and social accomplishments, tourist attractions, sports, festivals, etc. – can tend to soften hard political attitudes, make for good feeling, and tend to correct misinformation about the country.'[9]

With Mr Heath and President Nixon in office, the Foundation's main – and increasing – influence now is through its high-level lobbying. (Here again, its work closely overlaps with that of UKSATA.) The Foundation could scarcely restrain its glee after the 1970 British General Election: 'No British Government in history, no British Cabinet, has had more members with personal, detailed and recent knowledge of South Africa' the London director, Mr Roy McNab, reported in the eleventh Annual Report.

'Contact at high level has been maintained in London', he went on. One trustee dined with the Prime Minister at Chequers, others had talks with the Foreign Secretary and the Chancellor of the Exchequer. Even so, Mr McNab complained that there was no respite in England in the debate about South Africa. Because the arms issue was unresolved, it was permanently available for 'every new round of anti-South Africanitis'. In these conditions the London office had (according to the Director of the Foundation, Mr L. B. Gerber) 'to act with the greatest circumspection and delicacy to reveal behind the unsmiling mask the reality of Anglo–South African relations which are better than they appear'.

In the United States the Foundation's influence has been equally effective. Sir Francis de Guingand's important meeting with President Nixon has been discussed in Chapter 7. A year later, in the Report for 1970 the Foundation celebrated what it saw as a growing rift between parts of the State Department and the White House, with the White House supporting the idea of 'dialogue' and rejecting a policy of isolating the Republic. 'These acute differences of opinion, manifested within the Government emphasized the value of the Foundation's activities', the Report went on. To maintain its influence, it decided to move its office from New York to Washington. The Foundation naturally made great play in its American contacts with the argument that had already influenced the British Government – the alleged threat of Soviet penetration in the Indian Ocean. It provided several American journalists with 'factual background' on the issue, and used the scare in its other briefings.

The Foundation is sophisticated enough to realize that many aspects of South Africa's way of life are damaging to the country's international reputation. Like any good public relations organization, it sees the necessity for image-building. Hence its fostering of black Bantustan leaders. Hence, too, its decision, taken in late 1970, to make the most delicate of hints to the South African Government that some things could easily be changed without affecting apartheid. At its annual meeting in March 1971. Sir Francis made a few tentative suggestions: need there be quite so many arrests without trial; could job reservation be relaxed a litle faster; must so many pass-law offenders be sent to prison? The '*verkrampte*' Afrikaner press reacted strongly, as might have been expected, but the more far-sighted Afrikaner papers, like *Die Burger*, as well as the English-language press pointed out accurately that the Foundation was in the business of gaining friends for South Africa and fighting the tide of world hostility. If the contact people were overwhelmed the cold war would become a military situation, *Die Burger* said. The South African Government, with its own image-building policy, saw the value of Sir Francis's plea. A few months after his speech the Government 'modified' the pass-law system and said that fewer offenders would go to prison and that more would be sent to 'aid' centres. In reality, control over Africans remained as tight as ever.

The South African Government maintains its own propaganda apparatus, the Information Service. Not surprisingly, it focuses chiefly on the countries from which the Republic receives its main investments, particularly the United States and Britain. In the United States, for example, it has three offices, in New York, California and New Orleans. The South African Embassy in Washington also has an Information Officer.

In London the Embassy has a Director of Information, an assistant and four other attachés devoted full-time to information services. These officers take an active view of their duties. Besides the normal exhibitions and poster displays which any country's embassy puts on, the South African Information Service sends out as much propaganda as it can find outlets for. In the United States, for example, it sends postcards, return postage paid, to schools all round the country, offering a free subscription to the publication *South African Panorama* to any school library.

Since 1966 the South African Government has set up its own radio transmitter, the 'Voice of South Africa', at a cost of £2,330,000. Although broadcasts go out every afternoon to black Africa for nearly five hours a day, South

Africa's immediate neighbours are not the only targets for these transmissions. By January 1971, according to a two-page advertisement which Radio South Africa placed in the *Investors' Chronicle*, the English service was broadcasting sixteen hours a day.[10] Transmissions go to the Middle East, Europe, the USA, Canada, Australia and New Zealand. 'In countering ill-informed and hostile criticism,' the advertisement went on, 'Radio South Africa does not attempt to indoctrinate listeners, but seeks to provide facts and information that will enable the listener to draw his own conclusions . . . the South African society is a complex society – very much more complex than people abroad realize . . .' Radio South Africa has also started advertising in international magazines like *Time*, giving details of its wave-lengths and programme times.

The Information Service also puts out several publications, *South African Panorama*, *South African Scope*, *South African Summary* and *Business Report*. The main content of their propaganda varies from the direct untruth (for example, the claim that there were no 'Bantu' in South Africa when the white settlers arrived) to misleadingly incomplete statistics (for example, that there are more doctors per person in South Africa than any other nation, a statistic which evades the point that, although the ratio of doctors to white patients *is* the world's highest, the ratio of one doctor to every 10,000 African patients is one of the lowest in the world). The Government puts forward its claims for 'apartheid' as a solution to South Africa's problems. The propaganda talks of the several African 'nations' in South Africa and the photographs in the glossy publications concentrate either on Africans in tribal dress or on the 'growing Bantu middle class'. But Africans in tribal dress are as rare as Africans in neat suits with white shirts, holding down pleasant office jobs. The propaganda ignores the reality of an impoverished rural community and a miserably-paid, detribalized industrial proletariat.

In Britain the South African Ambassador has played a particularly active role in winning friends and influencing people. In 1969 he began a series of 'goodwill missions' to British cities. Once a month over a period of two years the Embassy sent out representatives, together with officials from South African Airways and the Tourist Corporation, to meet local aldermen, business people, industrialists and newspapermen. They had special talks with provincial editors. The *Cape Times* commented on the success of the programme: 'All this has been done in a period marked by demonstrations and emotional outbursts against South Africa. The going has not always been easy and it has been noted that the Ambassador has shown great courage in facing initial coldness, indignities and worse. In the end however good friends have been made in whole communities where South Africa has never had them before.'[11] Sir Arthur Snelling, the British Ambassador in South Africa, paid his own tribute to the programme when he arrived in Cape Town to take up his post. 'I will be very happy if I can win as many friends for Britain in South Africa as Dr Luttig has done for South Africa in extremely difficult circumstances,' he said.[12]

The South African Ambassador's visits were matched by a regular flow of British businessmen making goodwill visits to South Africa, either individually or on missions. In 1969 about fourteen British trade missions toured South Africa. In 1970 the number was due to be thirteen and the number would have been higher if British trade officials had not discouraged some of them.

A sudden pricking of conscience in the Department of Trade and Industry? No, simply a feeling that too many missions could be a nuisance, and become counter-productive. As Mr W. W. Wilson, Britain's acting Consul-General in Durban, commented: 'We have never made any bones about the importance of the South African market to us. However, we do not want to overdraw on goodwill by sending too many trade missions. About one a month is about as many as we can cope with.'[13]

THE BRITISH NATIONAL EXPORT COUNCIL

This rush of industrialists hastening to South Africa was made possible by generous financial assistance from the British National Export Council, which paid approximately half of each mission's expenses. Without this Government backing, many missions could not have afforded to go. When the BNEC decided to cut down its spending in the spring of 1971, six disappointed British missions, ranging from the Pottery Manufacturers' Federation and the Bristol and West of England Exporters' Club to the Hydraulic Association of Great Britain, postponed their trips.

It is easy to understand the popularity of these missions. British businessmen come to a country with a superb climate. They feel immediately at home in South Africa's English-speaking community, among people with similar outlook, traditions and sports. They are lavishly entertained. Many businessmen come again and again: Sir Isaac Wolfson, Chairman of Great Universal Stores, for example, visits South Africa every two years. Sir Isaac took time off from the English winter at the end of 1969 to bring his wife on the leisurely boat trip to South Africa. On arrival in Durban he gave as his view that the demonstrations against the Springbok rugby team were the work of a 'troublesome minority' which would have no effect on mutual trade.[14]

Comments like that are given ready publicity in the South African press. This flattering attention from the media also serves to make the visiting businessman enjoy his trip and feel a warm glow of self-importance. In February 1971 the Johannesburg *Star* reported the views of Sir George Harvie-Watt, a former Conservative MP and a director of Consolidated Gold Fields, Eagle Star Insurance and other companies with South African interests; he was also on a holiday from the English winter: 'The stupid statements,

H*

sweeping statements of minorities on South Africa don't reflect public opinion in Britain and have no effect on investment decisions.'[15]

British participation in South African trade fairs and industrial exhibitions has also increased markedly. At the Rand Easter Show in 1971 some sixty companies had stands. The British Government approved official participation in six exhibitions in 1971, twice as many as in the previous year.

Few of the British industrialists who come out on goodwill missions or business holidays bother to examine the way in which Africans are forced to live. They have little contact with Africans except on a master–servant, or employer–employee basis. They rarely visit the African townships, let alone the agricultural reserves from which the permanent pool of exploitable labour comes. How many of them take time to see the pass-law courts which deal with hundreds of thousands of Africans a year? Even if a businessman were to get into a serious conversation with an African, the chances of his hearing the view that foreign industrialists should withdraw from South Africa are minimal. To advocate trade or investment boycotts is illegal in South Africa, and can be treated as an offence under the Terrorism Act, punishable by death. The point was well made by the *Rand Daily Mail* in an article on the legal proceedings in Britain against Peter Hain, the Chairman of the 'Stop the Seventy Tour' Committee: 'Peter Hain could hang – here.'

Business contacts are a two-way matter. South African trade missions to Britain are almost as common as their counterparts in the other direction. The Durban Chamber of Commerce, for example, sent its first mission abroad in 1964 and since then has already sent ten to Europe. UKSATA's opposite number, SABRITA, sent a high-powered mission to Britain in the autumn of 1971, described by the *Financial Mail* as 'possibly the most influential group of South Africans ever to pack their bags for a trip together'.[16] One purpose of its mission, openly stated by its Chairman,

Mr W. R. Stephens, the Managing Director of ICI (South Africa), was 'to correct through high-level personal contact, some wrong impressions about South Africa'.[17] Like other less powerful missions, the SABRITA group toured Britain, being entertained by local Chambers of Commerce and polishing up South Africa's image at lunches or dinners given by mayors and local representatives.

At Government level a similarly easy and frequent exchange of contacts goes on. When the Conservative Government came to power in June 1970, the number of South African Ministers visiting Britain, officially or unofficially, was much increased. Within days of the election, Dr Hilgard Muller, the South African Foreign Minister, was in Downing Street. The Finance Minister, the Minister of Information, the Minister of Transport and the Chief of South Africa's Defence Forces all came to London within the next eighteen months, some of them more than once. In return Mr Heath got round the hypocrisy which had restrained any British Government from sending a Minister to South Africa for ten years for fear it would draw attention to British links with the country: he despatched Mr Anthony Grant, Junior Minister at the Department of Trade and Industry, to tout for new business.

There is no need to have a theory about conspiracy to see that the tie-up between commercial and political interests in both countries is bound to lead to a near-identity of views. British businessmen talk to South African businessmen. South African businessmen talk to the South African Government. The two Governments talk to each other. None of them talks to black South Africans. The circle is complete.

In many cases British businessmen are politicians at the same time. They move from boardroom to Cabinet Office with effortless regularity. At its best this is likely to mean that the British Government will ignore, or turn a blind eye to, the reality of apartheid. At its worst it produces a gradual

235

alignment of British policy with the vital interests of the South African Government. In the favoured analogy of Sir Alec Douglas-Home, that of 'bridge-building', it comes about that the real influence across the bridge is *from* South Africa *to* Britain and not in the other direction. And in any event, the close link between political and commercial interests in Britain produces an automatic acceptance of the fallacious argument that economic development in South Africa has brought and will continue to bring a softening of white supremacy. Some businessmen and politicians must know this to be untrue.

Throughout the 1960s the number of British Trade Ministers who had had links with companies with South African interests or who joined such companies later was remarkable. At the time of Sharpeville and immediately afterwards, when popular pressure for a withdrawal of British trade and investment in South Africa was strong, almost every Trade Minister was in this category.

From 1959 to 1961 the President of the Board of Trade was Reginald Maudling, a future director of Dunlop with its several South African subsidiaries. David Price, Parliamentary Secretary at the Board of Trade in 1962, had been an economic consultant for I C I for thirteen years, three of them as personal assistant to the Chairman. Lord Mills, Harold Macmillan's spokesman on trade in the House of Lords until 1962, became a director of E M I which has four South African subsidiaries. Lord Derwent who succeeded Lord Mills in the Lords in 1962, later became a director of the Yorkshire Insurance Company which had a South African subsidiary of the same name. He told the House of Lords on 27 May 1963, 'Her Majesty's Government have repeatedly made it clear that while they do not believe that the boycotting of South African trade would help those who suffer from this policy, trade between South Africa and Britain takes place because both countries find it advantageous.' Alan Green, Minister of State at the Board of Trade in 1962, had been a director of Scapa Dryers, linked with Scapa Dryers South Africa.

In the subsequent Labour administration, Harold Wilson appointed Lord Brown as Minister of State, Board of Trade, in 1965, with special responsibility for stimulating exports. Until his appointment Lord Brown was on the board of Associated Engineering which has interests in more than a dozen South African companies. In 1968 Edmund Dell, a former sales executive for I C I became Minister of State at the Board of Trade.

One of the few former Trade Ministers with no formal connections with South African companies is Edward Heath who, unlike most of his Cabinet colleagues, has never visited South Africa. But his attitude to the country was well illustrated when, as Lord Privy Seal, he introduced the South Africa Bill on 26 February 1962. The Bill was designed to ratify the various changes necessary after South Africa withdrew from the Commonwealth and became a Republic, but it did not, however, end South Africa's Commonwealth trade preferences. At no time in his speech did Mr Heath make any reference to the political situation in South Africa. For Labour, Christopher Mayhew commented, 'He set out to play the Bill down, as a non-political measure, just a mass of technicalities. . . . He showed no appreciation of the very important political and psychological context in which the Bill is presented. . . . The Lord Privy Seal's attitude, like the Bill itself, was a considerable victory for South African diplomacy.' It was fair comment. The nearest Mr Heath had come in his speech to an expression of emotion was when he said that relations with South Africa outside the Commonwealth would be like those 'with any other friendly foreign state with whom we share mutual interests in trade, defence and the relationship between our peoples'.

The most sensitive tie-up with South Africa comes via the eight Cabinet Ministers who held directorships in firms with South African connections (under parliamentary rules they had to resign them immediately they joined the Government). They are Anthony Barber, a director of British Ropes; Robert Carr, of the Metal Closures Group and Norwich Union Insurance; Lord Carrington of Barclays, Schweppes and the British Metal Corporation; Lord Jellicoe of James Templeton and Smiths Industries; Lord Hailsham of Wellman Engineering Corporation; Reginald Maudling of Dunlop; Peter Walker of the Adwest Group and Slater Walker Securities. Lord Eccles, now Minister of the Arts, though he is not in the Cabinet, was a director of Courtaulds. John Davies declared a large shareholding in Hill Samuel, a very substantial proportion of whose profits come from South Africa: in the early 1960s Mr Davies was Vice-Chairman of Shell-Mex and BP and a director of City Centre Properties, which has an associate company in South Africa.

Many a former Conservative Minister has gone easily from the Cabinet to the boardroom of a company with South African interests. Lord Watkinson, a former Minister of Defence, became Chairman of Cadbury-Schweppes and a director of its subsidiary, Schweppes (South Africa). Lord Erroll, a former President of the Board of Trade, joined the board of Consolidated Gold Fields Ltd. Selwyn Lloyd, a former Foreign Secretary and the present Speaker of the House of Commons, was for some years on the board of the Rank Organization which owns Rank Xerox (South Africa). Lord Boyd, a former Colonial Secretary became a Director of ICI, which has a 42·5 per cent interest in AE & CI.

The view that trade and investment with South Africa must be expanded at all costs is now so much part of the canon of Conservative thought that a genuine debate on the issue of apartheid is impossible; the small group of lobbyists who want to push Britain even further towards defending the South African *status quo* finds itself working on fertile ground. UKSATA, the South Africa Foundation, and South Africa House, with its contacts in London, have all helped to keep the debate moving steadily to the right. It is no surprise that the present Conservative Government has been effectively influenced by the numerically small but ideologically powerful Monday Club.

THE MONDAY CLUB

The Monday Club's support for white supremacy has been consistent since it was founded in 1961. Indeed, it was the reason for the group's foundation: a number of right-wing Conservative MPs came together in opposition to the effect of Mr Harold Macmillan's famous 'wind of change' speech before the House of Assembly in Cape Town. But it was not until the Unilateral Declaration of Independence in Rhodesia in 1965 that the Club grew considerably. 'The Monday Club was the first organization in this country to come out clearly and unequivocally against sanctions against Rhodesia', the Assistant Director, Mr Harvey Proctor, now says proudly.[18] The Club also believes that South Africa needs to be strengthened by the West 'to fight Communism'. One of its members, Mr Harold Soref put it like this: 'It is absolutely indispensable that together with South Africa and other countries we fight and contain Communism; the increasing danger in Africa can only be met by the West by strengthening South Africa to fight communism for our own future.'[19]

At the end of 1971 its membership included thirty-four Conservative MPs and thirty-five peers, including several members of the Government; Mr Geoffrey Rippon, who negotiated Britain's entry into the Common Market; Mr Julian Amery, the Minister of Housing and Public Works; Mr John Peyton, the Minister of Transport and Mr Vincent Goodhew, a Government Whip.

Two of the Club's members, Mr Goodhew and Mr John Biggs-Davison sat with two other well-known right-wingers, Sir Frederic Bennett and Rear Admiral Morgan Giles, on a sub-committee of the Conservative Commonwealth and

Overseas Council which has had a distinct influence on
Conservative policy on Southern Africa. The sub-committee,
known as the Cape Route Sub-Committee of the Working
Group on Defence outside NATO, produced a report
shortly before the 1970 General Election, and large parts of
this have now been adopted by the Government; they are in
almost complete alignment with South Africa's own thinking
on defence.

The report's main assumption was that the Russians are
planning aggression in Africa. It came to the conclusion that
Britain should arm South Africa. 'Acts of aggression below
the threshold of declared war might take place anywhere
along the South African coastline, *or in the hinterland* [authors'
italics] without necessarily calling forth the immediate
response which would result from an act of aggression in the
NATO area', the report said. 'The threat to security might
take the form of isolated warfare possibly through direct
Communist-inspired and assisted aggression against, for
example, Angola, Mozambique, Portuguese Guinea, Rhodesia and South Africa. . . . There could be attacks on British
ships and/or other forms of harassment well below the level
of declared war. . . . The Russians and possibly the Chinese
might obtain base facilities for warships of all types at
Zanzibar or again at Cape Verde.'

To avert all this, the Sub-Committee recommended that
Britain should act fast. A first step politically would be 'to
restore relations with South Africa, based on the recognition
of mutual interest, to encourage trade and sell arms for
external defence'. The second point was that Conservative
policy should support Mr Vorster's 'outward-looking'
policy of 'dialogue' with the economically weaker states to the
north: 'Tory policy should foster already existing trends
among the independent African states to encourage *détente*
between those states on the one hand and Portugal, Rhodesia
and South Africa on the other.' Within a few months of
the report's completion in February 1970 this small lobby

group had persuaded the Government to adopt its recommentations.

The trend of the report's thinking was revealed in its other recommendations: 'There should be a friendly re-examination of ways and means of utilizing the Anglo-Portuguese alliance to establish mutually valid and workable defence arrangements in the Southern Atlantic. It is pertinent in this context to think of naval port facilities at Beira (Mozambique), Lobito (Angola) and Cape Verde.' Finally, the report called for a regional pact for the defence of Southern Africa 'if the NATO area of commitment cannot be extended to this vital supply route'. The suggested participants would be Britain, South Africa, Argentina and Brazil.

The outstanding success of this right-wing, pro-South African lobby in bringing pressure on the Government is similar to the United Kingdom South Africa Trade Association's successful pressure on the Confederation of British Industry, again a case of fertile ground being well tilled. In 1967, when the Labour Government reaffirmed its arms embargo on South Africa, the CBI put out a strong statement: 'We can see no sense in handing over on a plate to our competitors trade that we so badly need. . . . The arms in question are wanted for external defence and have nothing to do with South Africa's internal problems. Nothing the Prime Minister said today justifies the blow to the whole of our export trade with South Africa.'

In subsequent months individual members of the CBI's staff tried to modify this. However, since no corporate member was prepared to raise the issue of investment in South Africa, even as an item for internal discussion, the militant views of the UKSATA lobby prevailed. In the autumn of 1970, when Mr Neil Wates, of the construction firm of Wates, announced at the end of a fact-finding tour that investment in South Africa was 'totally unacceptable' because it inevitably meant exploitation, the silent majority in the CBI cold-shouldered him. Finally the CBI Council

241

came round to a discussion of the problem when an article in the *Guardian* suggested that the CBI's Director-General, Mr Campbell Adamson, was changing his mind about the advisability of investment in apartheid. At the meeting Mr W. E. Luke, UKSATA's Chairman, immediately demanded an assurance that the CBI's 1967 statement stood, and that the policy of increasing trade and investment was still supported. Some 250 industrialists readily agreed that this was so after Mr Adamson, and indeed Mr Luke, said that they personally detested apartheid but that the issue must be left to individual members of the CBI to decide for themselves.

Once again UKSATA, and commercial self-interest in the boardrooms, had won. South Africa's lobbyists have no illusions about the futility of the usual rhetorical condemnations of apartheid when subsequent policy contradicts them. 'We have grown used to the fact that even our friends at the UN will take the "moral" vote against us. Even Tory leaders for instance feel constrained to make a moral judgement on us as a preface to their every declaration of friendship for us', said Mr Roy McNab, in a report to the South Africa Foundation's headquarters in Johannesburg.[20] For those who might have thought that the apartheid lobby was losing ground, he went on: 'Damaging a country's reputation is one thing, damaging its economy or defence is another. The more involved one country becomes with another, in economic terms alone, the less likelihood there will be of one taking steps to damage the other. . . . If you look at the real basis of the relationship between Britain and South Africa which is one of mutual self-interest and a recognition of where power lies in terms of economic and strategic strength then you will see this relationship is growing stronger.' Mr McNab did not need to elaborate; a seasoned observer of the British business scene, he knew what really matters.

11   Recruiting Immigrants for South Africa

> The shortage of skilled workers is invariably putting
> up white salaries. If there was more white emigration
> to South Africa, it would help – *M. L. Bexon, Director
> of Dunlop Holdings Ltd, in an interview with one of the
> authors*

Superficial reflection might suggest that emigration to South
Africa is one area in which British companies are not especially interested. It would be wrong. A casual inquiry by
letter to South Africa House about the prospects for would-be
emigrants produces an envelope with three enclosures. One is
a standardized reply from the Chief Immigration Officer,
thanking you for your interest and pointing out that the South
African Government offers grants of £70 towards every
immigrant's fare. The second is a preliminary immigration
questionnaire which includes the question 'Are you and all
members of your family European (White)?' The third item
is a glossy, illustrated booklet, called *Emigrating to South Africa*,
compiled and designed by Barclays International. Why a
British company Chairman Sir Frederic Seebohm, (member
of the council of the Institute of Race Relations until the
April 1972 shake-up) should produce an expensive booklet
for free distribution by the South African Government to
encourage white British citizens to leave this country for the
land of apartheid is a matter for some curiosity.

The booklet is a neat piece of propaganda. It uses the
word 'Bantu' instead of African throughout, and perpetuates
the, by now exploded, myth that Africans only arrived in
South Africa 'at about the same time as the first whites
were establishing themselves at the Cape'.[1] The centre of
the 88-page booklet is a lavishly-illustrated section on the

243

'New South Africans', with long profiles on four English
families who are now making wonderful homes for themselves
in South Africa. The Cardews from London have spent a
year in Johannesburg: 'One thing they are still finding hard
to get used to is the fact that they can now have servants.
"We can even afford a garden boy once a week," says Mr
Cardew. His wife who has never worked since they came out,
has time to make clothes for daughter Caroline and potters
around the garden while the maid does the cleaning and
cooking. "In England we would have to be earning twenty
thousand a year to afford two servants," says Mrs Cardew.'
Or there are the Cowpars from Liverpool, who are now
living in Port Elizabeth. Father works in the General Motors
assembly plant there while son Edward, so the Barclays Bank
booklet tells us, has joined the South African Police as a
student constable, and 'He votes the South African Police as
"great". He enjoys the work, and the camaraderie which
the Force provides.' His younger brother Paul says he is
keen to join the police too.

Advertising of this kind undoubtedly helps to attract people
to South Africa. Britain still provides more immigrants than
any other country, and the South African Government is
determined to maintain the flow. According to its latest
report, its Immigration Department had a staff of twenty-
nine people overseas in 1970.[2] Seventeen of these were in
England, seven were in West Germany, and five worked in
The Hague.

Thanks partly to their work, and to the strong links between
Britain and South Africa, 44 per cent of the country's
immigrants between mid-1968 and mid-1970 came from
Britain. As the Table shows, this is an increase on the percentage for the 1960s as a whole, when it was 32·7 per cent.
But this latter figure is perhaps misleadingly low. The item
for immigration from 'Africa' certainly includes a large
number of English-speaking colonists who moved south as
black Africa became independent. In absolute terms the

number of people going out from Britain to South Africa as immigrants was rising annually in the late 1960s. In 1966 13,130 people emigrated. By 1969 it had gone up to 19,000.[2]

ORIGIN OF IMMIGRANTS TO SOUTH AFRICA

	1961 to 30 June 1970	Percentage	July 1968 to June 1970	Percentage
Rest of Africa	113,456	33.0	16,060	19.4
United Kingdom	112,159	32.7	36,561	44.0
Netherlands	10,311	3.0	2.780	3.3
West Germany	22,829	6.7	6,659	8.1
Rest of Europe	65,999	19.2	16,381	19.8
Rest of World	18,674	5.4	4,419	5.4

Source: Reports of the South African Department of Immigration, 30 June 1961 to 1968 and July 1968 to June 1970.

One need look no further than the appointments columns of the national press to see that advertisements for jobs in South Africa abound. In one month (July) chosen at random last year the *Daily Telegraph* carried fifteen composite announcements of a variety of vacancies, and an appeal for eighty telecommunication engineers to work on South African Railways' scheme to modernize all their signalling and communications equipment. Many of the firms advertising for immigrants are British companies or their subsidiaries. In July 1971, for example, International Combustion Africa, a subsidiary of International Combustion Ltd, advertised for operating engineers; and United Transport Overseas Ltd, a subsidiary of United Transport, applied for a chief bus engineer. General Electric (South Africa) Ltd used all the attractions of the nearby Kruger National Park to entice electricians out from England. An advertisement in the *News of the World* in the summer of 1971 offered men two-year contracts, with free housing and fares paid, for electrical work on the railway line being built from Kaapmuinden to Phalaborwa in the Northern Transvaal. A recruiting team from GEC interviewed applicants in Britain and selected

245

thirty, some of whom were attracted, as the advertisement put it, 'to see the sights the tourists have to pay to see'.

Other firms help to swell the privileged white labour force without advertising. They simply transfer personnel from their UK staff to plants and subsidiaries in South Africa.

The South African Government itself runs an efficient recruiting operation (its head office in London is on the first floor of the building which houses the headquarters of Barclays International.) It also has links with a private organization known as the South African Immigration Organisation (Pty) Ltd, which has offices in regional centres in Britain. The technique here is the 'fishing expedition'; a general advertisement is put into British newspapers calling for craftsmen or skilled workers and offering a wide range of vacancies.

Increasingly now, because of the chronic shortage of white labour in South Africa, the Government encourages more dramatic methods, sending high-powered recruiting teams to Britain for specific vacancies. The procedure here is to put advertisements in local or national newspapers, take a room in a hotel for a few days and interview potential immigrants on the spot. In the last four years teams have come over from the South African Navy, the Natal Provincial Administration, the Johannesburg City Council, ISCOR, the South African Post Office and from many private companies. Most of the teams collaborate closely with the Government: as Mr J. P. Coetzee, the Managing Director of ISCOR put it, shortly before he despatched a five-man team to Europe to try to make up a shortage of 3,000 white workers (20 per cent of the labour force), 'We work hand in hand with the Immigration Department.'

The recent spate of redundancies in Britain caused by closures and mergers has been a godsend for South Africa. The run-down of the coal industry has been welcomed by the South African mines; in the *Derbyshire Times* in May 1971 the Anglo American Corporation put an advertisement for underground supervisors, fitters and electricians.[3] The corporation offered free passages to South Africa, subsidized housing (three-bedroomed bungalows for £1·35 a week) and basic wages for underground workers of £35·75 per week. Advertisements like these continue to be accepted by British newspapers, even though they deliberately ignore the fact that only white applicants need bother to reply; a black coal-miner, electrician or fitter is not eligible. In 1970 a South African recruiting mission succeeded in recruiting 1,000 British miners for the gold mines.[4] At the time of the Rolls-Royce crash in 1971, the local papers in Derby had a sudden spate of advertisements for jobs in South Africa. Dorman Long (Africa) Ltd announced vacancies for a range of skilled trades, from welders, fitters, and electricians to platers and spray painters. Tollgate Holdings Ltd, a South African bus company, had room for diesel mechanics and vehicle fitters, while an unnamed manufacturer offered jobs to machinists.

A fourth, rather more cryptic announcement[5] headed 'The Engineering Industry in South Africa' said simply 'There is an acute shortage of skilled personnel in all branches of the production engineering industry in South Africa.' It went on to say that 'Our Mr Eric Knos will be at the Midland Hotel, Derby, conducting interviews with prospective immigrants on Saturday, 27 February, in the afternoon and evening, all day and evening on Sunday and all day on Monday.' It was signed by PATRIA (Professional Artisan and Trade Recruitment and Immigration Agency) and gave an address in Earls Court. A visitor there would find an undistinguished and run-down looking rooming-house with the name 'Eric Knos' by one of the six bells. So much for this impressive sounding 'agency'.

The one-man recruiting mission is not an unusual device. Two years ago, under the headline 'The man who lured draughtsmen to South Africa', the Johannesburg paper, the *Weekly Star*[6] ran a profile of Mr Ray Vann who interviewed

140 skilled workers in Britain and brought over 35. His tips for other businessmen planning missions to Britain were these: recruiting officers should be immigrants from Britain themselves and they should be highly qualified in whatever trade they represent.

One-man missions are clearly useful. For one thing they allow a group of businesses to pool the costs of sorties into Britain for skilled workers. Equally importantly, they are relatively inconspicuous. As the latest report of the Department of Immigration put it, since most countries in Europe are dependent on immigrants themselves, 'The need for a discreet approach in those countries cannot be overemphasized.' The Department insists that no private firms should recruit abroad without first consulting it. Discretion is also desirable on occasion because of South Africa's image. After all, the United Nations General Assembly in a resolution in December 1968, 'requested all States to discourage the flow of immigrants, particularly skilled and technical personnel, to South Africa'.

Although the Labour Government in Britain instructed its delegate to abstain from voting on the resolution, some trade unions have since attempted to comply with the spirit behind it. In September 1969, DATA (the Draughtsmen and Allied Technicians' Association) for which Mr Ray Vann's 35 emigrants would have been eligible refused to take any advertisements for South Africa in its journal. During the same month the general secretaries of DATA and five other unions, the Mineworkers', the Post Office Engineers', the Public Employees', the Transport and General Workers', and the Firemens', wrote a letter to *The Times*,[7] expressing their concern at the number of skilled workers emigrating to South Africa. 'Statements by South African Cabinet Ministers', the letter said, 'show that these emigrants are an important part of the apartheid scheme. They help to maintain the industrial colour bar which helps to exclude the 15 million African, Coloured and Indian people from skilled jobs despite the needs of an expanding economy. They add, marginally but cumulatively, to the numerical strength of the privileged white elite. And they enjoy by reason of their colour the political, economic and social advantages which are denied to four-fifths of the population.' Britain, the letter went on, needed all the skilled manpower it could muster. 'It does not need the appearance, still less the reality of collaboration with a ruthless racist régime. South Africa needs skilled labour – and should be encouraged to find it in the ranks of its neglected non-white population.'

Unfortunately their concern was not shared equally by *The Times'* sister paper in the Thomson Organisation, the *Sunday Times*,[8] which six months later sold a whole page to the South African Government for one of its rare sallies into open advertising for immigrants. (In 1968 the *Sunday Telegraph* had gone one better and carried an advertisement put out by the Smith régime, headed 'Reach for the Top in Rhodesia' with opportunities for every type of skilled artisan in 'this progressive, peaceful country.')[9]

The union leaders who signed *The Times* letter have tried to translate their concern into action. In 1969 the annual conference of the Trades Union Congress passed a resolution calling on member unions to discourage emigration to South Africa. Some unions acted. DATA carried articles in its union journal exposing the apartheid system and warning workers who emigrate that they are exploiting black labour. The Transport and General Workers' Union in 1971 told its members to beware of recruiters who came looking for white bus-drivers to go out to Johannesburg City Council – in this case, the Johannesburg people were unwise enough to announce in advance that they were planning a big recruiting drive in Britain and Holland 'because of the common language advantages'. None the less, and in spite of the advance warning, the recruiting went on. In October 1971 the Annual Conference of the TUC passed a new resolution calling for more effective anti-recruitment publicity.

As long as South African recruiters are allowed to operate in Britain, with no restriction by the British Government, union campaigns will only have a limited effect. Whitehall has not lifted a finger even to reinforce its own foreign policy. In January 1968 the Labour Government, after much hesitation, decided to reaffirm its embargo on arms sales to South Africa. As a result the Hawker-Siddeley aircraft factory in Portsmouth, which builds the Buccaneers wanted by the South African Government, decided to lay off 1,200 skilled workers. The Atlas Aircraft Corporation in South Africa[10] immediately sent over a team to recruit as many of these dismissed men as it could, to go out to Johannesburg to build the Impala jet for South Africa's Air Force. To no one's surprise, the Government made no attempt, then or later, to prevent this recruiting or to invoke the Race Relations Act against what must have been discriminatory hiring.

South Africa's immigration policy is an integral part of the apartheid system. Apartheid is based on the exploitation of cheap black labour. Skilled jobs have to be reserved for white people if the psychological, economic and social basis of white supremacy is to be maintained. But up till now, the rapid expansion of the South African economy has created skilled jobs much faster than the natural growth of the white population has been able to fill them.

The Department of Immigration estimated in 1970 that in order to maintain an economic growth rate of $5\frac{1}{2}$ per cent a year, the country needed a net annual intake of 40,000 immigrants a year (which would produce 13,000 to 14,000 working men and women). The rate achieved has not been as high as that. No wonder that the Department is doing all it can via its overseas offices to step it up.

Immigration also obviously swells the white population and helps to maintain the proportion of whites to blacks in the country, and thus the strength of white supremacy. Currently immigration accounts for 37 per cent of the annual growth of the white population, the rest coming from natural increase. The influx of young mature adults is also leading to an increase in the birth-rate.

Immigration is a cheap way of obtaining skills for the economy. In October 1969, Mr Piet Weidemann,[11] the Deputy Secretary for Immigration, said that South Africa gained about 90 million pounds' worth of professional and technical skills every year in this way: that is what it would cost the country to train the 3,000 professional people and 7,000 tradesmen who arrive annually. The Minister of Immigration has said that it costs South Africa only £77 to recruit each new immigrant.[12]

Britain is a special target for South Africa's recruitment for obvious reasons. There is no problem of language, no difficulties in adjusting to the white society's political and cultural institutions. British immigrants are mainly Protestant. Denomination might not seem to be a particularly relevant qualification for a skilled machinist, but in South Africa's always suspicious society, these things matter. Right-wing Nationalists began to become restive when the number of Catholic immigrants from Portugal started to increase in the mid-1960s. Not only were these people Catholics but many of them were rather dark-skinned too. Between 1961 and 1967 more than 27,000 Portuguese emigrated to South Africa, a total exceeded only by Britain and Germany. In 1967 the Government started to scale down the number of immigrants coming in from Portugal, Greece and Italy, although the full scope of the new policy did not become evident until two years later when the Deuputy Minister of Immigration, Dr Piet Koornhof, told Parliament that the emphasis was being placed on immigration from 'countries of origin', a concept applying primarily to immigration from Britain, Holland and Germany. Dr Koornhof also listed Belgium, Austria, Switzerland and Scandinavia as 'countries of origin', and added proudly that in 1968, as a result of the special emphasis on recruiting from these countries, there had been an increase in the numbers from each of them;

Britain topped the list with an increase of 10·4 per cent. It was left to Mr Dirk Richard, the Editor of *Dagbreek*, a Nationalist Sunday paper, in an article in January 1969,[13] to put into the clearest language why British immigrants are preferred to Portuguese: 'The average South African', he wrote, 'would only have to glance at most Portuguese immigrants to say with a shake of his head "No, they are not our people. How on earth did they get into the country?" '

To ensure that immigrants are 'pure white', the South African Government takes four special steps. First, there is the question in the application form, asking for the immigrant to state that he is white. Secondly, 'very clear photographs' of the man and his family must be sent. Thirdly, the immigrants must before they leave appear before officials 'with experience in recognizing whether people are white'. Fourthly, on arrival in South Africa the immigrants are scrutinized by officials again.

In 1971 the first small but encouraging signs appeared that trade union pressure might be slowing the flow of immigrants to South Africa. The figures for the first half of 1971 showed a drop of 17 per cent in the number of new immigrants. The *Financial Mail* calculated that for the year as a whole South Africa's net gain, i.e. immigrants minus emigrants, would be down by 20 per cent. It foresaw that the total of new immigrants at 34,484 would be the lowest since 1962.[14]

There was no obvious reason for the development, which affected British immigrants particularly. Their proportion in the total flow of immigrants dropped from 46·1 per cent in 1969–70 to 43·8 per cent for January to July 1971. With rising unemployment in Britain it might have been expected that more Britons would be tempted South. There is, however, no direct correlation between levels of employment and rates of emigration. (In spite of West Germany's boom, for example, and very low unemployment, emigration to South Africa has been higher in the last few years than in the early 1960s.) The *Financial Mail* reported that some businessmen claimed that the London office of the Department of Immigration had become 'lax or obstructive (or both) in recruiting and processing immigrants'.[15] More pertinently perhaps, it also reported that South Africa's political image was 'becoming more important to prospective immigrants'. It was certainly true that the years 1969, 1970 and 1971 produced a growing campaign against apartheid, starting with the Springbok rugby tour.

The trade union campaign may have had some effect. In its annual report for 1970 the Natal Chamber of Printing said a recruiting mission from the South African Typographical Union had been sent abroad to remedy the tremendous shortage of white printers, and had reported that it was becoming progressively more difficult to persuade skilled men to emigrate to South Africa. The mission had learnt 'with dismay' that certain overseas trades unions were discouraging their members from emigrating. 'As immigration has always been the second most important source of labour for industrialists in this country members should readily appreciate the seriousness of the decisions.'

In January 1971 the *Rand Daily Mail* reported that some British trades unions were planning to 'black' members who went to South Africa, and who decided to come back. Returning emigrants would find themselves 'unemployable'.[16] In August 1971 the International Confederation of Free Trades Unions appealed to its unions in 57 countries to discourage members from emigrating to Southern African countries that practised apartheid.

How effective these measures will be remains to be seen. The 1971 drop in immigration to South Africa may be an aberration, or have other causes. In implementing their policies unions certainly face an uphill task. They are not helped by the regular bombardment from newspaper and company advertisements enticing people to go to South Africa.

If there were any lingering doubts that British firms which encourage or abet the influx of white workers into South

Africa are strengthening white supremacy, Dr Connie
Mulder, the Minister of Immigration, dispelled them in 1969.
He told delegates to the Orange Free State Nationalist Party
Congress that there were only two alternatives to bringing in
white immigrants from abroad. One was to accept a growth
rate for the economy of 3 per cent a year instead of 5 per
cent, which would mean economic retreat, devaluation and
unemployment. The other was to elevate the required number
of blacks to the status of skilled workers. But this would cut
across basic matters like job reservation and the industrial
colour bar. It would be the 'beginning of the end of separate
development'. 'The Government', Dr Mulder said, 'rejects
the idea.'

12 Western Trade Follows the South African Flag

> We are of Africa, we understand Africa, and nothing is going to prevent us from becoming the leaders of Africa in every field – *John Vorster*, *in* Newscheck, *8 November 1968*

In the last five years South Africa has started to go on to the offensive in foreign affairs. It has developed an 'outward-looking' foreign policy of trying to establish close economic and diplomatic ties with nearby African States. It has committed its security and police forces to operating beyond the country's borders, in white-controlled Rhodesia, Angola and Mozambique. Farther north, beyond the Zambezi, it is attempting to open a 'dialogue' with independent African States.

South Africa had virtually no foreign policy at all two decades ago, beyond the routine requirement of maintaining traditional links with the other white Dominions and with Britain. But after the Second World War, as Britain's African colonies fought for and won their independence, South Africa found itself increasingly obliged to defend itself before the bar of the United Nations. South Africa had been a founder member of the UN and had signed the UN Declaration of Human Rights without a qualm. It now faced growing demands that it put those rights into practice inside South Africa. As the pressure mounted for boycotts, sanctions, and eventually the use of force against South Africa's racialist system, Pretoria resisted tenaciously, mainly by enlisting the support or at least the pretended neutrality of the leading Western countries, particularly Britain and the United States. Time and time again, these countries, separately or together in agreement with

255

Portugal and frequently with France and Spain, refused to vote in favour of UN resolutions seeking to end racial oppression in the Republic. Even if the resolutions passed, South Africa knew that without the co-operation of the Western powers effective action to implement them was impossible.

By the end of the 1960s it was obvious that South Africa could count on a virtually limitless number of reprieves from the Western governments. At the same time private and corporate Western interests were enlarging their investment and trading stakes in the country. With their help the country was industrializing fast.

South Africa was strong enough to move out of its defensive posture and go on to the attack. Hence the 'outward-looking' posture. The Republic's ties with the former British High Commission territories, Botswana, Lesotho and Swaziland, had always been close since they were incorporated into a customs union with South Africa in 1910. The aim now was to create links with the next group of economically weak States, Malawi, Mauritius and the Malagasy Republic, and then move still further afield. Side by side with support of the African liberation struggle, the independent African States have from time to time stressed their readiness to talk to South Africa about ways of ending apartheid. In the Lusaka Manifesto in 1969, signed by fourteen East and Central African States and later endorsed by the Organization of African Unity, they referred to possibilities of discussing the chances of peaceful and non-violent change towards racial equality. Pretoria rejected them all. Conditions inside South Africa were not open to discussion, but Pretoria would talk about trade, aid and economic co-operation.

As the strongest economic power on the continent the offer was easily made. It had several objects: to win back for South Africa the diplomatic initiative, to make Pretoria look 'reasonable', while making the Africans who rejected this generous hand of friendship look 'extremist', and to undermine and split the united African front. The repercussions on African support for the liberation movements in Southern Africa were obvious. In 1966 when Lesotho and Botswana became independent, their Governments announced that they would not allow the liberation movements to operate against South Africa from their soil. Sir Seretse Khama, the Botswanan President, explained it thus: 'We fully appreciate that it is wholly in our interests to preserve as friendly and neighbourly relations with the Republic of South Africa as possible. Our economic links with the Republic are virtually indissoluble.'

Botwana's borders touch on independent Africa at only one fragile point across the Zambezi River. Otherwise she is surrounded by white-controlled States. Her economic links with South Africa have been forced on her by the circumstances of geography and her historical development before independence. As a part of the 'outward-looking' policy, Pretoria is now trying to forge similar 'indissoluble' links with other African States which still have the room to reject South Africa's embrace. Trade and diplomatic missions are busy probing outwards with offers of commercial agreements, loans and joint investment projects to any African country prepared to listen. In the white-ruled States to the immediate north, South African influence is steadily growing. And wherever the South African flag goes, British and other Western profit-seekers are not far behind. It is one more example of the way Western economic interests are helping to strengthen and expand the South African system.

From the Republic's point of view, the growing concern with the rest of Africa makes sound political, economic and strategic sense. The presence of Dr Banda at the same banquet-table in Pretoria as the country's white leaders is a small (and rather fashionable) price to pay for the huge benefits of having tame and docile neighbours. Just as

I

Pretoria has managed subtly to twist the emphasis of
'dialogue' to exclude any discussion of apartheid but to
include economic 'co-operation', so it is drawing attention
away from the treatment of Africans inside South Africa
towards relations with other African States. The Foreign
Minister, Dr Hilgard Muller, revealed part of the reasoning
behind the 'outward-looking' policy in 1968 when he said:
'We must simply accept that our relations with the rest of
the world are largely determined by our relations with the
African states.'

Part of the aim is also economic. Africa is South Africa's
natural market. As the emphasis of the South African economy
has shifted away from mining towards manufacturing, the
country has been faced by the need to ensure a growing
demand for new products. The white population is not yet
four million, and by the end of the century is still unlikely
to exceed six million. No country has sustained an economic
expansion with so small a market. As long as political and
economic restrictions prevent the Republic's Africans from
sharing equally in the country's development, they can
provide no adequate market. One of the commonest debat-
ing points now between South African industrialists and the
Government centres on the pace at which South African
purchasing power can be increased while ensuring continuing white supremacy. But nearly all are agreed that the safest
way of widening the market is by selling more goods to
Africans abroad.

Dr Verwoerd was the first Minister to propose the idea of
a Common Market in Southern Africa in 1963. Two years
later Mr Jan Haak, the Minister for Economic Affairs,
opened a conference on the theme 'A Common Market in
Africa – a Marketing Concept'. He argued that links similar
to those South Africa had with the High Commission
Territories be formed with other states. Since then a
number of Afrikaner economists and intellectuals have
elaborated on the long-term thinking behind the project.

In *The Third Africa*, a title chosen to distinguish the white
South from Arab and Black Africa, a former senior diplomat,
Eschel Rhoodie wrote in 1968 that 'the concept of a Common
Market formed part of the ultimate objective [of a community
of Southern African States] which is shared today not only
by a great many Afrikaners, politicians, diplomats, government officials, university professors, economists and students
but also by an increasing number of English-speaking South
Africans in all walks of life.'[1]

Praising Botswana, Lesotho and Swaziland for taking
stands at the UN and in the Organization of African Unity
which are 'quite contrary to the line the militant Afro-
Asian world had hoped for', Rhoodie says that what is now
taking place is 'the birth of a strong regionalism in which
racial affairs are taking a back seat'. He goes on to make
clear that the analogy with the European Common Market
breaks down on the issue of political integration. South
Africa is not about to welcome another thirty million
Africans into a union in which blacks would outnumber
whites even more heavily than they already do in South
Africa. Instead, the proposal is for economic interdependence,
but political independence. In another study of the project,
'The Concept of Economic Co-operation in Southern
Africa', three economists at the University of Pretoria,
Lombard, J. J. Stadler, and P. J. van der Merwe describe
the aim as 'systematic co-operation'. They oppose this to
South African 'isolation' on the one hand and 'integration'
on the other: 'The idea of systematic co-operation is to obtain
the best of both worlds of politics and economics respectively.'[2]

In a region where one country is so much stronger economically, militarily and diplomatically than the others,
obviously 'free market relationships' will soon allow economic penetration to undermine political independence.
Rhoodie reveals the fundamentally neo-colonialist goal of
South African policy when he writes that 'if allowed to
proceed unhindered developments could lead to the creation

of a new multi-national giant, the Europe of Africa, which will one day exercise a profound influence on developments in Africa, if not in the world.'[3]

The analogy therefore is less that of the Common Market in Western Europe than United States' relations with Latin America. Rhoodie himself makes the point: 'On its part South Africa dominates the Third Africa to the same, if not a greater extent than, the US enjoys pre-eminence in the Americas.'[4] Just as many Latin American Governments, even conservative ones like Argentina and Colombia, have frequently doubted the advantages for them of US hegemony in the Americas, Africans are right to be sceptical of Pretoria's intentions. The political pitfalls in 'systematic co-operation' are obvious. It is no accident, for example, that the South African concept of a Common Market always includes Zambia, one of the most militant critics of apartheid. The crudest expression of the Republic's intentions was provided by the journal *Africa South*[5] and should be a warning to all: 'Our economic and political objectives in Southern Africa are to harness all natural and human resources from Table Mountain to the border of the Congo river.'

An economic region in which a number of poor areas find themselves adjacent to an economically advancing area is rarely to the benefit of the poor areas. Without systematic planning, and Government intervention, and even often in spite of it, the tendency of market forces is for the poorer regions to become little more than exporters of labour to the advanced region. This has happened in Southern Italy, in Ireland, in Northern Scotland, and in South Africa's reserves and the poverty-stricken neighbouring territories. The gap between the centre and the periphery tends to widen. If the poorer regions have raw materials which need processing, the centre is likely to come in, extract them, and have them processed not in the region which could benefit from increased employment opportunities, but at the centre where a skilled labour force already exists. The best way for a poorer region to escape from the pull of a powerful centre is to develop its own industry and to produce for home consumption rather than for export.

South Africa itself has learnt this lesson. From being a source of raw materials to the Western world, South Africa took political steps to modify its 'peripheral' relationship with the major Western economies. It developed its own industrial base by setting up Government corporations in basic industries, by investing in infrastructure, and by forcing or enticing foreign capital to accept a measure of local participation and control. In relation to South Africa the neighbouring territories face the same problem. Even Rhodesia, whose white minority shares South Africa's political and strategic interests, has shown wariness about South Africa's potential power to halt its industrial development. The Unilateral Declaration of Independence put Pretoria into something of a quandary. It was bound, clearly, to support Rhodesia's efforts to set up infant industries and expand existing plants towards import substitution as a way of surviving sanctions. But at the same time it was worried that Rhodesia industry could be a threat to its own. Tariff barriers had to be raised when Rhodesian textiles started to enter the South African market at competitive prices.

Great dangers therefore confront the weaker states to the north who have none of Rhodesia's closeness to South Africa on most issues. South African domination of the area is already great. A customs union and common currency area exists between South Africa, Lesotho, Botswana and Swaziland. The results are not encouraging, as Robert Molteno has pointed out in *Africa and South Africa*.[6] South Africa treats the three countries as exporters of labour, agricultural produce, and raw materials, while it exports industrial goods to them. When the customs union was being re-negotiated in 1969, Pretoria tried to keep free entry for its manufactured goods into Botswana, Lesotho, and Swaziland, while demanding protection against theirs.

The attempt was partially rebuffed after a leak to the press. The three countries are allowed under certain circumstances to protect their industries but at the same time their manufactures cannot enter South Africa freely.

At the end of 1971 a two-man commission which looked into the Rand Zone recommended that they tie themselves even more closely to South Africa. It argued that they would benefit from membership of a large, gold-backed reserve pool and from the 'advice' of the South African Reserve Bank. Membership would also facilitate the entry of South African capital. The commission, made up of a Bank of England official and a Canadian Civil Servant, claimed that the three former High Commission Territories did well out of the customs union, but it was no coincidence that their recommendations met with support from the South African advisers in the Territories' Civil Service. They also created a deliberate alternative to the offer made to the territories of associated membership in the European Common Market.[7]

The 1967 trade agreement between Malawi and South Africa was another unequal affair. It provides for preferential entry by certain South African agricultural and manufactured goods into Malawi, but only by Malawian agricultural exports into South Africa. The most revealing evidence of South Africa's neo-colonial practice is seen in the fate of Namibia (South West Africa) after 50 years of South African rule. Namibia has been administered almost as a province of South Africa. It still has virtually no industry. Its economy is based on mining, agriculture, fishing and tourism.

The Namibian experience emphasizes that South African, and Western capital, although expanding northwards from the Republic, very rarely goes into industry. If it has done so, the investment has generally been tied to imports from South Africa. In Malawi, for example, a South African firm, Optichem, recently announced plans for building a fertilizer plant. The deal gave the company a five-year monopoly on all fertilizer imports into Malawi (from its South African holding company.)[8] The only manufacturing processes to be performed in Malawi were bagging and blending. Another instance is the new rail link being built in Malawi with a loan from Pretoria. The loan is tied to the use of South African steel for the track, and the Malawian Government is obliged to have the South African firm, Roberts Construction, build it.[9]

Western capital in the 'Third Africa' had always behaved in this way and has no difficulty now in adopting Pretoria's grand strategy without a murmur. It has gone almost exclusively into extractive industries. The exact amount of foreign investment in Southern Africa outside the Republic can only be estimated. In a recent article, 'Private and Overseas Investment in Southern and Central Africa', two British economists, Robin Murray and Colin Stoneman, produced an approximate minimum figure of 550 million pounds for the total of non-South African investment in the Southern African periphery.[10] South African investment in the area they estimated as 375 million pounds, though some of the components in their calculation were admitted to be out of date and therefore too low. The breakdown was as follows:

| | In Millions of Pounds | |
	South African investment	Non-South African investment
Rhodesia		200
Zambia	245*	100
Malawi		15
South-West Africa (Namibia)	96†	
Botswana, Lesotho Swaziland	25	120
Angola		85
Mozambique	10	30
Total	376	550

*1966   †1963

In many cases South African and foreign capital have gone in together. The vast bulk of the investment is in mining. In Botswana the magnet is diamonds, copper and nickel. Companies operating there are Harry Oppenheimer's De Beers, which is mining diamonds at Orapa, and Bamangwato Concessions Ltd, a subsidiary of Botswana Roan Selection Trust, which is spending over 40 million pounds in bringing a copper/nickel mine into operation at Selebi/Pikwe. Botswana RST is a mixed foreign and South African company: 30 per cent is owned by Roan Selection Trust, in which Oppenheimer has a minority holding, and 44 per cent by American Metal Climax.

In Lesotho the Bethlehem Steel Corporation of South Africa, a subsidiary of the American firm, is working with the British-owned Rio Tinto-Zinc Corporation in prospecting for diamonds at Letseng-la-Terai.

In Swaziland the Commonwealth Development Corporation has invested 24 million pounds in the Ngwenya iron-ore mine with the British company Guest Keen and Nettlefolds, and with Anglo American. Swaziland also has the Havelock asbestos mine, controlled by Turner and Newall.

In Namibia foreign and South African capital is completely intertwined in the race to exploit the country's rich mineral deposits. Two American companies, American Metal Climax (29 per cent) and Newmont Mining Corporation (29 per cent) have gone into partnership with South Africa's De Beers (2·5 per cent) and Britain's Roan Selection Trust to develop the largest mining complex in Namibia at Tsumeb. At Oamites the State-controlled Industrial Development Corporation is putting up a quarter of the capital for a copper and silver mine run by the Canadian mining house, Falconbridge. The big oil companies, Shell, BP and Caltex are prospecting in the territory or off its shore. Charter Consolidated, the international branch of the Anglo American Corporation, registered in London, has a

30 per cent interest in the South West Africa Company Ltd. Rio Tinto-Zinc of London is developing the world's largest opencast uranium mine at Rossing near Swakopmund, in collaboration with the Afrikaner-controlled company General Mining, and with the IDC. The capital cost of the mine will approach 60 million pounds.

Outside the immediate zone of the customs union the pattern is little different. In Mozambique Gulf Oil has invested 5½ million pounds. Lonrho owns 62·5 per cent of the pipeline connecting Rhodesia with the coast at Beira. (The pipeline was taken out of use when sanctions were imposed on Rhodesia, but the company received compensation for loss from the British Government.) Sena Sugar Estates, a long-established British company has a stake of over 5 million pounds. The ubiquitous Anglo American Corporation has 50 per cent of the cashew-nut business in Mozambique and 45 per cent of Mozambique Fisheries. Across the continent in Angola, Gulf Oil has another investment of over 15 million pounds at Cabinda.

In Zambia the bulk of the foreign investment is in the copper mines. When President Kaunda nationalized the mines in 1969 Anglo American through its subsidiary, Zamanglo, had an investment stake worth 143 million pounds.

South African capital has begun now to move into infrastructure projects, but it tends to favour schemes which have a substantial strategic, geographical and political value for the Republic, ones which the countries themselves might not have made their first priority, or even chosen at all. The rail link from Mpinde in Malawi to Nacala in Mozambique has already been mentioned. While Zambia is awaiting the construction of the railway outlet through Tanzania, and Botswana is building a new road connection northwards to Zambia, Malawi is accepting a 3·8 million pound loan from South Africa for a railway which will tie it firmly to the white-controlled South.

I*

Western capital has followed smoothly behind the South African. The most publicized scheme so far has been the Cabora Bassa dam in the Tete province of Mozambique. This vast hydro-electric scheme will supply power eventually to South Africa, Mozambique, and Rhodesia at a lower unit cost than South Africa's thermal power stations produce it now. The dam will help in irrigating a huge tract of Mozambique, in which the Portuguese aim to settle up to one million extra whites with the clear purpose of strengthening the colony against the liberation movement. South African security forces are already patrolling the area of the dam which is being built by ZAMCO, a consortium which is led by Anglo American. The British company, Guest Keen and Nettlefold's African subsidiary has set up a branch, GKN Mills, in Mozambique to manufacture equipment for the dam. African Explosives and Chemical Industries Ltd is putting up half the capital for a 3 million pound factory in Mozambique which will manufacture commercial explosives for the first time in the colony. Its partners are two Lisbon-based companies. Much of the factory's output will be used in building Cabora Bassa.[11]

In Angola a similar dam project at Kunene will link the colony with Namibia (South-West Africa) and produce electric power for Walvis Bay and Windhoek, the two main populations centres in the territory.[12] Along the Namibian coast South Africa is installing eight radar beacons to be supplied by Marconi South Africa, a subsidiary of the General Electric Company of London.

South African capital is also increasingly going into tourist development. This is yet another area where the white South will benefit more than the countries concerned. As South Africa's own beaches become more crowded, and as white consumers demand exotic holidays and release from their casino-less society, the Indian Ocean islands or the beaches of Lake Malawi begin to look inviting. Hotels are springing up on all the islands. The South African firm,

Koornhof Holdings, is spending over £250,000 on a hotel on Lake Malawi. Holiday Inns of South Africa, a subsidiary of the American chain, is planning to open hotels in the Malagasy Republic, in Mauritius and the Seychelles.[13] Tananarive, the Malagasy capital, already boasts its Hilton Hotel, controlled by Alda, a State-owned Israeli company, which operates the franchise in return for giving one-third of its profits to the American Hilton Corporation.[14] South Africa has extended Malagasy a loan to enlarge its airport. For Pretoria the islands have two long-term attractions: They are potential bases for operations in the Indian Ocean, and they will eventually, Pretoria hopes, bring tourists from Europe and the United States on tours combining the 'paradise islands' with South Africa and the game parks. One more small link will join it to the West.

South Africa's penetration of the surrounding region steadily proceeds, but the Government's long-term plans for the 'Third Africa' have never been clearly stated. The nearest approach to a blue-print comes in the study, 'The Concept of Economic Co-operation in Southern Africa' (see p. 259). It focuses particularly on South Africa's immediate neighbours, the former High Commission territories and Malawi, which all currently export labour to South Africa. Out of the proceeds of these labour earnings the countries import from South Africa goods which the Republic produces as a result of its own imports of capital, machinery and technical knowledge from abroad. The problem, as Lombard, Stadler and van der Merwe see it, is to reorientate this activity. They would like to cut down the flow of labour within the region and increase the flow of goods. Sean Gervasi, in 'South Africa's Economic Expansionism'[15] has shown that this would in practice mean that the area would become more self-sufficient. South Africa would export more of the goods to the periphery which these countries now import from outside the region; in return the Republic would take more of the goods which they can export, and thus make it less necessary for them to send their migrant labour to South Africa. The whole region would consequently expand, but with South Africa as the centre of an essentially neo-colonial system with a permanently dependent periphery.

Whether such a scheme has been thought through in detail by the South African Government is uncertain. Its own pronouncements on the subject tend to be good propaganda rather than hardheaded analysis. In an interview with a conservative American journal,[16] Mr Vorster has said: 'We are willing and anxious to assist other African states in coping with the tremendous problems of economic and social development that confront them. . . . And we recognize against this background that in many ways we have with respect to much of Africa south of the Sahara a responsibility for assisting in development. . . . Although we do not publicize it, we are in fact already doing quite a lot in this field.' Whatever this and other similar statements are meant to express, the reality of South Africa's dealings with the 'Third Africa' come nearer to the picture drawn by Mr Jan Haak, the Minister of Planning, when he addressed the Conference on the prospect of a Common Market in Southern Africa: 'South Africa believes that aid to developing countries should be directed to the promotion of trade. . . . An analysis of the economic structure and existing trade patterns of the countries in Southern Africa reveals that these countries produce products for which the Republic can offer a market, whereas in turn South Africa can provide their import requirements to a larger extent. South Africa would also be favourably disposed towards assisting these countries to improve their infrastructures.'[17] Rhoodie commented: 'South Africa has no intention of undertaking a one-sided foreign aid programme.' The University of Pretoria study remarked: 'To a large extent the Republic's economic ability to sustain a programme of political and economic viability for the new nations of this sub-continent depends heavily on the continuation of its trade and financial relations with Europe.'[18]

South Africa supplies approximately 80 per cent of the trade within the region. But there is still enough room for it to expand its exports to the region to make up for the goods which it imports from abroad – particularly in the countries outside the customs union.

Within the customs union, in 1964 South Africa provided 90 per cent of imports for Namibia and Lesotho, 83 per cent of Swaziland's, and 50 per cent of Botswana's. But it supplied only 27 per cent of Rhodesia's imports and 20 per cent of Zambia's. Elsewhere the picture worsens: Malawi took only 3·8 per cent of its imports from the Republic, Angola only 1·7 per cent and Mozambique 15 per cent.

Five years later, South Africa's penetration of these markets had increased considerably. In 1970 Malawi took 11 per cent of its imports from there, and South Africa had become the country's third largest supplier. Botswana's imports were up to 65 per cent (in 1968, the latest figure available). In Angola there was most room for expansion, and the South African Foreign Trade Organization ran a campaign to publicize the opportunities, particularly for exports of machinery, chemicals, and automobile components. By 1970 South Africa supplied 4 per cent of Angola's imports. Although this was still a very low share, South Africa had moved up the scale, from being the province's tenth supplier to being the seventh. No other country's exports were rising so fast.

The expansion into the Rhodesian market was probably the most outstanding of all, thanks partly to the imposition of sanctions on Rhodesia by the rest of the world. The Economist Intelligence Unit estimated that in 1969, 80–85 per cent of the country's imports came from South Africa.[19]

In purely economic terms, South Africa's main theoretical advantage in competing in the markets of Africa against the products of other Western countries or Japan, is the shorter distance. Transport costs from the Republic are lower than from Western Europe or elsewhere, and delivery dates can be shorter. This natural advantage has so far been out-weighed by three factors. In independent African countries, importers have shown a natural reluctance to 'buy South African', reinforced by the Organization of African Unity's trade boycott. In white-controlled territories, Angola, Mozambique and Rhodesia, and to a lesser extent in African ex-colonies, the old colonial patterns of trade with Britain, France or Portugal continue to play a role. Thirdly, South Africa's production costs are not always cheaper than those of the rest of the world. Its internal market is small. South African factories have not benefited from economies of scale. Compared with other industries in the Republic, manufacturing still has a relatively low African labour content, and white wages are high. In 1970 Africans formed 52·9 per cent of the work-force in manufacturing as a whole.

These problems are being tackled now. The policy of 'dialogue' is designed to overcome the barrier of African ill-will. The spread of South African diplomatic influence in the whole region south of the Zambezi is helping to alter the old colonial ways of trade and thought. Businessmen are urging the Government to allow them to employ more African labour and thus undercut white wages or at least hold down the rate of increase in over-all wage costs. In those industries which already have a large non-white labour force, South Africa is not only competitive in Africa by world standards – it can also operate effectively in overseas markets in spite of high transport costs. South African clothing and textiles, for example, which have a 90 per cent black labour force, are beginning to win a share of the British market.

The country's main target is still Africa; its aim is to displace other suppliers there. A Common Market or just a free trade area dominated by the Republic would give South Africa an extra edge through protected entry. Robert Molteno has estimated that if South Africa could dominate the other Southern African States (Rhodesia, Zambia, Malawi, Angola and Mozambique) as it dominates its customs-union 'partners' Namibia (South-West Africa), Botswana, Lesotho and Swaziland), on the 1964 figures it would increase its exports by 278 million pounds a year.[20] This would almost wipe out the average annual trade deficit which the Republic was running in the second half of the 1960s. This deficit, and the pressure on its foreign exchange reserves, have become grave economic issues. In November 1969 Mr Harry Oppenheimer rated the problem of finding a replacement for gold as a generator of foreign exchange as South Africa's 'main economic problem'[21] – more important than the shortage of skilled labour, about which he made more publicized comments.

South Africa's growing export potential has not escaped the attention of far-sighted foreign profit-seekers. Increasingly, the South African subsidiaries of British, American and other Western firms are producing for export. Satisfied with the 'stability' which the Western stake has helped to create in South Africa, some firms now are beginning to use the Republic as a base for expanding elsewhere in Africa. Inevitably this gives them a vested interest in supporting South Africa's foreign policy. It is no accident that the British Government has nailed its colours firmly to the mast of 'dialogue'. In September 1971 Sir Alec Douglas-Home told the UN General Assembly that he was 'glad to see that in spite of the deep feelings aroused by apartheid, which we share, the urge to dialogue grows, and is to some extent being practised there. In Africa, as elsewhere, neighbours have no choice but to live side by side: and ultimately dialogue must be resumed and must take charge.' Sir Alec's statements in New York were only the public expression of a policy already being promoted privately with considerable energy. When President Amin of Uganda saw Sir Alec in London in July 1971, the Foreign Secretary urged him 'to explore all the possibilities of a closer relationship with

271

South Africa', as the *Rand Daily Mail* reported. The British Government was 'known to be giving encouragement to all the African countries at present teetering on the edge of an approach to South Africa – or countries like Malawi, which had already committed themselves.

Three days after that meeting, the South African Minister of Information, Dr C. P. Mulder, at the end of a long over-seas tour, said that Western countries favoured a dialogue in Africa although they found it hard to express their real feelings because they had to take the UN into account.

In 1970 the United States for the first time endorsed the concept of dialogue between black Africa and Pretoria. The propaganda lobby, the South African Foundation, inter-preted this move with some satisfaction as a victory by White House advisers over the State Department's policy of isolating the Republic.[22]

A decade ago it would have been unthinkable for foreign companies to use South Africa as a base for expansion: Kenya or Nigeria would have been chosen as the base that was best, safest and most congenial for private enterprises. South Africa then was seen as a profitable but isolated market. Now, through dialogue, South Africa is hoping to be in a better position to house a company's African head office.

In 1970 the American computer firm Univac, a branch of the Sperry-Rand Corporation, set up a subsidiary in South Africa. This itself was significant since the company's links with other countries in Africa, where it has sold some machines, was through independent selling agents. A year later the company decided to use its South African offshoot for expansion into the rest of the continent. Its managing director, Mr Robin Lugard-Brayne, a plantation owner from Kenya and, appropriately, the nephew of the great British colonialist, Lord Lugard, was appointed regional general manager for Africa. The firm announced that in the first instance he would concentrate on South Africa's neighbours, Angola, Mozambique and Malawi, but that he would move to other countries later.

Plate Glass and Shatterprufe Industries, a South-African-owned company, had set up branches and sales outlets in sixty-five centres from Zambia to the Cape by 1970; a year before it had only operated in forty-eight centres. The company trades extensively in Malawi, Mozambique, Botswana and Zambia. Boots Pure Drug South Africa, a subsidiary of the British pharmacy chain, is expanding sales to Mozambique. McKinnon Chain (South Africa) Pty Ltd, a subsidiary of an American company, exports to Canada, Australia, New Zealand and the United Kingdom as well as to Mauritius and Mozambique. The Rhodesian branch of the company has been built up to meet the needs of the rest of the African market.[23] John Deare-Bobaas (Pty) Ltd, an American-owned manufacturer of agricultural implements saw its exports to nearby States, particularly Malawi, Mozambique and Angola, increase by 150 per cent between 1970 and 1971.

The McKinnon example demonstrates how the South African subsidiaries of Western companies are moving into the wider world market. As far as head offices in Western Europe or North America are concerned, the South African base is an integral part of their world operations, and often one of their most profitable outlets.

In 1970 the biggest multi-national corporation of all, General Motors, announced that its South African subsidiary would start exporting its passenger car, the Ranger, designed and developed in South Africa, to Europe. GM branches in Europe will make the engines but the body-parts and several styling items will be South African.[24] As wage costs increase in the West, the apartheid system of forced labour should help South-African-based industries to capture markets for other, unsophisticated consumer goods. It may even lead to South Africa undercutting Japan. In June 1971, for example, the Johannesburg *Sunday*

Times reported that a large South African electrical components firm, Allied Electric of Boksburg, was already exporting
parts for television sets and telecommunication equipment
to neighbouring African territories. It was exploring new
markets in Malagasy and Mauritius, had achieved success
in Zambia and Rhodesia, and could supply virtually the
entire demand in Swaziland and Lesotho. The firm, only
formed in 1964, had even won orders from Australia and
Taiwan. The *Sunday Times* reported that its advantage in
competing with established industries in Europe, America
and the Far East, was 'largely a matter of price'.[25]

As long ago as 1966, James Williams, the Managing
Director of the South African Foreign Trade Organization,
an export promotion body, singled out several sectors which
he believed had good prospects of expansion in Southern
Africa and the rest of the world.[26] They include clothing (at
that time exported mainly to Zambia and Rhodesia),
chemicals (fertilizer, synthetic rubber, explosives), electrical
machinery (mainly to the rest of Africa, and South America
and the Far East) and machinery in general, for which a
'dramatic' expansion of exports was anticipated to South
America, southern Europe and neighbouring African
territories. Williams also pointed out that in the past many
South African subsidiaries of foreign companies had been
precluded from exporting by their parent companies or by
franchise arrangements. It was 'encouraging to note' that
this ban was being dropped, and that many corporations
were now looking to their South African subsidiary to supply
some of their world market needs.

As South Africa begins to cast covetous glances farther
afield for trade outlets, South African capital is also on the
look-out for investment openings overseas. Several Western
corporations are now encouraging their South African
subsidiaries to use their profits as a source of funds for
expansion in third markets. Other companies are linking
up with South African capital in joint ventures in other parts

of the world. This development is one more factor binding South Africa more closely to the Western economic system. Many industrialists have tried to stimulate it for political reasons, including Mr John Davies, the Secretary of State for Trade and Industry. In 1967 Mr Davies was Director-General of the Confederation of British Industry when the Government decided to maintain its ban on the sale of arms to South Africa. The CBI reacted bitterly and a defiant Mr Davies was sent to try to drum up extra trade with South Africa. While there, he discussed with South African businessmen the possibility of their putting up capital, with British firms supplying the expertise, for joint projects in South America and the rest of Africa. The scheme, designed to embarrass the British Government, was no doubt partly inspired by the CBI's President, Sir Stephen Brown, who had issued a fierce statement denouncing the arms ban 'as a cynical and depressing example of attributing high moral purpose to a political compromise of the most unpleasant kind'.[27] Sir Stephen is Chairman of the Stone-Platt group whose South African subsidiary Stone-Stancor (Pty) Ltd has since used its parent company's technical experience to fulfil several export orders to South America and elsewhere.[28]

The South African Foreign Trade Organization has also pushed the idea of joint ventures, suggesting that in some projects, particularly mining, South Africa could supply the technical knowledge as well as the capital. In 1969 General Mining, the Afrikaans-owned mining house, won what was believed to be, according to the journal *News-Check*, 'the largest international construction contract ever awarded to a South African company'. Worth about 9 million pounds, it was for a 10-mile tunnel in a large irrigation scheme in southern Peru. The contract was in association with Roberts Construction Co. *Newscheck* commented that it 'would certainly also indirectly give rise to many other contracts in which South African mining and constructional engineering knowhow will be made use of in other parts of the world. In this manner the exportation of knowhow which invariably will be accompanied by exports of South African equipment and materials will become a growing source of foreign exchange earnings.'

Latin America, as both these examples suggest, is becoming a particularly promising area for South African initiatives of this kind. The Republic is slowly waking up to the relative proximity of this vast market. By 1971 the financial and business press was full of articles encouraging South Africans to look west. In shrewd anticipation of an explosion of business there, Barclays National Bank became in October 1971 the first of the leading South-African-based banks to open its own offices in Latin America.

South African capital has started to move into Europe. In 1971 a South African property company for the first time undertook a central city development in Europe. The Summit Real Estate Development Corporation was building on a site in the financial district of Paris. The construction firm, LTA, set up an international subsidiary, LTA International, which intends to raise capital on the money markets of Europe. Charter Consolidated has been in many ways the pace-maker and symbol of South African capital expansion. Forty per cent of Charter's investment income is South African. The rest is subscribed from all over the world, with the United Kingdom providing 14 per cent. But almost 20 per cent of its assets are in the UK, 3 per cent on the Continent of Europe, 20 per cent in North America and 12 per cent in Australia. In Britain, Charter has a 25 per cent interest in Ferranti, a 25 per cent stake in Elevators and Engineering, and a 37·5 per cent stake with ICI in establishing Cleveland Potash, a mining venture in Yorkshire. Other South African industrialists have been encouraged to set up plants in Ireland to take advantage of duty-free access to the British market for goods manufactured in Ireland.

The export of South African capital to Britain and the

rest of the Western world brings Britain's involvement in South Africa ironically but logically full circle. The apartheid system is now fully integrated into the world economy. To what extent South African capital will continue to expand into Europe is not yet clear. That is for the future. The immediate issue now is South Africa's expansion in Africa, and its creation of a sphere of influence there. South Africa claims that its neighbours' political independence is being respected. But the Republic's economic domination of the sub-continent and its penetration of its neighbours' markets inevitably restrict their freedom of manoeuvre. Pretoria is trying to build up new 'geopolitical relations' like those which forced Botswana, for example, to deny access and facilities to the liberation movement. South Africa will then have widened the economic *cordon sanitaire* around its borders. In the process it will also have strengthened the apartheid system by finding markets abroad and delaying the day when it has to concede Africans inside South Africa greater economic power.

By an uncanny piece of insight, J. A. Hobson in his book *Imperialism* foresaw seventy years ago the pattern that is now emerging. Assessing the choices open before Britain's 'self-governing colonies', i.e., the Dominions, Hobson recommended that Britain 'encourage and aid them in a policy of annexation and the government of lower races'.[29] He went on: 'Independently of the centralized imperialism which issues from Great Britain these colonies have within themselves in greater or lesser force all the ingredients out of which an imperialism of their own may be formed. The same conspiracy of powerful speculators, manufacturing interests and ambitious politicians, calling to their support the philanthropy of missions and the lust for adventure which is so powerful in the new world, may plot the subversion of honest self-developing democracy in order to establish class rule, and to employ the colonial resources in showy enterprises of expansion for their own political and

277

commercial ends. Such a spirit and purpose have been plainly operative in South Africa for many years past.'

That was in 1902. In 1972 the process of expansion which Hobson predicted is well and truly under way. No one can say how far or how successfully it will progress. Zambia is currently in the front line of South Africa's outward thrust. Malawi has already succumbed. Much will depend on how firmly the African states to the north of the Zambezi resist the call for 'dialogue'. Much will depend, too, on how eagerly Western companies follow the South African flag northwards, and continue to aid – and profit from – the expansion of its power.

13 Conclusion

> Even if a multi-racial society could be brought about
> by either military or economic coercion, would that
> be in our interest or in the interest of anyone else?
> Would we like to see the white entrepreneurial class
> in South Africa driven out of the country . . .? –
> *George W. Ball, former US Assistant Secretary of State*,
> The Discipline of Power

Several conclusions ought by now to have emerged. Principal
among them is the interpenetration of Western and South
African business interests. This has deepened over recent
years, especially since the beginning of the 1960s. Trade in
both directions is worth many hundreds of millions of pounds
a year. Capital flows are increasing.

Britain's investments in South Africa constitute over ten
per cent of its foreign assets and produce over 13 per cent
of its direct foreign investment income. For its part, South
Africa is heavily dependent on Britain for capital, technological knowledge, goods, markets for her exports, and
for political and moral support in the face of world condemnation. As Britain enters the 1970s and British capitalism
goes into decline, with a fierce rise in unemployment and
a falling rate of profit at home, the natural reaction of British
capital is to invest abroad.[1] (This although the decline of
British capitalism has itself been due to long years of imperialism during which the flow of investment was abroad, rather
than into the development of British industry.) Since the
end of the Second World War, among the great corporations
which supply the capital for export, there has been a shift
in direction from under-developed to more developed countries and economies. The interpenetration of Britain's

economy with South Africa's is likely to become even more inextricable. Other Western countries, notably the United States and Western Germany, are following the British pattern. In crucial sectors it is with American corporate assistance, and in some instances, leadership, that South Africa has developed into the major industrial power on the African continent and is achieving integration into the Western economic system, itself dominated by the United States. For although the total percentage of the United States' investment in South Africa is small as a proportion of its total foreign investment, it has been applied there to areas critical to the development of an industrial society. Between South Africa and foreign capital there has grown a close and mutual dependence, based on the crucial role played by the Southern African periphery in the maximization of profit for imperialist capital.

There are those in Britain who, out of their antipathy to apartheid and Britain's involvement in it, have reasoned that it is not even in Britain's own short-run business interests to continue this economic involvement.[2] Their argument is that while both countries derive benefit from the various economic links, the balance of advantage is very much in South Africa's favour, and – judging the relationship on economic and not on moral grounds – Britain is compromising itself for very little gain through a relationship that harms it financially on balance (as in the case of Commonwealth preferences, which are not reciprocated) and in the potential long-term effect on Britain's relationship with black Africa. It is suggested that it would be in Britain's economic interests to review the relationship with South Africa. This critique of Britain's unprofitable economic links with apartheid, not on political or moral grounds but on economic ones – which thus sets out to challenge investors and traders on their own territory – is, regrettably, of doubtful validity.[3] There can be little doubt that investment in apartheid and economic links with South Africa are profitable to Britain (or, rather,

Conclusion

to British capital for the argument is not that the interests of one are the same as the other). It is these very economic ties that were responsible throughout the 'sixties for the futility of United Nations' decisions to act against apartheid. Resolutions ringing with moral condemnation are on record in abundance; meaningful pressure against South Africa was made impossible by the simple political refusal by the major powers of the West to coutenance action lest the government of white control be replaced by a régime, perhaps more just and rational, but less accommodating to the requirements of private investment and Western strategy.

Britain and the West profit from apartheid without doubt. This is the indictment which is central to this book: British and Western involvement are by now so deeply grafted into the politics and economics of apartheid that attempts to 'reform' business in its relations with South Africa, while admirable from a moral view, must end in failure. It is not a matter of amputating a leg or an arm from business; the whole body of economic involvement is corrupt.

Nor is it a matter of piecemeal reforms of business or labour practice while the South African system as a whole remains unchanged. The much-vaunted reform programmes of men like Harry Oppenheimer have as their goal, not the abolition of the exploitation of cheap labour, but the substitution of a more conventional class-based meritocracy for the one presently determined by race and colour; labour exploitation will persist. This is fully recognized by the Oppenheimer school of thought. A leading Anglo American Corporation executive has, in fact, argued – at a meeting with the Manchester Chamber of Commerce[4] – that the 'basic dualism' of the South African economy was 'normal and inevitable' in a developing country. The speaker was Mr M. C. O'Dowd, an alternate director of Anglo American and Chairman of several of its gold-mining companies, who was on tour in Britain with a South Africa–Britain Trade Association mission. He argued that wage levels for the (white) skilled were set by international standards as it was possible for skilled workers to emigrate to advanced countries. Wage levels for the (black) unskilled were set by South Africa's internal supply and demand situation. He then said:

It is not clear that racial discrimination has significantly altered the proportions of the population in each category. What it has done is to give priority to Whites in entry to the available skilled jobs. Had there been a non-racial free-for-all, the composition of the skilled and unskilled labour forces would obviously be some-what different, but there is no reason to suppose that the skilled minority would be larger or that the gap in the standard of living between the two would be less.

Even under apartheid, Africans might well be permitted – as indeed they are to some extent – to filter into enclaves formerly preserved for whites. But as long as State machinery and the capitalist economic order continue to control the mass of the unskilled labour force, and as long as the curbs on free move-ment of African labour, on bargaining power and trades union organization remain, together with the differences in right of access to education, to trade skills and to the general opportunities of life, then the huge gap between white prosperity and black poverty, even poverty to the point of destitution, will persist.

Moreover, even if British or American businesses in South Africa decided overnight to pay equal wages for equal work, commendable as such an isolated reform of employment practice might be, it would in the long run be to the dis-advantage of African workers, and would produce unemploy-ment. For any disturbance of the cheap labour system would lead to a great mechanization of industry, and African workers would invariably be the first to be dismissed. The history of white politics is one of the manipulation of the state and its legislative machinery by whites to protect themselves from being supplanted or threatened by Africans. Isolated reforms will be limited in their efficacy, or even abortive, in the absence of over-all changes which undermine the economic and political basis of the cheap labour system in South Africa. This is not to argue that labour should not press its claims and that business should not be indicted for unjust labour practice; it is to argue that isolated reforms however well-meaning will be ineffective, for single improvements under the forced labour economy only deepen the gulf between the developed and the under-developed society, between white and black.

The problem for South Africa has always been how to change the tyranny of race, colour and class that is apartheid and who will make that change? At the close of the last century and the beginning of this the old Cape liberal theory argued that if Africans could demonstrate their 'civilized' qualifications for the franchise (through education and property tests), they would be allowed to share it. Since that time until now Africans have acquired more and more education and property qualifications, despite every conceivable obstacle placed in the way of both, and they were entitled to less and less of the franchise until the vote for them was abolished altogether. There is probably no technique of struggle that has not been tried in South Africa – from patient, long-suffering petitioning on African grievances and claims, to conventional methods of mass organizing, to the non-violent protest advocated by Gandhi, to the use of the general strike for political as well as economic demands, and inevitably, as police repression closed every avenue of protest against the African majority, to the decision to carry out acts of sabotage, and then, when these brought no response except still further repression, to begin the slow movement towards popular armed warfare or guerilla struggle.

The Government repression of the 1960s, typified by the Sharpeville shooting, ended the politics of protest and the politics of confrontation began; it is significant that it was only then that the air began to fill with arguments for change, not by revolution or struggle, but by reform; with arguments not for disengagement from apartheid and its isolation and weakening by boycotts or sanctions, but for bridge-building or 'transmission lines for change', or for 'creative persuasive contact'. The reasons vary. Some people say that the white front is splitting, or can be split, and that Africans will find allies among the powerful white groups if only they will have patience and wait for the contradictions in the white structure to break it down. A variation of this view sees apartheid as an Afrikaner creation and the English-speaking element, derived from a more liberal tradition, acting as a safety-valve or a corrective of the more aggressive Afrikaner nationalism. Yet another variation sees the presence of a powerful class of reforming industrialists, principal among them Mr Harry Oppenheimer, whose interests are said to be essentially incompatible with the economic rigidities of apartheid.

It is true that white politics in South Africa have thrown up dissension and even schism, and so too have Afrikaner politics, as witness the split on the eve of the 1970 general election between the die-hard *'verkramptes'* and the more pragmatic Vorster-led *'verligtes'* or 'enlightened'. But a long view of white politics before and after Union in 1910 reveals that, on all basic questions concerning the place of the African majority, the principal white parties, whether based on predominantly English- or Afrikaans-speaking electorates, have moved in step, and that in many practical respects the two white parties have operated in a white coalition against the black disfranchised majority. It was to be confirmed again in Rhodesia that the exclusion of the majority from the vote leads inexorably to a steady, virtually unopposed move to the right among whites. Any differences between white parties or white politicians have been on minor, even trivial aspects of apartheid and neither of the white parties, whether in government or opposition, have sought to alter the essential nature or the objectives of apartheid.

284

This is not to say that there have been no significant changes in the social and economic bases of white politics; however, *in toto*, these have served to narrow the differences between the two blocs of white power rather than to accentuate them. In the beginning, Afrikaner power was based on land in the rural *platteland* and included a significant number of poor-white workers, whereas the United Party, largely English-speaking and British-oriented, rested on mining and industrial interests capitalized by British investment, and had a predominantly urban voting constituency. After the 1930s Afrikaner nationalism set out to mobilize itself to compete with British-derived capital and English-speaking political power. By marshalling middle-class savings and organizing purchasing power, Afrikaners created for themselves a base for the emergence of an Afrikaner sector of capitalism, however small in the beginning its share of industrial and commercial activity. When the Nationalist Party came to power in 1948, political control of the State apparatus consolidated the gains made by Afrikaner capital and extended them under the aegis of the powerful State-controlled sector. After the 1960s Afrikaners were being encouraged to join the boards of major South African companies. Afrikaner and Nationalist State capital has increasingly created an identity of interest with British-based capital interests, and together they run an economic establishment on the basis of reciprocal interest. It has been possible to trace a conflict in earlier years between the interests of mining capital, for which the migratory labour system was devised, and the needs of industry, but mining capital has gone increasingly into industry – Anglo American's industrial holdings rank third in its assets, for example – so that divisions between mining and industrial interests are blurred now, too.

That traditional political conflict in South Africa has largely resolved itself into a working alliance of capital, both internal and foreign, and apartheid has well suited all interests as a system of intense exploitation of labour resources. Apartheid, far from being a doctrine peculiar to Afrikaner needs, is an economic instrument, organically connected with the various sources of capital control in South Africa, and with the operations of international capital in the country. The rebellious *verkrampte* group represents the minority tendency among Afrikaner nationalists, not yet adjusted to the changed nature of capital in South Africa. Vorster's policies, on the other hand, like his 'outward-looking policy' towards Black Africa, are proof of the convergence of the interests, and therefore the political tactics, of white capital.[5] Various disequilibria will undoubtedly continue to develop, like the present shortage of skilled manpower and the over-production of consumer goods in so restricted a market. But though it needs certain controlled adjustments, apartheid will not crack from purely economic pressures. Differences between the white parties about how to handle distortions in the economy will continue to be secondary to the far greater difference between the interests of a white ruling group and a black oppressed class.

Since its formation in 1959 the Progressive Party, backed financially by Harry Oppenheimer and represented in the South African Parliament by a single member, Mrs Helen Suzman, has put itself forward as an alternative to the compromises arrived at by the two main streams of white power in the Nationalist and United Parties. But the qualified franchise proposed by the Progressive Party would allow fewer blacks to vote than participated in the 1886 Cape Colony election. As for the advocated reforms of the industrial colour bar, these are not calculated to end the colour bar in industry but to permit a controlled upward movement of blacks such as would remove some curbs on production – and consequently on profit. The paternalist solution is also to encourage a small, urban, native lower middle class to help to weaken militant black organizations.

To this solution the Nationalist Party is adamantly opposed. 'Separate development' based on migratory labour remains the basis of the economy and any 'development', whether of the African people as a whole or of an elitist traditional or middle class, must take place in the Bantu homelands or Bantustans.

Some people with long records as bold critics of the system have recently argued that one should think again about the Bantustans in the hope that these government-created territorial authorities may show more vitality and heterodoxy than their manipulators intended.[6] In other words, that the Bantustans may turn against Pretoria's intentions.

The salient facts about the Bantustans are well known. Their share of South Africa's economic output is negligible, perhaps only two per cent of the Gross National Product. They are overcrowded and over-stocked with cattle, depressed areas of peasant subsistence agriculture debilitated by centuries of land hunger and migrant labour. In the Transkei, the best-developed Bantustan, which is supposed to be a self-governing territory, the Legislative Assembly consists of forty-five elected members and sixty-four Chiefs, all of whom are Government servants, appointed by, paid by and liable to be dismissed by Pretoria. The Assembly's powers are extremely limited and the Transkei is subject at all times to the overriding control of the South African Government and its white bureaucrats. On the other hand, there are signs that the Government has refined its conception of the Bantustans in an attempt to devise a neo-colonial solution for use inside South Africa and to improve her image in her 'outward-looking' policy. After all, a certain kind of independence – political self-government without any economic means for real freedom of decision-making and development – has made small and weak African States peculiarly susceptible to a variety of neo-colonial pressures. The Bantustans are to be used to spread abroad the deception that apartheid is changing for the better. Inside South Africa they will be used as a way to shift the centre-point of political protest from the cities to the stagnant and fragmented tribal areas, where it can smother peasant protest under the weight of a revived traditional tribal authority, served by a tame administrative elite. This is an attempt to deflect African protest from the white Government to the Bantustans.

It is an interesting development, because the ideal of self-government has already encouraged some Africans, and may encourage others, to make more militant demands in the Bantustans than they can legally make in 'white' South Africa. Some opponents of apartheid, therefore, see in the Bantustans the possibility of giving direct aid to Africans and they urge investors not to withdraw from South Africa but to re-route their investments into the Bantu homelands. It is highly unlikely that this will have a reforming, let alone revolutionary, effect. The examples of Lesotho and Swaziland are hardly inspiring: their emergence into political independence has had absolutely no impact on white supremacy in South Africa.

The one difference between the Transkei and Lesotho is that its people are more closely integrated into the South African labour system. This is a double-edged weapon. On the one hand it means they are more subject to direct exploitation and the other techniques of control On the other hand, if political and industrial radicalism were to come to the surface in the urban areas of South Africa, inspired by a militant self-governing Bantustan, it could paralyse the apartheid system. It takes little imagination, however, to see that the South African Government would act early to prevent that happening. The 'geo-political realities' which force Botswana and Lesotho to deny open and unequivocal support to the liberation movement would operate equally in the Bantustans. It has to be remembered that a state of emergency has been in force ever since the Transkei became 'partially self-governing' in 1963.

The Bantustans are a dead end. They may create a few problems for Pretoria because, like any new development in the apartheid system, they have some internal contradictions.

But these are minor compared to the over-all advantages which the Bantustans offer white South Africa. They are certainly too small to justify support for the Bantustans as a way of undermining apartheid.

The government is already taking measures for the most rigorous control of all investment in decentralized industry, whether in the border areas or the Bantustans. Decentralization itself has become part of official planning for three ends: (1) to check the flow of African labour to the main industrialized centres of white population (and so to limit in one more way the development of an articulate and organized black urban proletariat); (2) to build industry in areas where costs can be kept as low as possible; and, (3) coincidentally, to help the predominantly Afrikaner areas to acquire an increased share of the national income.[7] For the greater part these decentralized industries will be sited in the border areas which adjoin the Bantustans in recognition of their function as reservoirs of cheap labour. A White Paper on Decentralization of Industries issued by the South African Government in June 1971[8] explains the controls to be operated by Government over the establishment and operations of new industry. If the enterprise is to be based in a controlled (white) area it may be established and expanded there, with the proviso that the Government will not guarantee the required African labour quota. (This is 'because the Government's policy in connection with the control of Bantu into the White areas remains unchanged'.) If you cannot run your factory with the officially stipulated ratio of white to black workers – which is to be reduced after June 1973 – you will be directed to a border area or a Bantu homeland. A Decentralization Board will vet all plans for new enterprises and decide where they many operate, and how many workers of what colour they may employ, and will then refer the enterprise through the eight Government ministries and four statutory authorities whose approval is needed not only for establishment procedures but also for detailed operations.

These ministerial departments will closely control the de-centralized growth points which are not in the Bantustans but near them as border areas; the tendency – not least in the interests of industry and investors and the principles that impel them to start new enterprises – must undoubtedly be not to encourage but to stifle industrialization in the Bantustans proper. These in any case suffer from built-in obstacles to development in the form of an almost total absence of infrastructural development, and the prohibitive cost problems that must flow from that. (For instance, in the six years during which the Bantu Development Corporation spent about 6 million pounds, it succeeded in creating only 945 new employment openings in the Bantustans.)

The problem of ensuring reforms for Africans and in African areas, despite the over-all context of apartheid controls, brings us back to the most serious misconception of all about changing apartheid for the better without overturning it as a system. This is the view of economic determinism which argues that growth through increased trade and investment are needed to help moderate South Africa's policies 'under the familiar and acculturating influence of urbanization and industrialization'.[9] This book has tried to demonstrate how South Africa's steady economic expansion has intensified the application of repressive legislation, and also how techniques of labour control and exploitation, though refined, remain essentially intact.

In South Africa industrialization has been interwoven with a system of racial exploitation. Indeed, a comparative survey of patterns of race relations in industrializing societies, including the United States, shows that an industrial revolution adapts itself to pre-existing patterns of racialism. So the conventional view that industrialization operates naturally to undermine a pre-existing race system is not borne out by the facts. 'While industry may alter the social order it may leave the race system embedded in that order, essentially intact, and (it) may reinforce that order.'[10]

This book shows conclusively, the authors believe, that racialism, far from being an impediment to capitalist economic growth, is an essential factor in it; that the impoverishment of the African wage-earner is in turn a function of white prosperity.[11] If this peculiarly South African form of 'underdeveloped development' has grown out of the distortions of the economy and of the society created by racialism, then real development will require the radical restructuring of the society 'which can only be carried out under the hegemony of those who are the present "objects" of underdevelopment'.[12]

There is a relatively new but central phenomenon of South African growth, and that is its role as an expansionist power on the continent of Africa. South Africa, once a colony of Britain, is embarking on a role as a colonist. South Africa, the largest recipient by far of foreign investment, both direct and indirect, has now become the most significant investor in neighbouring southern African countries.[13]

Several theoretical issues have yet to be explored before the full political consequences can be appreciated. Is South Africa still a satellite power or is it, expanding and expansionist, becoming a metropolitan power in its own right? The Anglo American Corporation in the Oppenheimer empire, for example, depends neither on strictly British or South African capitalism but is almost an independent economic 'super state' centred in Southern and Central Africa. Anglo American is the most prominent of the multi-national corporations with an interlocking system of holdings and directorships that spreads across the sub-continent and the South African companies are playing an increasingly central role in. The Oppenheimer group, built in the first instance on the mineral wealth of Southern, and then of Central Africa, is gradually losing its territorial identity, especially since the creation of Charter Consolidated, which is involved in Canadian, Malaysian and Mauretanian mining, French industry and Australian merchant banking. Under the head-ing 'More Like a Government than a Company', the *Investors' Chronicle* commented on Anglo American's international diversification: 'Its shares are proof against all but the most far-reaching economic trends. They are really an investment in the Western capitalist system.'[14]

In Southern Africa as a whole the pattern of foreign investment has two main aspects. On the one hand there is an increasing integration between the economies of Southern Africa themselves. The large companies that have straddled the area up to now, the Anglo American group, American Metal Climax, Rio Tinto-Zinc, and more recently Lonrho, are slowly integrating all their activities, consolidating themselves economically as well as financially. On the other hand, there is a weakening in the area of the old colonial powers, Britain and Portugal, and a diversification of economic relationships through trade with the United States, Germany, Italy, Japan and, to some extent, France. The 'internationalization' of Southern Africa and the growing strength of South African corporation interests coincide with the striking change in South African foreign policy from isolationism to expansionism[15] and, at the same time, with the closer integration of South African, British and European economic interests and political strategy.

South Africa's expanding influence and its assertive sense of long-term strategy, occurring as they do side by side with Britain's decline as an imperialist power and its enforced cession of her Southern African sphere of interest, explain many things about British policy towards apartheid. Conservative Party policy has, after all, like Mr Vorster's, been explicit. Indeed the attempt to surrender to Ian Smith speaks for itself. So does the confidential defence planning document on defence planning prepared before Britain's last general election by the Conservative Commonwealth and Overseas Council, which is steadily working itself out in official Government policy.

Those who make policy in Britain, the United States and

Western Europe know only too well that South Africa is the key to their role in Africa. They recognize South Africa not merely as a trading partner, a profitable outlet for investment and an increasingly important source for minerals, but as a strategic force on the continent and a brake on radical change. Most importantly, South Africa's own reasons for expansion and an aggressive strategy against independent Africa coincide happily with the interests of Western investors and Western powers in general. They are anxious to avoid confrontation with liberation movements; above all, they want a political climate in Southern and Central Africa which penetration by outside capital can be pursued without opposition.[16]

Ostensibly, of course, the concern is strategic. When he was still Shadow Foreign Secretary in 1968, Sir Alec Douglas-Home discussed a plan with South African leaders for putting the Cape route under the protective wing of NATO. A number of similar proposals found their way into the issues of specialized military journals, some issued from NATO headquarters and others published in NATO member-states.[17] The theme is frequently echoed in the United States. Thus Dean Acheson, former Secretary of State, told a US Congressional inquiry[18] that it was sheer idiocy to sever relations with South Africa, that Africa's greatest hope of stability and development lay 'with the competent, highly-developed people who rule South Africa'. He then proceeded to link the defence of the Cape route with the threat of a Russian penetration into the Mediterranean and the Indian Ocean.[19]

A Russian military threat in Southern Africa President Kenneth Kaunda regards as a bogey-man: 'To me the military threat is not the Soviet Union nor China. The threat here is South Africa. The Caprivi Strip is only a few miles from here. . . .'[20] It was from the Caprivi Strip, where South Africa maintains an airfield and a base, that South African forces went into Zambian territory on a punitive expedition in 1971. There has been a working alliance in the military field since the early 1960s between South Africa and Portugal, and later, Rhodesia. The three countries meet regularly to plan a unified defence and intelligence programme. The last reported meeting of their security chiefs was in February 1971 when the head of BOSS, the South African external security service, was present. On this occasion discussion appears to have centred on the situation in the Tete province of Mozambique where a new guerilla offensive is in full swing. South African para-military forces have been active in Rhodesia and in Mozambique; South African helicopters regularly patrol southern Angola, and fly over southern Tanzania and Zambia from the Caprivi Strip base and from Malawi airfields. The immediate need of the white powers is to maintain the white circle as far as the Zambezi, and perhaps even a little farther north, certainly in Malawi and in the longer run even in Zambia. The strategic calculations have been made; it is a matter of seizing timely opportunities.

The old dividing line between the two Africas is being dissolved, not as independence advances southwards into the southern colonies but as white power moves north into areas considered 'de-colonized' but now vulnerable to a new domination, and one especially inimical to any principles of independence and development.

Britain has ceded her 'sphere of influence' to apartheid, only to join this aggressive scheme as an accomplice. That unholy alliance of white powers, South Africa, Portugal and Rhodesia, is in the process of being enlarged to an alliance with Western business and Western political and strategic policy. Foreign business might have had small, even naïvely apolitical beginnings, but business and political involvement with apartheid are forging ever stronger Western links with the indefensible apartheid policies and their aggression northwards into the rest of Africa.

Can anything be done? Can business be expected to

change its role? If business cannot or will not act on its own, what can Western governments be brought to do through pressure? Who will act?

The kind of remedies offered by a reformist or more liberal capitalism – the suggestion that British business offer South Africa the example of a more enlightened wage policy – ignore several pertinent factors that the authors tried to stress. Piecemeal changes will alter very little and will soon be swallowed by the rapacious system; society already manipulates its labour mechanisms without any significant improvement in the conditions of the majority of Africans; apartheid is indeed capable of flexibility, but its flexibility enables it to avoid meaningful change, not to open the way to it. Harry Oppenheimer makes the intention plain:

I suggest that we should not worry about the existence of the colour bar. What we should worry about is its rigidity. . . . I plead, therefore, for flexibility in industrial labour organization. We must not allow the dead hand of convention, whether expressed in a colour bar or an outmoded technique, to impede development. A caste system is not dangerous so long as it expresses a social reality and similarly the existence of an industrial colour bar need not, at our present stage, prevent our progress so long as it is not rigid but can be adapted to changing conditions.[21]

If reform of the system from within will not work, what then?

It is unrealistic to argue that companies – with eccentric exceptions possibly – can be expected to withdraw from South Africa on their own initiative. It is equally unrealistic to expect that Western governments will withdraw support for apartheid. The association is far too profitable; it is also, despite the moral outcry at the offensiveness of blatant racialism, a quite congenial working relationship for several issues considered important to Western strategy.

Only when forces inside South Africa, aided, possibly, by favourable international circumstances, effect a change in the control of the South African system will Western governments perhaps consider changing sides and trying to join the winning one.

Is such an internal change imminent and who will produce it? Experience of apartheid from the inside, far more than theoretical knowledge of it, leads inescapably to the conclusion that it is not racialism as such that is the oppressor but a system of South African capitalism, incorporating a particularly virulent strain of racial oppression, and one that is an increasing part of a world economic system. How this realization grows into action, and then into commitment, for revolutionary liberation, and what the instruments of this liberation will be, are part of another story altogether. If this book has produced only one more argument for supporting the South African freedom struggle rather than the illusion that the apartheid Establishment, with the help of outside investors, will reform itself, that is enough.

Trade with apartheid, investment in apartheid, have wide-ranging consequences for deepening British and Western complicity in all apartheid's schemes. The defeat of the apartheid system will in turn have profound consequences for the liberation, not only of the South African people, but of the African continent as a whole. It will have an equally profound significance for those in Britain and the West generally who have come to understand how inextricably corporations and politics intertwine and who consequently realize that the committed search for radical solutions in Britain, in the West and in South Africa is the same search.

As for South Africa, it is clearly trying to play in Africa the role that the United States is playing in Latin America and in Asia. The analogy is far from strained; Mr Vorster himself has used it. But for South Africa, as for the United States, the very expansion of its financial and military power may lead to fresh sources of conflict. The dispersal of military strength and counter-insurgency resources across the sub-continent could commit South Africa to fighting guerrilla warfare halfway across Central and Southern Africa in its own interests and those of its business allies. The outward movement of economic resources will build client States and client economies, but these will in time be challenged by peoples disenchanted and discomfited by the economics of dependency. So even as South Africa expands with the help of its western allies it produces fresh sources of conflict for itself and for them. The parallel with the United States needs to be closely followed through. Economic expansionism seems to offer nothing but advantages for the dominant power, till the cost and the strain of policing the area of expansion become counter-productive even of profit. If the United States now faces defeat in Vietnam and elsewhere in Asia, for how long will South Africa succeed in Africa?

Chapter Notes

2 THE FOUNDATIONS OF THE PARTNERSHIP

1 South African Reserve Bank: *Annual Economic Review*, 1971
2 South African Reserve Bank: *Quarterly Bulletin*, December 1971
3 Ralph Horwitz: *The Political Economy of South Africa*, Weidenfeld & Nicolson, London, 1967, p. 359
4 J. C. du Plessis, 'Foreign Investment in South Africa' in Litvak and Maule, *Foreign Investment: The Experience of the Host Countries*, Praeger, New York, 1970
5 J. Davis, 'US–South African Relations: Strategic and Economic Considerations' African Studies Assoc., Denver, 1971
6 *Sunday Times*, Johannesburg, 4 April 1971
7 *Financial Mail*, Johannesburg, 26 March 1971
8 *Trade and Industry*, figures for 1960–65; *Business Monitor*, Miscellaneous Series, Overseas Transactions, M4, Department of Trade and Industry, 1971, figures for 1966–68
9 *Trade and Industry*, Board of Trade, 26 January 1968
10 Anglo American Corporation Annual Report, 1971
11 Letter to the authors
12 Supplement to the *Financial Mail*, Johannesburg, 19 June 1970
13 A memorandum from ICI to the authors
14 Industrial Development Corporation, Annual Report and Accounts, 1970
15 ibid.
16 *Financial Times*, London, 5 November 1971
17 *Financial Times*, London, 15 November 1971
18 International Monetary Fund, *Balance of Payments Yearbook*, November 1969

19 Hansard, 26 February 1962
20 House of Assembly Debates 5 May 1971 and *Rand Daily Mail*, Johannesburg, 25 June 1971
21 *African Express*, October 1970
22 *Star*, Johannesburg, weekly airmail edition, 20 November 1971
23 Sean Gervasi and Gilad Lowenstein, 'Southern Africa in the World Economy', unpublished paper, Oxford University, January 1972
24 South African Reserve Bank, *Annual Economic Report*, 1971
25 South Africa's deficit on current account was 144 million pounds in 1969 and 496 million pounds in 1970. South African Reserve Bank, *Quarterly Bulletin*, September 1971
26 South Africa's gold and foreign currency reserves fell by 34 million pounds in 1969 and a further 154 millions in 1970. South African Reserve Bank, *Quarterly Bulletin*, September 1971

3   THE BLACK POOR GET POORER
1 Figure given by Deputy Minister of Bantu Administration, House of Assembly Debates 3 June 1969, quoted in Muriel Horrell, *South Africa's Workers*, South African Institute of Race Relations, 1969, p. 17
2 Dr Francis Wilson, paper given at National Conference on Productivity and Employment, organized by the *Financial Mail*, Johannesburg, 1971
3 A. Hepple, *South Africa: Workers under Apartheid*, International Defence and Aid Fund, London, 2nd ed., 1971, p. 57
4 Hepple, op. cit., p. 57
5 *The Times*, 30 April 1971
6 *Financial Mail*, Johannesburg, 40 May 1968
7 Hepple, op. cit., p. 54
8 *Guardian*, 14 July 1971

9 *Natal Mercury*, 22 April 1967

10 Ian Hume, 'Notes on South African Wage Movements', *South African Journal of Economics*, Vol. 38, No. 3, September 1970

11 John Sackur, 'Casualties of the Economic Boom in South Africa', *The Times*, 26 April 1971

12 *Financial Mail*, Johannesburg, 18 April 1969

13 Sackur, op. cit.

14 *Star*, Johannesburg, 28 February 1971

15 *Rand Daily Mail*, Johannesburg, 1 October 1970

16 *Sunday Times*, Johannesburg, 25 July 1971

17 Ida Briggs, 'Malnutrition', *Sash*, March 1971, published by the Black Sash, Johannesburg

18 ibid.

19 *X-Ray*, August 1971, published by the Africa Bureau, London

20 *Financial Mail*, Johannesburg, 10 May 1968. Sackur, op. cit., quotes a figure of 'about £53'.

21 Selwyn Lloyd, 'South Africa: Time for Reappraisal', *Reader's Digest*, 11 September 1970

22 Billy Nannan, 'Discrimination and Segregation in South African Education', in *Objective: Justice*, Vol. 3, No. 3, 1971, published by the UN, p. 31

23 *Financial Mail*, Johannesburg, 9 October 1970

24 Neil Wates, 'A Businessman looks at Apartheid', special article published by UN Unit on Apartheid, October 1970

4 THE FLOATING COLOUR BAR

1 Sean Gervasi, *Industrialization, Foreign Capital and Forced Labour in South Africa*, UN ST/PSCA/Ser.A/10, p. 7

2 Martin Legassick, 'South Africa: Forced Labour, Industrialization, and Racial Differentiation', mimeographed, 1971

3 ibid.

4 ibid.
5 Harold Wolpe, 'Class, Race, and the Occupational Structure in South Africa', paper presented at the World Congress of Sociology, September 1970
6 *Financial Mail*, Johannesburg, 18 April 1969, reporting on research by Market Research Africa
7 *Rand Daily Mail*, Johannesburg, July 1968
8 A. Hepple, *South Africa: Workers Under Apartheid*, 2nd ed., published by the International Defence and Aid Fund, London, 1971, p. 55
9 Barbara Rogers, *The Standard of Living of Africans in South Africa*, UN Unit on Apartheid, Notes and Documents, November 1971
10 *Sunday Times*, Johannesburg, Business News, 17 January 1971
11 *Star*, Johannesburg, 14 August 1971
12 *Rand Daily Mail*, Johannesburg, 31 March 1970
13 *Rand Daily Mail*, Johannesburg, 14 April 1969
14 *Star*, Johannesburg, 29 May 1971
15 *Rand Daily Mail*, Johannesburg, 11 September 1971
16 *Star*, Johannesburg, 15 February 1971
17 *Financial Mail*, Johannesburg, 23 July 1971
18 Harold Wolpe, op. cit.
19 *Financial Mail*, Johannesburg, 15 March 1968
20 *Rand Daily Mail*, Johannesburg, 6 October 1970
21 *Financial Mail*, Johannesburg, 10 May 1968
22 *Financial Mail*, Johannesburg, 3 July 1970
23 Hepple, op. cit., p. 59
24 *Star*, Johannesburg, 26 November 1970

5 THE PLACE OF FOREIGN CAPITAL

1 *News from South Africa*, New York, 25 March 1970
2 South African Reserve Bank, *Quarterly Bulletin*, December 1964, December 1967 and September 1971

3 *Trade and Industry*, Department of Trade and Industry, 7 April 1971

4 *Survey of Current Business*, US Department of Commerce, October 1971

5 J. C. du Plessis, 'Foreign Investment in South Africa' in Litvak and Maule, *Foreign Investment: The Experience of Host Countries*, Praeger, New York, 1970

6 Anglo American Corporation, Annual Report, 1970

7 du Plessis, op. cit.

8 State of South Africa, *Year Book*, Johannesburg, 1971

9 Standard Bank, *Annual Economic Review: South and South-West Africa*, July 1971

10 Anglo American Corporation, Annual Report, 1970

11 'Top Companies', Supplement to *Financial Mail*, Johannesburg, 16 April 1971

12 'Survey of South Africa', *The Banker*, September 1971, p. 48

13 ibid., p. 39

14 Barclays Bank DCO, Report and Accounts, 1971

15 Statement by John Thomson, Chairman of Barclays Bank at Annual General Meeting, 1 April 1970

16 'South Africa', Supplement to *Financial Times*, 27 June 1970

17 *Financial Times*, London, 29 November 1971

18 'South Africa', Supplement to *Financial Times*, London, 14 June 1971

19 Ralph Horwitz, *The Political Economy of South Africa*, Weidenfeld & Nicolson, London, 1967, p. 328

20 *Newscheck*, Johannesburg, December 1970

21 'Phase III Ahead: The South African Motor Industry', Special Survey by the *Financial Mail*, Johannesburg, 13 March 1970

22 *Financial Gazette*, Johannesburg, 17 June 1967

23 Horwitz, op. cit., p. 352

24 ibid.

25 'Textiles', Supplement to *Financial Mail*, Johannesburg, 9 February 1968

26 ibid.

27 *Today's News*, South African Embassy, London, 25 November 1971

28 *Financial Mail*, Johannesburg, 23 April 1971

29 'Chemicals', Supplement to *Financial Mail*, Johannesburg, 2 August 1968

30 ibid.

31 *Los Angeles Times*, 8 January 1968

32 'Oil', Supplement to *Financial Mail*, Johannesburg, 5 March 1971

33 UN Report, Doc. A/6868, New York, November 1967, p. 17

34 *Financial Mail*, Johannesburg, 28 May 1971

35 *Star*, Johannesburg, 13 March 1971

36 'US Corporate Activity in South Africa: An Analysis of Thirty-One Major Corporations', Council on Economic Priorities, Washington DC, September 1970, p. 47

37 *Financial Mail*, Johannesburg, 20 November 1970

38 *Financial Mail*, Johannesburg, 15 October 1971

6 THE PATTERNS OF THE PAST

1 E. J. Hobsbawm, *Industry and Empire*, Weidenfeld & Nicolson, London, 1968. Chapter 7 gives a good account of Britain's role in this period

2 Werner Scholte, *British Overseas Trade from 1700 to the 1930s*, Blackwell, Oxford, 1952

3 A. K. Cairncross, *Home and Foreign Investment*, CUP, Cambridge, 1953

4 S. H. Frankel, *Capital Investment in Africa*, OUP, London, 1938

5 William Plomer, *Cecil Rhodes*, Peter Davies, Edinburgh, 1933

6 ibid.

7 Frankel, op. cit., p. 81

8 Estimates quoted by A. K. Cairncross, op. cit., p. 185. They were made by the *Economist* in February 1884 and by Sir George Paish in the *Journal of the Royal Statistical Society*, 1911

9 Sheila Van Der Horst, *Native Labour in South Africa*, new ed., Frank Cass, London, 1971, p. 205

10 A. S. J. Baster, *The Imperial Banks*, P. S. King & Son, London, 1929, p. 239

11 Ralph Horwitz, *The Political Economy of South Africa*, Weidenfeld & Nicolson, London, 1967, pp. 264–5

12 C. S. Richards, 'Problems of Economic Development in the Republic of South Africa', *South African Journal of Economics*, March 1962

13 Frankel, op. cit., estimated that of the total of 45 million pounds invested between 1932 and 1936, 24 millions came from abroad

14 Frankel, op. cit., p. 93

15 The British South African Explosives Company merged with the Cape Explosives Company, which was owned by De Beers, in 1924 and the two companies formed African Explosives and Industries. The company changed its name to African Explosives and Chemical Industries in 1944. See *The Dynamite Company* by A. P. Cartwright (Macdonald, London, 1965) for the history of AE & CI and ICI's participation in it.

16 Eric Rosenthal, *As Pioneers Still: An Appreciation of Lever Brothers' Contribution in South Africa, 1911–1961*, Lever Bros., Durban, 1961

17 *Newscheck*, Johannesburg, 'Siemens at 75', 17–30 April 1970

18 South African Reserve Bank, *Quarterly Review*, September 1971

19 ibid.

20 *Industrialization, Foreign Capital and Forced Labour in South Africa*, UN document ST/PSCA/Ser.A/10, New York 1970

21 Standard Bank *Annual Economic Review: South and South-West Africa*, July 1971
22 A. R. Conan, 'The Changing Pattern of International Investment in Selected Sterling Countries', *Essays in International Finance*, No. 27, International Finance Section, Princeton University, Princeton, 1956
23 The South African Reserve Bank conducted its first survey of South Africa's liabilities in 1957. It published annual figures for net new overseas investment in its *Quarterly Bulletin of Statistics*
24 Conan, op. cit. In Rhodesia the proportion was 45 per cent
25 Sir Theodore Gregory, *Sir Ernest Oppenheimer and the Economic Development of Southern Africa*, OUP, Cape Town, 1962, quoted on p. 571
26 South African Reserve Bank, *Quarterly Bulletin*, December 1969
27 *Who Owns Whom*, 1963, 1968 and 1971
28 Michael Barratt Brown, *After Imperialism*, Heinemann, London, 1963
29 du Plessis, 'Foreign Investment in South Africa', in Litvak and Maule *Foreign Investment: The Experience of Host Countries*, Praeger, New York, 1970, p. 198

7 SOUTH AFRICA'S OTHER FRIENDS
1 South Africa Foundation, Annual Report for 1969
2 Quoted in *Sechaba*, African National Congress of South Africa, February 1967
3 *Sunday Times*, Johannesburg, Business News: supplement on West Germany, 21 March 1971
4 *Financial Mail*, Johannesburg, special supplement on Japan 30 October 1970

8 THE COMPANIES: IMAGE AND REALITY
1 In a letter to Timothy Smith, Assistant for African Affairs,

Council for Christian Action, United Church of Christ, quoted in *Economic Priorities Report*, Vol. 1, No. 5, October/November 1970, Council on Economic Priorities, Washington DC

2 *Financial Mail*, Johannesburg, 23 April 1971

3 Speech circulated to the press by UKSATA

4 Timothy Smith, 'The American Corporation in South Africa: An Analysis', United Church of Christ, New York, 1971

5 Smith, op. cit.

6 *Sunday Times*, 18 April 1971

7 Quoted in fact-sheet on RTZ published by the Anti-Apartheid Movement, 1971

8 *Sunday Times*, Johannesburg, 31 January 1971

9 ibid.

10 Council on Economic Priorities, op. cit.

11 John Kane-Berman and Dudley Horner, 'Report on the Polariod Experiment', South African Institute of Race Relations, November 1971, p. 5

12 Smith, op. cit., p. 18

13 *Rand Daily Mail*, 30 July 1971

14 US State Department memo, 1971, p. 6

15 Denis Herbstein, unpublished notes

16 *Financial Mail*, Johannesburg, 9 July 1971

17 Muriel Horrell, *South Africa's Workers*, South African Institute of Race Relations, 1969, p. 78

18 *Financial Mail*, Johannesburg, 9 July 1971

19 ibid.

20 Smith, op. cit., p. 46

21 'Barclays in Africa: Some Facts': statement by Barclays Bank, 23 September 1971

22 Memorandum to one of the authors

23 Council on Economic Priorities, op. cit., p. 30

24 ibid., p. 31

25 ibid., p. 31

26 Council on Economic Priorities, op. cit., p. 12

27 *Financial Mail*, Johannesburg, 16 July 1971
28 *Guardian*, 12 May 1971
29 *Optima*, September 1970, p. 37
30 Chairman's Statement to A.G.M., 16 May 1968
31 Statement issued by Palabora Mining Company, August
     1971; *Rand Daily Mail*, Johannesburg, August 1971;
     Sunday Times, Johannesburg, 29 August 1971
32 Interview with Sir Val Duncan by one of the authors
33 State of South Africa *Yearbook*, Johannesburg, 1971
34 Interview with Sir Val Duncan by one of the authors
35 'Survey on Britain', Supplement to *Sunday Times*,
     Johannesburg, 28 March 1971
36 ibid.
37 Leyland South Africa, Annual Report, 1970
38 'Survey on Britain', Supplement to *Sunday Times*,
     Johannesburg, 28 March 1971
39 Interview with Denis Herbstein
40 ibid.
41 Memorandum in Support of the Union's Proposals for
     Increased Wages and Improved Working Conditions
     submitted by Western Province Motor Assembly
     Workers' Union, August 1969
42 ibid.
43 ibid.
44 Information supplied by Jack Heeger to Denis Herbstein
45 *Guardian*, 1 April 1971
46 *Sunday Times*, Johannesburg, 10 January 1971
47 African Explosives and Chemical Industries, Annual
     Report, 1970
48 A. P. Cartwright, *The Dynamite Company*, Macdonald,
     London, 1965
49 *Financial Mail*, Johannesburg, 25 June 1971
50 Denis Herbstein, unpublished notes: figures supplied by
     ICI South Africa
51 Figures supplied to one of the authors, January 1972
52 Denis Herbstein, unpublished notes

53 Stewarts and Lloyds and Dorman Long both refuse to reveal wage-rates paid to their African employees. Stewarts and Lloyds employs 9,100 workers and is twenty-first in the list of South Africa's leading companies; Dorman Long employs 10,000 workers and ranks eighteenth in the list
   Sunday Times, Johannesburg, 17 January 1971
   Rand Daily Mail, Johannesburg, 15 May 1971
   Sunday Times, Johannesburg, 3 October 1971
54 *Financial Mail*, Johannesburg, 25 December 1970
55 Interview with one of the authors
56 Interview with Denis Herbstein
57 Information supplied to Denis Herbstein
58 Interview with Denis Herbstein
59 Official transcript of GEC-English Electric A.G.M., Pratts New Agency, London, 15 September 1971
60 Information supplied to Denis Herbstein
61 *Sunday Times*, Johannesburg, 6 December 1970
62 Industrial and Commercial Agreement, Iron, Steel, Engineering and Metallurgical Industry of South Africa: Main Agreement and Schedules, p. 132, *Government Gazette*, 4 September 1970
63 Denis Herbstein, unpublished notes
64 General Motors, press release quoted in the *Washington Post*, 30 June 1970
65 J. M. Roche, Chairman of General Motors Company, quoted in 'Chrysler, Ford and General Motors in South Africa', the Council on Economic Priorities, October/November 1970
66 'US Corporate Activity in Southern Africa', Council on Economic Priorities, Washington DC, September 1970, p. 24
67 'Chrysler, Ford and General Motors in South Africa', op. cit., p. 27
68 ibid., p. 26
69 ibid., p. 27

70 'US Corporate Activity in Southern Africa', op. cit.
71 ibid.

9   EXPERIMENTS AND FAILURES

1 Statement reproduced in *Polaroid and South Africa*, published by the Africa Research Group, Cambridge, Mass., March 1971
2 *Star*, Johannesburg, 21 November 1970. Quoted in *Polaroid and South Africa*, op. cit.
3 Quoted in *Polaroid and South Africa*, op. cit.
4 *Financial Mail*, Johannesburg, 22 January 1971
5 *Wall Street Journal*, 22 September 1971
6 *Daily Telegraph*, 28 January 1971
7 *Financial Mail*, Johannesburg, 22 January 1971
8 Dudley Horner and John Kane-Berman, *Report on the Polaroid Experiment*, South African Institute of Race Relations, November 1971
9 Quoted in Horner and Kane-Berman, op. cit., p. 3
10 Quoted in Horner and Kane-Berman, op. cit., p. 5
11 *Observer*, 24 January 1971
12 *Rand Daily Mail*, 1 September 1971
13 ibid.
14 *Rand Daily Mail*, 10 September 1971
15 *Rand Daily Mail*, 21 September 1971
16 Horner and Kane-Berman, op. cit., p. 10
17 *Financial Mail*, Johannesburg, Special Survey, 'Inside the Anglo Power House, 4 July 1969
18 Harry Oppenheimer, 'A Reassessment of Rhodes and his Relevance to the Problems of Africa Today', *Optima*, September 1970, p. 106
19 *Economist*, 29 June 1968: A special survey on South Africa, 'The Green Bay Tree'
20 *Rand Daily Mail*, 28 April 1970
21 Oppenheimer, op. cit., p. 103
22 *Rand Daily Mail*, 11 August 1971

23 *Sunday Times*, Johannesburg, 25 June 1963
24 *Financial Mail*, Johannesburg, 26 March 1971
25 *Rand Daily Mail*, 17 September 1971

10   BUSINESS PLAYS POLITICS
 1 *South Africa, Apartheid, and Britain*, published by the
   Labour Research Department, London, May 1970, p.
   17
 2 *Guardian*, 18 April 1968
 3 *Rand Daily Mail*, Johannesburg, 3 June 1970
 4 *Rand Daily Mail*, Johannesburg, 11 April 1970
 5 South Africa Foundation, Johannesburg, Tenth Annual
   Report, 1969, p. 22
 6 Speeches circulated to press by U K S A T A, 19 October
   1970
 7 *Sunday Times*, Johannesburg, 11 September 1971
 8 John Laurence, *Seeds of Disaster*, Gollancz, London, 1968,
   p. 143
 9 Laurence, op. cit., p. 147
10 *Investors' Chronicle*, 29 January 1971
11 *Cape Times*, 13 April 1970
12 *Rand Daily Mail*, Johannesburg, 15 January 1970
13 *Natal Mercury*, 26 March 1970
14 *Daily News*, Natal, 5 January 1970
15 *Star*, Johannesburg, 27 February 1971
16 *Financial Mail*, Johannesburg, 17 September 1971
17 ibid.
18 *Anti-Apartheid News*, London, March 1971
19 ibid.
20 *Newscheck*, Johannesburg, 20 March 1970

11   RECRUITING IMMIGRANTS FOR SOUTH
     AFRICA
 1 Leo Marquard, *The People and Policies of South Africa*,
   Oxford University Press, 1969, p. 1

2 Report of the Department of Immigration, Pretoria, 1970
3 *Derbyshire Times*, 28 May 1971
4 *The Times*, 2 January 1971
5 *The Times*, 24 February 1971
6 *Weekly Star*, Johannesburg, 1 November 1969
7 *The Times*, 1 September 1969
8 *Sunday Times*, London, 29 March 1970
9 *Sunday Telegraph*, London, 31 March 1968
10 *South Africa in World Strategy: a Special Survey*, published by the Director of Information, South African Embassy, London, June 1969
11 *Sunday Times*, Johannesburg, 5 October 1969
12 *Today's News*, published by Director of Information, South African Embassy, London, 6 May 1971
13 *Sunday Times*, Johannesburg, 29 June 1969
14 *Financial Mail*, Johannesburg, 5 November 1971
15 *Financial Mail*, Johannesburg, 5 November 1971
16 *Rand Daily Mail*, 19 January 1971

12 WESTERN TRADE FOLLOWS THE SOUTH AFRICAN FLAG

1 Eschel Rhoodie, *The Third Africa*, Twin Circle Publishing Co., Cape Town, 1968, p. 1
2 J. A. Lombard, J. J. Stadler and P. J. van der Merwe, 'The Concept of Economic Co-operation in Southern Africa', University of Pretoria, 1968
3 Rhoodie, op. cit., p. 3
4 ibid.
5 *Africa South*, February 1968, p. 4
6 Robert Molteno, *Africa and South Africa*, Africa Bureau, London, 1971, p. 12
7 *Financial Times*, 29 December 1971
8 Molteno, op. cit., p. 9
9 Molteno, op. cit., p. 10
10 Murray and Stoneman, 'Private and Overseas Invest-

ment in Southern and Central Africa', mimeographed article, 1970, p. 3

11 'Cabora Bassa and the Struggle for Southern Africa', Programme to Combat Racism, World Council of Churches

12 'Kunene Dam Scheme', Programme to Combat Racism, World Council of Churches

13 *Financial Mail*, Johannesburg, special survey, 'The Indian Ocean Beckons', 18 June 1971

14 ibid.

15 *Sechaba*, Vol. 5, No. 6, June 1971

16 US News and World Report, quoted by Rhoodie, op. cit., p. 197

17 Rhoodie, op. cit., p. 217

18 Lombard, Stadler and van der Merwe, op. cit., p. 34

19 Annual Supplement for 1969 of the Economist Intelligence Unit's *Quarterly Economic Review of Rhodesia, Zambia and Malawi*, quoted in Sean Gervasi, 'Industrialization, Foreign Capital and Forced Labour in South Africa' Table D2, UN ST/PSCA/Ser.A/10, 1970

20 Molteno, op. cit., p. 20

21 Oppenheimer in *Survey of Race Relations in South Africa*, 1969, p. 88

22 South Africa Foundation, *Annual Report*, 1970, p. 6

23 Norman Herd (ed.) *Industrial South Africa*, 1967

24 *Today's News*, South African Embassy, London, 30 September 1970

25 *Sunday Times*, Johannesburg, Business Section, 10 January 1971

26 *Cape Times*, supplement: Annual Review of the South African Economy, 12 February 1966

27 *The Times*, 21 December 1971

28 United Kingdom South Africa Trade Association, *Bulletin*, May 1971, Part II, p. 7

29 J. A. Hobson, *Imperialism*. James Nisbet & Co., London, 1902

13 CONCLUSION

1 Andrew Glyn and Bob Sutcliffe, 'The Critical Condition of British Capital', *New Left Review*, 66, March–April 1971. Though not presenting figures of British investment in South Africa as such, Glyn and Sutcliffe show that direct investment overseas has risen from averages of around 220 million pounds in 1959–63 and 280 million pounds p.a. 1964–7 to 410 million pounds in 1968 and 531 million pounds in 1969. They add: 'Figures for the first three-quarters of 1970 suggest that the 1969 level will at least be maintained. Even after allowing for the effects of devaluation on their sterling value, profits earned abroad on direct investment more than doubled between 1962 and 1969.'

2 Barbara Rogers, *South Africa's Stake in Britain*, Africa Bureau, June 1971

3 See the critical review of Rogers (op. cit.) by Peter Nicholson in *Anti-Apartheid News*, July–August 1971, in which the method of calculating the rate of return on investment in South Africa is criticized, also the attempt to estimate Britain's deficit with South Africa

4 *Rand Daily Mail*, Johannesburg, 6 October 1971

5 This alliance of capital interests was illustrated at an early point by the congenial presence as trustees of the South African Foundation of Mr Harry Oppenheimer, Mr Charles Engelhard and Mr Anton Rupert, Afrikanerdom's most successful industrialist

6 See an interview with and an article by Alan Paton in *The Times*, 22 July 1971 and 30 July 1971

7 Stanley Trapido, 'South Africa as a Comparative Study of Industrialization', *Journal of Development Studies*, Vol. 7, No. 3, April 1971

8 *X-Ray*, October–November 1971, Vol. 2, No. 3, published by the Africa Bureau summarizes the White Paper on the Report by the Inter-Department Committee on the Decentralization of Industries, June 1971

9 Lawrence Gandar's *Sunday Times* Weekly Review, 27 June 1971. A more systematic and theoretical exposition of this view is contained in M. C. O'Dowd's, *The Stages of Economic Growth and the Future of South Africa*

10 Herbert Blumer, 'Industrialization and Race Relations', in *Industrialization and Race Relations*, Guy Hunter (ed.), OUP, 1965

11 See also the work of Harold Wolpe, S. Trapido, Martin Legassick and F. Johnstone, in particular Wolpe's 'Industrialism and Race in South Africa' in S. Zubaida (ed.) *Race and Racialism*, Tavistock Publications, London, 1970; 'Class, Race and the Occupational Structure', Institute of Commonwealth Studies Seminar paper, December 1970; Johnstone's 'White Prosperity and White Supremacy in South Africa Today' in *African Affairs*, April 1970; S. Trapido's 'South Africa in a Comparative State of Industrialization', Institute of Commonwealth Studies Seminar paper, September 1970; and Legassick's 'Development and Under-development in South Africa' Chatham House, 11 March 1971; and 'South Africa: Forced Labour, Industrialization and Racial Differentiation', mimeographed 1971

12 M. Legassick, 'Development and Under-development in South Africa', 11 March 1971, p. 14

13 R. Murray and C. Stoneman, 'Private Overseas Investment in Southern and Central Africa', London, unpublished, 1970

14 *Investors' Chronicle*, 26 November 1971

15 Anton Rupert, the leading Afrikaner industrialist has written: 'In the belief that the multi-national corporation, even more than the geographically confined "local" business undertaking, has responsibilities far beyond the mere attaining of profit objectives, the multi-national entrepreneur seeks to establish bridges of

partnership, such as those erected by our group between capital and educational capital and sport, capital and art, capital and culture. For these reasons too we are seeking ties of better understanding with our neighbour states' – 'International Business Partnership – the Multi-National Concept', in *South African International*, Vol. 1, No. 2, October 1970

16 Sean Gervasi, 'The Significance of South Africa's Economic Relations with the Western Powers', mimeographed, Anti-Apartheid Movement, London, 4 July 1971

17 Statement by S. Minty before the UN Special Committee on Apartheid, 20 May 1970

18 *South African International*, December 1969, published by the South African Foundation

19 The American Committee on Africa writes in 'Apartheid and Imperialism: A Study of US Corporate Involvement in South Africa', *Africa Today*, Vol. 17, No. 5, September–October 1970: 'It makes as much sense today to talk about the defence by sea of South Africa and Western bases there as it did to defend Singapore by sea in 1941.'

20 *Observer*, 11 October 1970

21 'The Future of Industry in South Africa', address given by Harry Oppenheimer, 1950

Appendices

APPENDIX 1   British firms with subsidiaries or associate
                       companies in South Africa (as listed in *Who
                       Owns Whom*, 1971)

A.C.E. Machinery (Holdings)
AD International
A.P.V. Holdings
Aaronson Bros.
Aberdare Holdings
Acrow (Engineers)
The Adamson Alliance Co.
Adwest Group
Affiliated Music Publishers
Air Holdings
Albright & Wilson
M. L. Alkan
Allied Breweries
Allied Colloids Manufacturing
    Co.
Allied Suppliers
Amalgamated Power Engineer-
    ing
The Anchor Chemical Co.
Anderson Mavor
Armitage Shanks Group
Armstrong Equipment
Ashe Chemical
Aspro-Nicholas
The Associated Biscuit
    Manufacturers
Associated Book Publishers
Associated Engineering
The Associated Octel Co.
The Associated Portland
    Cement Manufacturers
Automotive Products
    Associated
Averys

BBA Group
BPB Industries
BTR Leyland Industries
Babcock & Wilcox
Baker Perkins Holdings
Bank of London and South
    America
Barclays Bank
Baring Brothers & Co.
Barrow Hepburn & Gale
Barton & Sons
Geo. Bassett Holdings
Bay Hall Trust
John Beales Associated Cos.
Bear Brand
Beaumont Properties
Beautility
Beckett, Laycock & Watkinson
Beecham Group
Bestobell
Bifurcated Engineering
Birmid Qualcast
Black & Edgington
Blackwood Hodge
Blundell-Permoglaze Holdings
Blythe, Greene, Jourdain & Co.
The Bolton Textile Mill Co.
Bonochord
Boosey & Hawkes
Boots Pure Drug Co.
Bovril
The Bowater Paper
    Corporation
C. T. Bowring & Co.

Bowthorpe Holdings
Bradley & Craven
Bray Gibb (Holdings)
The Brent Manufacturing Co.
Bridgend Investment Trust
Brightside Engineering
  Holdings
The British and Common-
  wealth Shipping Co.
British–American Tobacco Co.
The British Electric Traction
  Co.
British Insulated Callender's
  Cables
British Leyland Motor
  Corporation
British Match Corporation
British Mohair Spinners
The British Oxygen Co.
The British Petroleum Co.
The British Printing
  Corporation
British Ropes
British Steel Constructions
  (Birmingham)
British Steel Corporation
British Vita Co.
J. Brockhouse & Co.
H. Bronnley & Co.
Brooke Bond Liebig
Brown Bayley
The David Brown Corporation
John Brown & Co.
Building Industries Services
H.P. Bulmer
Bunzl Pulp & Paper
The Burmah Oil Co.
Bydand
C.C.L. Systems
Cable Trust
Cadbury Schweppes
Caledonia Investments
W. Canning & Co.
Caravans International
Carpets International
Cavenham Foods
Centrovincial Estates

Chamberlain Phipps
Chambon
Charter Consolidated
The Charterhouse Group
The Chloride Electrical
  Storage Co.
Chubb & Son
C. & J. Clark
Clarke & Smith Industries
Clarke Chapman–John
  Thompson
Clarke, Nickolls and Coombs
Clarkson International Tools
Clayton Dewandre Holdings
Clayton, Son & Co.
H. Clegg & Co.
Coates Brothers & Co.
Coats Patons
A. Cohen & Co.
The George Cohen 600 Group
J. Collett
William Collins & Sons
  (Holdings)
Commercial Union Assurance
  Co.
Commonwealth Development
  Corporation
Commonwealth Development
  Finance Co.
Consolidated Gold Fields
Consolidated Tin Smelters
Cope Allman International
Copperad Holdings
Cornelly Equipment Co.
Wm. Cory & Son
Court Line
Courtaulds
Crabtree Electrical Industries
Crown House
Cussons Group
Davidson & Co.
Davy-Ashmore
Dawson & Barfos
Joseph Dawson (Holdings)
Decca
Delta Metal Co.
Desoutter Brothers (Holdings)

The Dickinson Robinson Group
The Distillers Co.
Dorman Smith Holdings
Doulton & Co.
Dowty Group
Drake & Cubitt Holdings
Dunlop Holdings
Duport
F. Dupre
EMI
E.R.F. (Holdings)
Eagle Star Insurance Co.
East Asiatic Rubber Estates
East Rand Consolidated
East Sussex Engineering Co.
Ebonite Container Co.
Electrical & Industrial Securities
Ellerman Lines
B. Elliott & Co.
George Ellison Holdings
Emu Wool Industries
English Calico
The Ever Ready Co. (Great Britain)
Explosives & Chemical Products
Federated Paints
Frank Fehr & Co.
J. H. Fenner & Co. (Holdings)
Denis Ferranti Meters
Firth Cleveland
Thos. Firth & John Brown
Fisons
A. B. Fleming (Holdings)
Fodens
Foseco Minsep
W. & G. Foyle
The Fram Group
Alex Fraser & Son
Thomas French & Sons
W. & C. French
Dorman Smith Holdings
Norman Frizzell & Partners
Gandy
W. H. Gaze & Sons

Geest Industries
General Accident Fire & Life Assurance Corporation
The General Electric Co.
Gestetner Holdings
Glaxo Group
Globe Investment Trust
Glynwed
Goblin (B.V.C.)
The Gourock Ropework Co.
Great Universal Stores
N. Greening & Sons
Green's Economiser Group
Gripperrods Holdings
Grundy (Teddington)
Guardian Royal Exchange Assurance
Guest Keen & Nettlefolds
S. Guiterman & Co.
Guthrie & Co. (UK)
The Guthrie Corporation
G. N. Haden & Sons
A. W. Hainsworth & Sons
Hayleybridge Investment Trust
Hall Engineering (Holdings)
Hall-Thermotank
James Halstead (Holdings)
Hamilton Star
L. Hammond & Co. (Holdings)
C. & J. Hampton
Hargreave Investment Co.
Harris & Sheldon Group
Harrisons & Crosfield
Derek Hartle
Hawker Siddeley Group
Quinton Hazell (Holdings)
Head, Wrightson & Co.
P. C. Henderson
A. & S. Henry & Co.
Arthur Hentzen & Co.
Alfred Herbert
Heywood Williams Group
Hickson & Welch (Holdings)
Hield Brothers
Highams
Hill, Samuel Group

H. R. Holfeld (Belfast)
Hopkinsons Holdings
Hover-Air
Alexander Howden (Holdings)
James Howden & Godfrey
Howe Richardson Scale Co.
Robert Hudson
Hudson's Bay Co.
Hunslet (Holdings)
Hunting Gibson
Hutchinson
Illingworth, Morris & Co.
Imperial Chemical Industries
Inchcape & Co.
Industrial & Commercial
  Finance Corporation
Industrial Inspection
  (International)
Insulation Equipments
International Combustion
  (Holdings)
International Compressed Air
  Corporation
International Computers
  (Holdings)
International Distillers &
  Vintners
Ernest Ireland
William Jacks & Co.
Isaac Jackson (Holdings)
Jessel Securities
Gordon Johnson-Stephens
  (Holdings)
H. & R. Johnson-Richards
  Tiles
Johnson, Matthey & Co.
Kangol
Keep Brothers
George Kent
Kleinwort, Benson, Lonsdale
LRC International
John Laing & Son
Laird Group
James H. Lamont & Co.
Lamson Industries
Laporte Industries (Holdings)
Laurence Scott

Harold Laycock (Bradford)
  Holdings
Lead Industries Group
Legal and General Assurance
  Society
Lep Group
Limmer Holdings
Lindustries
Lines Bros.
Lister & Co.
F. H. Lloyd Holdings
Lloyds & Scottish
Thomas Locker (Holdings)
Lockwoods Foods
London Merchant Securities
London Shop Property Trust
Lonrho
Lopex
The Low & Bonar Group
Lowe & Carr
Joseph Lucas (Industries)
Edward Lumley & Sons
McKechnie Brothers
Macmillan (Holdings)
Management Selection
  (Group)
Manbre & Garton
Manders (Holdings)
Marchwiel Holdings
The Marconi International
  Marine Co.
Marks & Spencer
Marley
Marshalls (Halifax)
Mather & Platt
Matthews Wrightson
  Holdings
May & Hassell
Melbray Group
Mercury Securities
The Metal Box Co.
Metal Closures Group
Metal Traders
Midland Aluminium
Midland Electric
  Manufacturing Co.
Mills & Allen

Minet Holdings
Mitchell Construction Holdings
Mitchell Cotts Group
Mobbs & Lewis
Molins
The Monotype Corporation
Montagu Trust
The Morgan Crucible Co.
Motor Rail
D. & W. Murray
Nairn & Williamson (Holdings)
National & Grindlays Bank
National Employers' Mutual General Insurance Association
Isaac Naylor & Sons
Negretti & Zambra
James Neill Holdings
Newey & Tayler
Newman-Tonks
Newton, Chambers & Co.
James North & Sons
Norvic Shoe Co.
Norwich Union Life Insurance Society
Ofrex Group
Oldham International
A. Oppenheimer & Co.
The Orion Insurance Co.
Samuel Osborn & Co.
Ozalid Co.
P–E Holdings
Pancreol
Parkinson Cowan
Pearl Assurance Co.
S. Pearson & Son
Pegler-Hattersley
The Peninsular & Oriental Steam Navigation Co.
Perivale Gutermann
Permali
G. D. Peters & Co.
Petrocarbon Developments
Phillips Electronic & Associated Industries
Phoenix Assurance Co.

Photo-Me International
Pilkington Brothers
Pilkington's Tiles
Sir Isaac Pitman & Sons
The Plessey Co.
Portals Holdings
Powell Duffryn
F. Pratt Engineering Corporation
Price, Forbes (Holdings)
Pritchard Cleaners (Holdings)
Prodorite
Provincial Insurance Co.
Purle Brothers Holdings
RCF Holdings
R.F.D. Group
Rabone Petersen & Co.
Racal Electronics
Randalls Group
The Rank Organization
Ranks Hovis McDougal
Ransome Hoffmann Pollard
Ransomes Sims & Jefferies
Readson
Reckitt & Colman
Redland
Reed International
Reeves & Sons
Renold
Rentokil Group
Revertex Holdings
Reyrolle Parsons
The Rio Tinto-Zinc Corporation
Road Machines (Drayton)
Rockweld
Rotaflex (Great Britain)
Rotary Hoes
Rotork Controls
Roussel Laboratories
Rowntree Mackintosh
Royal Insurance Co.
The Royal Sovereign Pencil Co.
The Ruberoid Co.
Rubery Owen Holdings
Walter Runciman & Co.
Rush & Tompkins Group

SGB Group
Sadia
Sagit Trust Co.
Sale Tilney & Co.
George Salter & Co.
Sanderson Kayser
Sanderson Murray & Elder
    (Holdings)
Saunders Valve Co.
Scapa Group
Scholefield, Goodman & Sons
Schreiber Wood Industries
Sears Holdings
Second Consolidated Trust
Seddon Diesel Vehicles
Selection Trust
Selincourt
Senior Economisers (Holdings)
Serck
Sheffield Twist Drill & Steel Co.
The 'Shell' Transport &
    Trading Co.
Siebe Gorman & Co.
Simon Engineering
Sirdar
Slater, Walker Securities
Smith & Nephew Associated
    Cos.
Smith & Wellstood
A. E. Smith Coggins (Holdings)
Smiths Industries
Somic
Sound Attenuators
South African Distilleries &
    Wines
The South West Africa Co.
Spear & Jackson International
Spooner Industries
Staflex International
Standard & Chartered Banking
    Group
Staplegreen Insurance
    Holdings
Starch Products
Staveley Industries
The Steel Group
The Steetley Co.

Stein Atkinson Stordy
Steinberg & Sons (London &
    South Wales)
Stenhouse Holdings
Stone-Platt Industries
Storey Brothers & Co.
Stothert & Pitt
Stroud, Riley & Co.
Sun Alliance & London
    Insurance
Bernard Sunley Investment
    Trust
Swan Hunter Group
T.P.T.
Tanganyika Concessions
Tarmac Derby
Tate & Lyle
Taylor Woodrow
Tecalemit
Telephone Rentals
The Thomson Organization
Thorn Electrical Industries
Thomas Tilling
Tobacco Securities Trust Co.
Towles
Town Centre Properties
Toye & Co.
Tozer Kemsley & Millbourn
    (Holdings)
Trafalgar House Investments
Transport Development Group
Transport Holding Co.
Trust Houses Forte
Tube Investments
Turner & Newall
Twinlock
Twyfords Holdings
Unigate
Unilever
The Union International Co.
United City Merchants
United Dominions Trust
United Transport Co.
United Wire Group
Universal Grinding
Urwick, Orr & Partners
Vantona

L

Vapormatic Co.
Vernon & Co. (Surgical
  Dressings)
Vickers
Walker, Crosweller & Co.
Thomas Walker
Andrew Weir & Co.
The Weir Group
The Wellcome Foundation
The Wellman Engineering
  Corporation
Allen West & Co.
Westbourne Publications
Westinghouse Brake & Signal
  Co.
George Weston Holdings
Whessoe
Whitbread & Co.
F. Whiteley & Co.
James Wilkes

Wilkinson Sword
W. Williams & Sons
  (Holdings)
Willis, Faber & Dumas
  (Holdings)
Willows Francis
George Wills & Sons
  (Holdings)
Wilmot Breeden (Holdings)
George Wimpey & Co.
Thomas Witter & Co.
Wolf Electric Tools (Holdings)
Rudolf Wolff & Co.
A.C. Wood & Son
Wood Hall Trust
Woodall-Duckham Group
Francis Woodcock (Engineers)
Woolcombers (Holdings)
Yarrow & Co.
A.C. Young & Co.

APPENDIX 2 Top South African industrial companies in
which British companies have a shareholding

SOUTH AFRICAN COMPANY	RANKING NUMBER	BRITISH COMPANY
African Explosives & Chemical Industries (A)	2	Imperial Chemical Industries
Premier Milling	9	Associated British Foods
Leyland Motor Corporation of South Africa	10	British Leyland Motor Corporation
Sentrachem (A)	14	British Petroleum
Oudemeester (A)	15	South African Distilleries & Wines
Stewarts & Lloyds (A)	19	British Steel Corporation
Federale Kunsmis (A)	21	Fisons Commonwealth Development Corporation
African Oxygen	25	The British Oxygen Co.
Pretoria Portland Cement Co. (A)	29	Charter Consolidated

The Metal Box Co. of South Africa	32	The Metal Box Co.
Dorman Long (A)	36	British Steel Corporation
The Carpet Manufacturing Co. (South Africa) (A)	38	Carpets International
The United Tobacco Cos. (South)	39	British-American Tobacco Co.
Woolworths (Holdings) (A)	45	Marks & Spencer
Dunlop South Africa	46	Dunlop Holdings
Alexander Sagov Holdings (A)		Carrington & Dewhurst Group
Swaziland Sugar Milling Co.	52	Lonrho
Mitchell Cotts South Africa	54	Mitchell Cotts Group
Slater Walker South Africa	59	Slater, Walker Securities
Illovo Sugar Estates	60	Tate & Lyle
Everite (A)	66	Turner & Newall
	70	South African Distilleries & Wines*
Tapsa (A)	71	Carpets International
L. Suzman (A)	75	Slater, Walker Securities
White's Portland Cement Co.	77	Associated Portland Cement Manufacturers
Lion Match	94	British Match Corporation

(A) Associate company.

*South African Distilleries & Wines is a British-registered company listed in the *Financial Mail*'s list of leading South African companies.

Source: 'Top Companies', supplement to *Financial Mail*, Johannesburg, 16 April 1971; *Who Owns Whom*, 1971.

APPENDIX 3 Industrial classification of British firms with
subsidiaries or associate companies in South
Africa

CLASSIFICATION	NUMBER OF COMPANIES
Engineering (including cutlery, foundries, hand tools, instruments and shipbuilding)	175
Chemical and process industries (including cosmetics, fertilizers, films and photographic papers, paints, pharmaceuticals, plastics, rubber processing, soap, vegetable and marine oils, welding and industrial gases	41
Textiles (including spinning and weaving, bleaching, dyeing, finishing, converting and printing), clothing, footwear (including rubber footwear), rags, furs and waste	41
Chemists, brokers and auctioneers, dairies, distribution (wholesale and retail), merchants, motor distributors	36
Miscellaneous: abrasives, belting and fire hose, brushes, buttons, cork manufacturers, glass, instruments, office accessories (including files, pens, pencils), oilcloth and linoleum, optical goods, perambulators, pottery, refractories, rope, shopfitters, tanners and leather goods, toys, travel goods, upholstery, wood-working and furniture (excluding office and other metal furniture	29
Building and contracting, building materials, civil engineering, roadmaking and timber distributors	24
Insurance companies and insurance brokers	24
Advertising and publicity, canals, car hire, catering, cold storage and refrigeration, colleges and correspondence courses, docks, dyers and cleaners, garages, harbours, holiday camps, hotels and warehousing, recreation, renting and relay of radio and television, renting of telephone equipment, service industries and entertainments, sports goods, transport (land and air but excluding shipping), travel agencies, undertakers and cemetery proprietors, wharves	22
Mining and metals (ferrous, non-ferrous and precious metals and non-metallic minerals), rolling and fabrication	21

Paper (including wallpaper), packaging, printing and publishing   20

Banks, finance and discount houses, investment trusts   21

Confectionery, drink (including breweries, distilleries and soft drinks), food and tobacco   19

Industrial holding companies   19

Property and estate companies   9

Shipping   6

Cocoa, petroleum products, rubber, tea, timber, wheat   5

TOTAL   512

Source: *Who Owns Whom*, 1971.

APPENDIX 4   British Members of Parliament listed in the 1971 *Directory of Directors* as holding directorships in groups which have South African subsidiaries or associate companies

MP	COMPANY IN WHICH THE DIRECTORSHIP IS HELD
S. Scholefield Allen (Lab., Crewe)	J. A. Irving & Co. (Deputy Chairman), subsidiary of Transport Development Group, which owns The Square Grip Reinforcement Co. (South Africa) (Pty)
Daniel Awdry (Con., Chippenham)	BET Omnibus Services, subsidiary of The British Electric Traction Co., which has six South African subsidiaries
Sir Frederic Bennett (Con., Torquay)	Arawak Trust Co. and Kleinwort Benson Lonsdale (Europe) SA, associates of Kleinwort, Benson, Lonsdale which has a South African associate J. L. Clarke & Co.: Commercial Union Assurance Co. which owns Commercial Union Assurance Co. of South Africa
Thomas Boardman (Con., Leicester SW)	Allied Breweries which owns John Harvey & Sons (South Africa) (Pty): Chamberlain Phipps which has five South

325

	African subsidiaries and one associate company
Rt. Hon. John Boyd-Carpenter (Con., Kingston-upon-Thames)	Trust Houses Forte which owns Forte's (South Africa) Pty
Bernard Braine (Con., SE Essex)	Purle Brothers Holdings which has two South African associates
John Cronin (Lab., Loughborough)	Racal Electronics which has one South African subsidiary and one associate company
David Crouch (Con., Canterbury)	Pfizer, subsidiary of Pfizer Inc., which has South African subsidiaries
Sir Geoffrey de Freitas (Lab., Kettering)	Laporte Industries (Holdings) which has a South African associate Peroxide Chemicals (Pty)
Edward du Cann (Con., Taunton)	Barclays Unicorn, Barclays Bank (London Board), Barclays Bank Trust Co., subsidiaries of Barclays Bank which owns Barclays National: Cammell Laird & Co., subsidiary of Laird Group which owns Cable Belt Pty
Nicholas Edwards (Con., Pembroke)	William Brandt & Sons, subsidiary of National & Grindlays Bank, which owns Hadfields (South Africa) Pty
Geoffrey Finsberg (Con., Hampstead)	GUS Transport and Fanfare Displays, subsidiaries of Great Universal Stores, which has three South African subsidiaries
Sir John Foster (Con., Northwich)	Sir Isaac Pitman & Sons (Chairman), which has a South African associate Pitman Publishing Co. South Africa
Hugh Fraser (Con., Stafford and Stone)	Sun Alliance & London Insurance, which owns Protea Assurance Co.
Alan Green (Con., Preston South)	Scapa Group, which has two South African subsidiaries
Alan Haselhurst (Con., Middleton and Prestwick)	Vitafoam and British Vita International, subsidiaries of British Vita Co. which has six South African subsidiaries

John Hay (Con., Henley)	Rediffusion London, Rediffusion (North West), International Library Service and Walport, subsidiaries of The British Electric Traction Co., which has six South African subsidiaries
Douglas Jay (Lab., Battersea North)	Flag Investment Co., subsidiary of Slater, Walker Securities, which has twelve South African subsidiaries
Toby Jessel (Con., Twickenham)	Jessel Securities, which has four South African subsidiaries
Sir John Langford-Holt (Con., Shrewsbury)	James North & Sons, which has a South African associate James North (Africa) Pty
Rt. Hon. Geoffrey Lloyd (Con., Sutton Coldfield)	Mersec Holdings, an associate of the British Electric Traction Co. which has six South African subsidiaries and of Mercury Securities which has a South African associate company, Employee Benefit Plans (Pty)
Rt. Hon. Selwyn Lloyd (Speaker, Wirral)	The Rank Organization, which has two South African subsidiaries and one associate company: Sun Alliance & London Insurance which owns Protea Assurance
John Osborn (Con., Hallam)	Samuel Osborn & Co. and Samuel Osborn (South Africa) (Pty). Samuel Osborn & Co. has four South African subsidiaries
Sir Richard Thompson (Con., Croydon S.)	Rockweld, which has one South African subsidiary and one associate company
Jeremy Thorpe (Lib., N. Devon)	Rediffusion (South West), subsidiary of The British Electric Traction Co. which has six South African subsidiaries
John Tilney (Con., Wavertree)	John Holt & Co., subsidiary of Lonrho, which has eleven South African subsidiaries
Peter Trew (Con., Dartford)	Rush & Tompkins Group, which has one South African subsidiary and one associate company

Mark Woodnutt (Con., Isle of Wight)	Charles Churchill, subsidiary of Tube Investments, which has twenty South African subsidiaries

Sources: *Directory of Directors*, 1971; *Who Owns Whom*, 1971.

APPENDIX 5 Directorships in companies with South African subsidiaries or associate companies held by members of the Council of United Kingdom–South Africa Trade Association

COUNCIL MEMBER	COMPANIES IN WHICH DIRECTORSHIP IS HELD
Sir Nicholas Cayzer	Air Holdings British & Commonwealth Shipping Co. (Chairman) Sun Alliance & London Insurance
W. E. Luke	Lindustries (Chairman) Powell Duffryn
Sir Robert Adeane	The British Electric Traction Co. Decca Mercury Securities Newton, Chambers & Co. The Ruberoid Co. Second Consolidated Trust (Chairman)
C. W. Bell	Coats Patons (Chairman)
J. P. Berkin	National & Grindlays Bank The 'Shell' Transport & Trading Co.
Sir Raymond Brookes	Guest Keen & Nettlefolds (Chairman)
R. H. Dent	Charter Consolidated
Lord Fraser of Lonsdale	Sun Alliance Insurance Co.
G. E. Graham	Unilever
Keith Graham	British Overseas Airways Corporation (Chairman)*

Sir Cyril Hawker	Head, Wrightson & Co.
	Standard & Chartered Banking Group (Chairman)
The Rt. Hon. The Viscount Leathers	Wm. Cory & Son (Chairman) Laporte Industries (Holdings)
J. Donald McCall	Consolidated Gold Fields (Chairman)
A. F. Macdonald	The Distillers Co. (Chairman)
Ian W. Macdonald	Lloyds & Scottish (Chairman)
D. F. Martin-Jenkins	Ellerman Lines (Chairman)
Sir John Mellor	Prudential Assurance Co.*
Sir Eric Millbourn	National Employers' Mutual General Insurance Association
	Tozer, Kemsley & Millbourn (Holdings)
A. J. M. Miller	Bestobell (Chairman)
	Nairn & Williamson (Holdings)
Sir Alec Ogilvie	Powell Duffryn (Chairman)
	Westinghouse Brake & Signal Co.
Sir John Reiss	Associated Portland Cement Manufacturers (Chairman)
Sir Frederic Seebohm	Barclays Bank DCO (Chairman)
Peter W. Seligman	A.P.V. Holdings (Chairman)
Sidney Spiro	Charter Consolidated (Deputy Chairman)
	Barclays Bank DCO
	Rio Tinto-Zinc
	Selection Trust
Sir Charles Wheeler	George Wimpey & Co.
	Guest Keen & Nettlefolds
	Phoenix Assurance Co.
	Rudolf Wolff & Co.
Col. W. H. Whitbread	Whitbread & Co. (Chairman)
	Barclays Bank
	Eagle Star Insurance Co.
Roy Wright	Rio Tinto-Zinc (Deputy Chairman)
Sir Eric Yarrow	Yarrow & Co. (Chairman)

* Companies which do not have separate South African subsidiaries, but which have important South African interests.

Source: *Directory of Directors*, 1971.

L*

TABLE 1: SOUTH AFRICA: FOREIGN LIABILITIES, 1970 (IN MILLIONS OF RANDS)

	Sterling Area	Dollar Area		Western Europe	All other places	Total
		International Organizations	Other Dollar Area			
DIRECT INVESTMENT						
Central Government and banking sector						
Long-term	160	—	3	5	—	168
Short-term	67	—	8	16	7	98
Total	227	—	11	21	7	266
Private sector						
Long-term						
Shares, nominal value	451	—	125	122	7	705
Reserves	1214	—	377	196	7	1794
Branch and partnership balances	136	—	30	10	—	176
Mortgages, long-term loans, debentures etc.	220	—	53	77	10	360
Real estate	5	—	—	1	—	6
Total long-term	2026	—	585	406	24	3041
Short-term	392	—	79	159	6	636
Total	2418	—	664	565	30	3677
TOTAL DIRECT INVESTMENT	2645	—	675	586	37	3943

NON-DIRECT INVESTMENT

Central government and banking sector						
Long-term	66	1	42	207	1	317
Short-term	54	110	18	56	2	240
Total	120	111	60	263	3	557
Private sector						
Long-term						
Shares	407	–	44	230	6	687
Mortgages, long-term loans, debentures etc.	93	12	56	290	13	464
Total long-term	500	12	100	520	19	1151
Short-term	106	–	20	37	4	167
Total	606	12	120	557	23	1318
TOTAL NON-DIRECT INVESTMENT	726	123	180	820	26	1875
TOTAL FOREIGN LIABILITIES	3371	123	855	1406	63	5818

Source: South African Reserve Bank, *Quarterly Bulletin*, December 1971.

TABLE 2: SOUTH AFRICA: NET CAPITAL INFLOW, 1961-70 (IN MILLIONS OF RANDS)

1961	1962	1963	1964	1965	1966	1967	1968	1969	1970
−129	−88	−80	−41	255	141	162	459	180	557

Source: South African Reserve Bank, *Quarterly Bulletin*, September 1971.

TABLE 3: UNITED KINGDOM: NET DIRECT INVESTMENT IN SOUTH AFRICA, 1961-69 (IN MILLIONS OF POUNDS)

1961	1962	1963	1964	1965	1966	1967	1968	1969
9	15	34	33	44	35	47	43	70

Source: Board of Trade *Journal*, July 1968 and Department of Trade and Industry, *Business Monitor*, Miscellaneous Series, Overseas Transactions, M4, 1971.

TABLE 4: UNITED STATES: NET DIRECT INVESTMENT IN SOUTH AFRICA, 1960-70 (IN MILLIONS OF DOLLARS)

1960	1961	1962	1963	1964	1965	1966	1967	1968	1969	1970
−37	18	53	54	56	62	72	65	26	63	109

Source: United States Department of Commerce, *Survey of Current Business*, October 1968, October 1969 and October 1971.

TABLE 5: SOUTH AFRICA: NET CAPITAL FLOW AND GROSS
DOMESTIC INVESTMENT, 1961-70 (IN MILLIONS OF RANDS)

	Gross domestic investment	Net capital inflow	Proportion of gross domestic investment formed by net capital inflow (percentage)
1961	1163	−129	−11.1
1962	1147	−88	−7.7
1963	1513	−80	−5.3
1964	1758	−41	−2.3
1965	2198	255	11.6
1966	2104	141	6.5
1967	2691	162	6.0
1968	2339	459	19.6
1969	2945	180	6.1
1970	3642	557	15.6

Source: South African Reserve Bank, *Quarterly Bulletin,* September
1968 and September 1971.

TABLE 6: UNITED KINGDOM: AVERAGE RATES OF RETURN
ON DIRECT INVESTMENTS IN SELECTED COUNTRIES, 1965-8
(PERCENTAGE)

	1965	1966	1967	1968
Overseas Sterling Area	9.4	8.6	8.5	8.6
Australia	8.0	6.6	6.9	6.9
South Africa	12.7	12.8	12.4	11.7
India	7.7	6.1	7.5	6.6
Malaysia	14.8	14.9	11.3	11.3
Kenya	8.2	9.8	8.6	9.5
Ghana	9.8	7.5	7.8	11.0
Nigeria	6.7	6.0	4.3	6.3
Canada	6.5	6.3	5.9	5.9
United States	11.9	12.5	11.7	12.0
Total, all areas	8.7	8.4	8.3	9.0

Source: Department of Trade and Industry, *Business Monitor,*
Miscellaneous Series, Overseas Transactions, M4, 1971.

TABLE 7: UNITED KINGDOM: DIRECT INVESTMENT EARNINGS IN SELECTED COUNTRIES, 1964-9 (IN MILLIONS OF POUNDS)

	1964	1965	1966	1967	1968	1969	Average 1964-66	Average 1967-69	Proportion of total, 1969 percentage
Australia	53	61	55	62	76	98	56	79	15
South Africa	62	57	60	65	76	86	60	76	13
India	21	25	18	18	20	21	21	20	3
Malaysia	22	22	24	18	22	28	23	24	4
Kenya	2	4	5	4	6	7	4	6	1
Ghana	7	6	5	5	7	7	6	6	1
Nigeria	8	8	8	5	7	11	8	8	2
Canada	32	37	40	41	50	42	36	44	6
United States	42	49	68	72	86	94	53	84	14
EEC	13	19	25	25	65	83	19	58	13
Total, all areas	370	400	429	438	568	650	400	552	

Source: Department of Trade and Industry, *Business Monitor*, Miscellaneous Series, Overseas Transactions, M4, 1971.

TABLE 8: UNITED KINGDOM: NET DIRECT INVESTMENT TO SELECTED COUNTRIES, 1964-9
(IN MILLIONS OF POUNDS)

	1964	1965	1966	1967	1968	1969	Average 1964-66	Average 1967-69	Proportion of total, 1969 percentage
Australia	77	56	49	54	80	116	61	83	21
South Africa	33	44	35	47	42	70	37	53	13
India	14	16	2	10	9	9	17	9	2
Malaysia	6	5	3	13	1	0	5	5	0
Kenya	0	−3	−3	−2	2	10	−2	3	2
Ghana	0	8	3	3	3	9	4	5	2
Nigeria	−5	7	−1	−2	3	24	−4	8	4
Canada	3	19	19	33	30	36	14	33	7
United States	31	22	42	51	84	53	32	63	10
EEC	37	32	50	30	73	104	40	72	19
Total, all areas	263	308	276	281	410	547	282	413	

Source: Department of Trade and Industry, *Business Monitor*, Miscellaneous Series, Overseas Transactions, M4, 1971.

TABLE 9: UNITED STATES: AVERAGE RATES OF RETURN ON DIRECT INVESTMENT IN SOUTH AFRICA AND ON TOTAL OVERSEAS INVESTMENT, 1965-70 (PERCENTAGE)

	1965	1966	1967	1968	1969	1970*
South Africa	19.1	20.6	19.2	17.2	16.8	16.3
Total, all areas	11.1	10.4	10.1	10.8	11.4	11.0

*Preliminary data

Source: United States Department of Commerce, *Survey of Current Business*, October 1971.

TABLE 10: UNITED KINGDOM: VALUE OF PRIVATE DIRECT
INVESTMENT IN SELECTED COUNTRIES, 1969
(IN MILLIONS OF POUNDS)

		Proportion of total (percentage)
Australia	1083	18
South Africa	656	11
India	287	5
Malaysia	173	3
Kenya	64	1
Ghana	68	1
Nigeria	118	2
Canada	722	12
United States	653	11
EEC	733	12
Total, all areas	6132	

Source: Department of Trade and Industry, *Business Monitor,*
Miscellaneous Series, Overseas Transactions, M4, 1971.

TABLE 11: VOLUME OF UNITED KINGDOM—SOUTH AFRICAN
TRADE, 1962-70 (IN MILLIONS OF POUNDS)

	*UK exports to South Africa**	*UK imports from South Africa**
1962	157	151
1963	207	166
1964	239	183
1965	265	181
1966	247	192
1967	262	220
1968	266	272
1969	293	302
1970	333	258

*Excluding Namibia (South-West Africa)

Source: Central Statistical Office, *Annual Abstract of
Statistics,* 1971.

TABLE 12: SOUTH AFRICA: DIRECTIONS OF TRADE, 1970

	Imports (in millions of Rands)	Per-cent-age	Exports (in millions of Rands)	Per-cent-age
AFRICA	131	5	264	17
EUROPE				
United Kingdom	561	22	446	29
West Germany	372	15	109	7
France	89	4	40	3
Italy	104	4	42	3
Netherlands	59	2	35	2
Belgium	34	1	56	4
Switzerland	50	2	5	0
Sweden	45	2	8	1
Other Europe	78	3	52	3
AMERICA				
Canada	70	3	28	2
United States	424	17	129	8
Other America	22	1	19	1
ASIA				
Japan	221	9	181	12
Other Asia	189	7	39	3
OCEANIA				
Australia	60	2	13	1
Other Oceania	5	0	3	0
OTHER	33	1	74	5
TOTAL	2547		1543	

Notes: Figures are rounded. Exports exclude gold bullion.

Source: Standard Bank, *Review,* January 1972.

TABLE 13: COMPOSITION OF SOUTH AFRICA'S IMPORTS AND EXPORTS, 1970 (IN MILLIONS OF RANDS)

	Imports	Exports
Animal and animal products	30	34
Vegetable products	61	148
Animal and vegetable fats, oils and waxes	14	9
Foodstuffs	47	152
Mineral products	144	234
Chemicals	160	59
Plastics	99	12
Leather and leather products	15	39
Wood and wood products	35	2
Paper	87	33
Textiles	240	96
Footwear etc.	15	1
Stone, cement and glass	30	8
Precious stones and metals	18	215
Base metals	200	262
Machinery and parts	705	84
Vehicles, aircraft and parts	467	28
Photographic, surgical, measuring equipment etc.	98	7
Miscellaneous manufactured goods	24	1
Works of art, antiques etc.	4	1
Other unclassified goods	54	117
Total	2548	1543

Note: Figures are rounded.

Source: Republic of South Africa, *Monthly Abstract of Trade Statistics,* compiled by the Department of Customs and Excise, January-December 1970.

Index of Companies

Adwest Group 238
AEG Telefunken 139–40; AEG South Africa (Pty) 140
AEI Henley Africa (Pty), see GEC–English Electric
African Cables & Telephone Manufacturers of South Africa (Pty) 188
African Explosives & Chemical Industries 27–9, 31, 66, 101, 103, 173–6, 200, 206, 238, 266
African Oxygen (Afrox), see British Oxygen
African Triangle 88
G. & L. Albu 116
Alcan Aluminium 133
Alda 267
Alexander Sagov Holdings 100–1
Allied Electric 274
Allied Investment Corporation 94
Allis Chalmers 28
AMCOR 179
American Metal Climax 130, 199, 264, 292
American–South African Investment Corp. 94, 131, 133, 167, 223
Amoco 104
Anglo American Corp. 32, 66, 76, 85, 90, 100–1, 116, 120, 125, 132, 141, 177–8, 203, 205, 210–12, 246, 264–6, 281, 285, 291–2
Anglo-Transvaal Consolidated Investments 87–8, 116, 133, 183
Armaments Development & Production Corp. of South Africa 223
Associated British Foods 31, 156; Premier Milling 31, 156, 200
Associated Engineering 237
Associated Manganese Mines of South Africa 223
Associated Portland Cement 156, 217; White's Portland Cement 156
Atlas Aircraft Corporation 250

Australian & New Zealand Bank 166

Baldwins, see British Steel Corp.
Bamangwato Concessions, see Roan Selection Trust
Banco Comercial de Angola 91
Bank of Africa, see Barclays Bank
Bank of Ireland 166
Barclays Bank 90, 120, 160, 200, 238; Bank of Africa 121; Barclays Bank DCO 13, 89, 91, 121, 160, 201–4; Barclays Bank International 89, 94, 201, 217, 227, 243–4, 246; Barclays National Bank 89, 92, 276; National Bank 120–1
Thos. Barlow & Sons 94, 132, 167, 223
Barlow–Weyerhauser 227
Benguela Railway Co. 166
Berkshire International 199
Bestobell 199
Bethlehem Steel Corporation of South Africa 264
Birfield Ruberowen, see Guest Keen & Nettlefolds
Boart & Hard Metal Products 132
Bolt Manufacturers Africa, see Guest Keen & Nettlefolds
Boots Pure Drug South Africa 273
Borg-Warner South Africa, see Guest Keen & Nettlefolds
Bowater Paper Corporation 32; Mondi Paper Co. 32
British & Commonwealth Shipping Co. 33, 217
British Calico Printers' Association 99
British Home Stores 166
British Leyland Motor Corp. 31, 97, 156, 168; British Leyland International 168; Leyland Motor Corp. of South Africa 31, 98, 167–72

341

344

O'Kiep Copper Co. 167
Optichem 262
Otavi Mining Co. (Pty) 140

Palabora Mining Co., see Rio
Tinto-Zinc Corporation
Pearl Insurance 95
Phoenix Assurance Co. 95
Pilkington Bros. 156
Placid Oil 104
Plate Glass & Shatterprufe In-
dustries 273
The Plessey Co. 32, 107, 217
Polaroid Corporation 20, 130,
159, 193–8, 200; Frank &
Hirsch 194–6
Premier Milling, see Associated
British Foods
Protea Holdings 200
Protea Assurance Co., see Sun
Alliance & London Assurance
Co.
Public Utility Transport Cor-
poration (PUTCO) 169

Raleigh Cycles 227
Rand Mines 94, 115, 132
Rand Selection Trust 132
Rank Organization 238; Rank
Xerox 199; Rank Xerox (South
Africa) 238
Reed International 79, 161; Reed
Corporation of South Africa 79
Rio Tinto–Zinc Corporation 11,
14, 33, 140, 151–2, 159, 162–5,
167, 264–5, 292; Palabora Min-
ing Co. 11, 163–5, 167; Rio
Tinto (Rhodesia) 165–6; Ros-
sing Uranium 33, 165, 265
Roan Selection Trust 264; Bot-
swana Roan Selection Trust
264; Bamangwato Concessions
264
Robert Hudson 156, 158
Roberts Construction Co. 263, 275
Rolls-Royce 10, 218, 247
Rossing Uranium, see Rio Tinto-
Zinc Corporation
Rothmans 223, 227
N. M. Rothschild & Sons 34, 111,
165

Royal Bank of Canada 120
Royal Insurance Co. 94
Russell Holdings 200

Safmarine 33, 217
Samson Holdings 200
Sanlam 93, 168
Scapa Dryers 237; Scapa Dryers
South Africa 237
Schlesinger Organization 94
Schweppes, see Cadbury
Schweppes
Selection Trust 165
Sena Sugar Estates 265
Sentrachem 33, 101–2
Shell 104–6, 136, 264; Shell-
Mex 238
Sidcor 100
Siemens 124, 138–9
Slater Walker Securities 238
Smiths Industries 220, 238
SNIA Viscosa 175
SOEKOR 39
South Africa Tourist Corporation
232
South African Airways 232
South African Associated News-
papers 200
South African Breweries 94, 156,
167, 200
South African Coal, Oil & Gas
Corporation 39, 103, 123, 223;
SASOL Marketing Co. 167
South African Eagle Insurance
Co., see Eagle Star Insurance Co.
South African Forest Investments
132
South African Immigration Orga-
nisation (Pty) 246
South African Industrial Cellulose
Corporation 100, 175
South African Manganese 223
South African Mutual Life Assur-
ance Society 93–4
South African Nylon Spinners 100,
173–4
South West Africa Co. 265
South West African Lithium
Mines (Pty), see Kloeckner &
Co.

General Index

Adamson, Campbell 242
Albu, George 110
Amery, Julian, MP, 239
Anderson, P. H. 94
Andrews, C. B. 167
Angola 30, 102, 130, 137, 139, 240–1, 255, 265–6, 269–71, 273, 294
Apartheid, attempts to reform 10, 12, 14, 21–2, 284; critics 203–5, 215, 249, 253, 260, 280–1, 288; economic basis of 9, 11, 15–19, 41, 53, 63, 79–80, 131, 179, 250, 285–6, 290, 296; erosion of 59, 61, 153, 220–1
Archibald, Hugh 181
Arms, embargo 36, 214–16, 218, 220, 241, 250, 275; sales 13, 36, 135, 200, 219; armaments industry 17, 28, 36, 175, 204

Baillieu, E. L. 166
Bamford, H. F. Y. 223
Banghart, M. D. 167
Banking 9, 81–3, 89–93, 120–1
Bantu Wages and Productivity Association 50, 67, 207–9
Bantustans 21, 42, 50, 61, 65, 99, 104, 226, 287–90, 229
Barber, Anthony, MP 224, 238
Baring-Gould, Francis 110
Barlow, C. S. 94, 167, 223
Barnato, Barney 110–13, 116
Beit, Alfred 112–13
Bennett, Sir Frederick, MP 239
Berman, O. J. 194
Bexon, M. L. 152, 159, 181, 243
Biggs-Davison, John, MP 239
Borckenhagen, C. L. F. 223
Border areas 77–9, 99, 164, 180–2, 198, 205, 290
Botha, M. C., 51
Botswana 21, 91, 256–7, 259, 261, 264–5, 269, 271, 273, 277
Boyd, Lord 238

British Government 9, 200, 228, 234–5, 250, 265, 271–2; British policy 21–22, 292–3, 235–6; Conservative Government 178, 214–15, 217, 219, 235, 239; Labour Government 213–16, 218–19, 241, 248, 250, 275
British investment in South Africa 9, 15, 23, 25–33, 124–5, 279–80; company case studies 162–88; early estimates of: (1870) 110, (1884) (1911) 116; return on 29–30; sectoral breakdown 81–4; banking 81–3, 89–92, 120–1; building 84; chemicals 84, 101–3; computers 106–8; distribution 81–3; engineering 82–4; food processing 84; insurance 81–3, 93–5; mining 81, 83–5, 88, 109, 114–16, 120; motor industry 97–8; oil 103–6; textiles 84, 99–101; and South African expansion 21, 37, 257, 263–6, 271–7
British National Export Council (BNEC) 217, 219, 233
British United Industrialists 213
Brookes, Sir Raymond 161, 185–6
Brown, Sir Stephen 275
Brown, Lord 237
Building industry 68–70, 84
Byers, Lord 14

Cabora Bassa 91, 137, 139, 174, 185, 266
Callard, Jack 173
Campbell-Pitt, W. L. 67
Carr, Robert, MP 238
Carrington, Lord 238
Cayzer, Sir Nicholas 104, 217, 220–1
Chemicals 26, 84, 101–3; petrochemicals 39
Clitheroe, Lord 166
Coetzee, J. P. 246

347